The Responsible Scientist

The Responsible Scientist

A Philosophical Inquiry

JOHN FORGE

University of Pittsburgh Press

7/09

Published by the University of Pittsburgh Press, Pittsburgh, Pa., 15260
Copyright © 2008, University of Pittsburgh Press
All rights reserved
Manufactured in the United States of America
Printed on acid-free paper
10 9 8 7 6 5 4 3 2 1
ISBN 13: 978-0-8229-4349-5
ISBN 10: 0-8229-4349-2

Library of Congress Cataloging-in-Publication Data

Forge, John, 1946–
  The responsible scientist : a philosophical inquiry / John Forge.
      p. cm.
  Includes bibliographical references and index.
  ISBN-13: 978-0-8229-4349-5 (cloth : alk. paper)
  ISBN-10: 0-8229-4349-2 (cloth : alk. paper)
    1. Scientists—Professional ethics. 2. Research—Moral and ethical aspects. 3.
Research—Social aspects. I. Title.
  Q147.F667 2008
  174'.95—dc22

                                    2008030472

To Edwina-Pearce, and to Sarah,
who each helped me in her own way
to write this book.

Contents

Preface

I began to think about science and responsibility when I decided to teach a course on science and ethics at Griffith University, where I worked in the "STS group." Our mission, as they say, was to teach scientists about the wider domain, about how their work affects matters beyond the laboratory. I decided to teach a course on science and ethics because the course that I had previously been in charge of—about nuclear issues, including nuclear weapons and nuclear strategy—had been rendered somewhat out of date by the end of the Cold War. It seemed to me that some of the resources of a small group dedicated to educating scientists needed to be redeployed. Some of the ideas expressed here—what I call the "wide view" of responsibility, for example—had their origin in that course. I am most grateful to my students for listening and responding to what I had to say. Other ideas, such as the "two-tier system" of responsibility, were worked out independently of any teaching. In one sense, then, this book is a systematic working out of the theory that I put forward in that course, and in another sense it is rather more.

I am a philosopher who has worked all his life in departments of science and technology studies and of the history and philosophy of science, and it is likely that this book will draw on more than technical philosophy, as regards both responsibility and ethics. In fact, in trying to reach the right audience, I have attempted to do as little "pure philosophy" as possible, preferring to leave such issues to one side and concentrate on what I take to be more central matters. I have no intention of denigrating philosophy as it is practiced by many, but I prefer to represent what I am doing as a kind of applied philosophy.

In addition to the students mentioned above, I would like to thank various audiences who have earlier received some of the ideas expressed here: in Kansas City (twice); in Bariloche, Argentina; in Rytko, Poland; in Pittsburgh; and in Brisbane, Melbourne, and Sydney, Australia. I would also like to thank Phil Dowe, Bernard Gert, Sarah Graham, Jim Moore,

Sverre Myhra, David Oldroyd, Monica Seini, Michael Selgelid, Jack Smart, and, above all, Hugh Lacey, whose comments and suggestions on drafts of the chapters were most helpful. Jane Oldroyd was kind enough to draw the figures for me. Finally, I owe a great debt of gratitude to all the people at the University of Pittsburgh Press, though I ought to single out Cynthia Miller, who edited the manuscript and much improved it.

The Responsible Scientist

Science and Responsibility

N A DRAMATIC STATEMENT OF THE IMPACT OF THE
Industrial Revolution, Paul Mantoux claimed that a man living at the
dawn of that era—let us say, in the 1770s—would have had more in common with a Roman legionnaire in Britain fifteen hundred years earlier
than he would with his own grandson. Perhaps this is something of an
exaggeration, but nevertheless, the Industrial Revolution did give rise to
immense and unprecedented changes in the social and economic circumstances of the nineteenth century. Another economic historian,
W. W. Rostow, described the Industrial Revolution as the "takeoff" into
sustained economic growth and saw all the period's other changes—
social change, for instance—as consequences of continuing increases in
the output of goods and services. Rostow believed, moreover, that one
of the causes of the Industrial Revolution was the role played by *science*.
If this is understood to entail the systematic application of science to
production, then I do not agree: the innovations in the "leading sector,"
textiles, were technical changes that owed little if anything to scientific
theory.[1] On the other hand, a kind of inquiring spirit and willingness to
innovate were prevalent among British entrepreneurs, and if that can be
put down to the effects of the Scientific Revolution, then a broader view
of the role of science—one that emphasizes its contributions to the
"ethos" of the time—is less obviously wrong. However, in order to sustain the Industrial Revolution and maintain economic growth, new
leading sectors were needed, and here there was a substantial role for
scientific theory.

There is therefore a clear, indisputable sense in which science is

1

responsible for the particular material circumstances in which we find ourselves, for without science the process of industrialization would have died out, and with it economic growth.[2] While Rostow's view of science as one of the *causes* of the Industrial Revolution suggests an obvious interpretation of what it means for science to be responsible for our material circumstances, science is not just a "thing": it is something people do. This leads, then, to another understanding of responsibility, as a relationship between people, such as scientists, and outcomes. Many would accept that some outcomes, such as improved material circumstances, are good things. However, science also has a darker side, most evident in regard to weapons of mass destruction. If scientists are responsible for the greatly improved material circumstances rooted in the eighteenth century, then they are also responsible for providing the means to utterly destroy the societies built on that wealth.

No one can deny that science affects us, in part by making certain technologies possible, and these technologies in turn give rise to artifacts and services—such as the many things that together make up our "material circumstances" and the weapons that threaten them. But it is possible to deny that *scientists themselves* are responsible for these outcomes. It is possible to claim that scientists are only responsible for the research that they do and that it is up to others to use this research. This claim most plausibly sits with those scientists who undertake research "for its own sake," not with those whose work is "applied." One of my aims here, however, is to determine the extent and limits of responsibility even for those basic or "pure" scientists whose scientific labor is performed "for its own sake." To this end, then, I will examine the relationship between pure and applied research and conclude that the nature of the work, its *content*, does not distinguish between the two. Rather, the work's *context*, determined by its aims, and so on, marks the difference. This determination is important, for if applied research has as its aim some application, but if its content is not intrinsically different from that of pure research, then the latter could also have some application as its end. Pure research is therefore not so simply divorced from applications and outcomes.

This becomes even clearer when "outcome" is understood to comprise something else, other than the impact of technology. Science taken as a *body of ideas* also affects us and the way we live. The Scientific Revolution of the seventeenth century, which inaugurated the scientific ethos, demolished the age-old worldview that the earth is the center of the universe. This worldview had been a cornerstone of Aristotle's physics and was incorporated into a technical astronomy by Ptolemy, but eventually the combined weight of theories and evidence, produced by a succession of great scientists from Copernicus to Newton, was enough to overthrow it. However, if the earth was no longer the center of the universe, then neither were we: the human race no longer dwelled at the very heart of God's creation, but on an outer branch of a small galaxy in the unimaginable immensity of space. The significance of this rude eviction for people who were accustomed to unquestioningly accepting the teaching of religious authorities is hard for us to imagine. While there is no strict or logical connection between the theories of Aristotle and Ptolemy and the religious and psychological constructions based on their ideas, those constructions were nevertheless a fact of life. Galileo, for one, was well aware of this. But if *in fact* the earth does indeed go around the sun, and not the other way around, then it might be supposed that there can be nothing wrong with saying so— that it is never wrong to discover the *truth*, whatever disruptions this causes to people's cherished beliefs. I will examine this seemingly obvious proposition later, but here I will simply reiterate the fact that science, as a medium of ideas and not just as the foundation of technology, affects our lives and that, moreover, discovering the truth is the avowed intention of the *pure* scientist.

Yet another way to discuss responsibility and the scientist—of secondary interest here, since it is not connected with outcomes—focuses on what we might call "responsible practice," or the proper way for a scientist to conduct himself in the course of scientific research undertaken *within* a particular institution or company.[3] In a university, for example, responsible practice might encompass honest reporting of experimental results; respect for colleagues; consideration of junior members of the department, including students; conformity to the particular goals of the university; and other such matters *internal* to the research community. Responsible practice then, more or less, has to do with *research ethics*. Whether scientists working in industry abide by such ethics is moot, as were the norms, identified by Robert K. Merton, for instance, that were supposed to identify the social structure of the scientific community (Merton 1973). The point here is that while internal questions about science and responsibility exist, these questions are distinct from external ones, and my interest is focused exclusively on these external questions: on the responsibility of the scientist for outcomes that reach beyond the scientific community. In other words, this book is not about research ethics.

What it is about are the circumstances under which a scientist is responsible for an outcome and how that should influence his work. Being a philosopher, and hence inevitably thinking and writing like one, I'm inclined to say that it is about the *conditions* under which a scientist is responsible for an outcome. As my interest is in outcomes, not just research, I want to try to give a unified account of the responsibilities of all scientists engaged in what has been called the "research system," the system that comprises all forms of scientific research. The present project is perhaps further complicated by the fact that there are two kinds of outcomes: those resulting from technology and those from science as ideas. It may be that these different outcomes give rise to different sorts of responsibility. I want to argue here, however, for a *wide* account of the responsibility of the scientist for outcomes. Take what might be thought of as an obvious or "standard" view of the matter: that scientists, like other persons, are responsible for what they intend to do.[4] In this view, if a scientist engaged in pure research intends only to write a scientific paper, then, no matter what eventually results, he is responsible only for publishing the paper. I reject this standard view. Suppose, for instance, that the scientist's paper provides the basis for weaponizing anthrax in a new and more potent form, because it describes a microbiological method for making spores smaller and more difficult to detect, even though the scientist does not intend his method to have any particular application.[5] When questioned, our scientist might respond that while he foresaw that his method could be used for weaponizing purposes, this was not his intent, so he is not responsible. Most of us (I hope) would see this response as weak and judge the scientist responsible on the grounds that he did indeed foresee how his work could potentially be used. I would like to widen the scope of responsibility still further to include both *foreseen* outcomes—those that the scientist has considered—and *foreseeable* ones—those that he should have considered.

In the above example, we can imagine the microbiologist so wrapped up in his work and so neglectful of world affairs that he simply did not consider the potential applications of his work. Do we still hold him responsible for the development of a more effective biological weapon? Compare this example with one suggested by Jonathan Bennett: A canoe has been booby-trapped by explosives strapped to the bottom. It is hired out and its occupants killed. The person who hired out the canoe could have easily learned it was booby-trapped simply by turning it over—he was evidently in a position to know about the explosives—

but did not do so (Bennett 1995, 48). One would not hold the canoe owner responsible for the deaths of the unfortunate occupants, *provided* that he had no reason to suspect that the canoe was booby-trapped. But if it was poorly maintained and sank for that reason, then one *would* hold him responsible. If, further, it had been damaged by the last people who used it, and the owner did not know, then one again might well hold him responsible. Thus, we *do* hold people responsible for things that they do not but could have known *if* those are the sorts of things that they *should have* taken care to know about.

A related question is whether any special demands are placed on scientists that require them to "look ahead" and see where their work might lead. This amounts to asking whether scientists have yet another kind of responsibility, one that looks ahead ("forward-looking" responsibility) rather than behind ("backward-looking" responsibility). Any person who hires anything out to the public, whether a canoe, a house, or a power tool, has this kind of responsibility: they must ensure that their property is in good condition and that it will not harm those who use it. Special responsibilities of this kind are also attached to some types of work, typically those of professionals—what is sometimes called *role-responsibility*. Doctors, lawyers, teachers, and engineers, for example, are expected to take care in certain situations where (and because) they have especial competence. Thus, when considering responsibility for outcomes, we need to ask whether the outcomes have taken place already or are anticipated in the future. When such a question is asked about science, and when the outcomes at issue have not yet eventuated, the suggestion is that there are certain things that scientists should and should not do. Professionals, such as doctors and lawyers, have codes of conduct that enjoin them to act in certain ways in relation to their clients. Similarly, engineers operate under some less specific demands, such as the expectation that they should only engage in "socially responsible" projects. But is there anything comparable for scientists? This question is of central concern.

Ethics and Responsibility

While there are a number of divisions within the field of ethics, not all of them strictly defined, it is the relationship between responsibility and *normative* ethics that is relevant here. For present purposes, normative ethics can be taken to mean the study of what constitutes morally right actions, decisions, and behavior—this statement must be qualified with "morally" because there are other ways to classify what we do as right. A moral code is therefore a set of moral standards, often referred to in the literature as *rules*, that codify what counts as right and wrong action, and one task of normative ethics is to generate and justify such codes. By "moral standard," I mean a statement that prescribes or proscribes certain actions, and so on, and as such, a set of moral standards indicates what should be done, not necessarily how people generally behave. A moral code stated within the (so-called) consequentialist framework will subordinate right and wrong actions to the states of affairs to which they give rise, in the sense that what counts as right action is a function of how it results in a better or worse state of affairs. The consequentialist thus focuses attention on good consequences rather than on the quality of the actions that are their causal antecedents. While I would prefer to remain neutral and not to opt for consequentialism or any rival, it is more convenient for the moment to talk about good and bad outcomes rather than the right and wrong actions that give rise to them. This does not entail a commitment to consequentialism, which I reject in favor of a straightforward moral system known as common morality (Gert 2004) (see chapter 8).

In their main uses, "responsibility" and its cognate terms take a direct object: for example, "P is responsible for X," where P is a person and X an outcome.[6] Using what is sometimes called the "accountability" view of responsibility, I am going to say that this means that P is open to praise or blame when he is responsible for X. Suppose, in the case under consideration, that X is judged to be a bad outcome and that thus, presumably, P is open to blame in regard to X. X is judged to be a bad outcome according to some (moral) standard, and therefore some standard must be available for this statement to be true or false. I assume, in other words, that if the state of affairs for which P is responsible is a bad one, then this implies that there are standards according to which it is bad (although I do not believe that these standards are grounded in any "objective" goodness or badness). In a world without standards, without ethics, there would be no responsibility.[7] All talk of responsibility therefore presupposes the existence of standards for the appraisal of actions and outcomes.

One useful way to understand a statement is to turn it into a question, which here gives us, "Is P responsible for X?" And to identify the *topic* of a question and so know how to answer it, it is helpful to inquire about the topic's *contrast class*. For example, in this case there might be several outcomes, and hence the question becomes whether P is responsible for X or for Y or perhaps Z. Or alternatively, the question might be whether P is *responsible* for X or if X was just the result of something that P happened to do. Again, someone can only be responsible for something if that something is good or bad—responsibility for things that are not important (or not important in the right way) is not an issue (see chapter 3). Thus, to address this topic, it is necessary to uncover the prevailing set of moral standards. Determining whether an outcome is good or bad may or may not be relatively easy to do. For instance, if there is general and well-founded agreement that X is bad, beyond all doubt— for instance, if X is a state of affairs in which innocent people are harmed with no compensating good, what I will call "gratuitous harm" —then judging X to be bad is uncontroversial. However, the status of X could be contested—as, for example, in recent debates over human cloning or stem-cell research using fetal tissue substrates.

Does this mean that the study of science and responsibility belongs to normative ethics, perhaps as the subbranch "science and ethics"? Along with the field of research ethics, mentioned earlier, there exists the field of bioethics, concerned with moral questions that arise in the life sciences. One might then identify the study of science and responsibility with what is left over—namely, with moral issues that arise without the (non–life sciences part of the) scientific community. However, this formulation is not quite correct either. To illustrate: if we suppose that X, Y, and Z are all bad outcomes, then asking which of them P is responsible for is not to ask whether they are morally significant (which is presupposed); it is simply to ask which of them P is responsible for. But the contrast class can also contain the subject of the question: is it *P*, as opposed to Q or R, who is responsible for X? In both cases, the question is whether P is responsible for X—whether, in other words, X *belongs* to P. This question has nothing to do with moral evaluation or judgment of X, though the *presupposition* is that X is morally significant.

According to the wide view of responsibility, X belongs to P rather than to Q or R (assuming these are exclusive alternatives) if it was P who brought X about—who did X—and if P intended, foresaw, or should have foreseen that his actions would lead to X. To see that it is P who satisfies this list of conditions is to see how things were at the time X came about: did P do the crucial piece of research that led to X? Did he realize where his work was going? Untangling these matters might not be straightforward: while, for example, it might be easy to see that P's research led to outcome X, there might be problems in deciding whether P could have foreseen X. In other instances, it might be clear that P did indeed intend to bring about X. For real-life examples, the kind of detailed historical work conducted by professional historians of science and technology would seemingly be relevant. To decide these matters, in other words, is not to do ethics, or at least it is not *just* to do ethics. Moreover, I wish to argue that the limits of responsible action are wider than the limits of intentional action (intentional in the sense of what the agent intends). This project, again, is not a matter of (just) doing normative ethics, of deciding on a suitable set of moral standards to govern the actions of scientists. It does, however, entail an account of how the things we bring about are related to the responsibility that we have for them, always with the assumption that we are moral agents.

It would thus be a mistake to view this project of giving an account of scientists' responsibility as reducing to the task of coming up with a moral code for science, a list of demands that scientists should fulfill. Until we know just what scientists can be blamed or praised for, we can't fix what science should or should not bring about, a concern that comes much closer to "applied ethics" (see part 3). Further, some specific areas in which scientists are charged with special responsibility must be pinpointed—such areas as research into making and improving weapons, things that I think they have a responsibility *not* to do. One might suppose that such responsibilities are responsibilities to *society* rather than (or superseding) responsibilities to individuals. This view would suggest that the issues are not (exclusively) about scientists as moral agents, which would *distance* the present project from applied ethics. I do not agree with this viewpoint, however. Rather, in discussing where the responsibilities of scientists lie, I believe it is possible to begin to see what these responsibilities might actually be.

Varieties of Responsibility

First of all, scientists have a *social* responsibility. Since World War 2, there have been calls for scientists to be socially responsible—to be aware that their work may carry consequences beyond the boundaries of their institution or community and then to act accordingly. Suppose we substitute, for the nebulous idea of society, those *individuals* who make up society—people—and refer the responsibility of the scientist to them. Then we have another kind of responsibility, the one implicit in the previous section—namely *moral* responsibility, in particular the responsibility of one person to another.[8] Calls for scientists to be morally responsible sound different, and more weighty, than calls for them to be socially responsible. However, it is clear that both enjoin the scientist to realize that his work can have consequences for others.[9] And again, it would appear that some minimum condition for morally responsible research is that no one is worse off as a result of the work in question without compensating greater benefit—this is the prohibition on gratuitous harm. If, on the contrary, someone is worse off as a consequence of a research program, then it would seem that the scientist is obliged to "respond" to that person, to explain his actions. Even this brief sketch of social and moral responsibility shows that the latter can be engaged with more directly. Indeed, it is difficult to see how someone could act in a socially responsible way without thereby being morally responsible. In terms of the minimum condition here, it is difficult to see how someone could refrain from harming society without, on balance, refraining from harming its individual members.[10] This reflects a *reductive* view of social responsibility, in which societal welfare is an aggregate of individual welfare. There are, therefore, grounds on which to suppose that if the conditions under which a scientist is morally responsible for his research were fixed, and if his moral responsibilities were clear, then considerable progress would thereby have also been made toward providing an account of science and social responsibility.

A third kind of responsibility—*legal* responsibility, or legal liability—makes citizens subject to the law of the land, which *prohibits* them from doing certain things—the law only very occasionally imposes positive duties.[11] Breaking the law—engaging in those proscribed practices—implies that the offender is liable to punishment or penalty. Further, legal responsibility, like social and moral responsibility, has a "forward-looking" aspect. For example, a landlord's legal responsibility to maintain his property to a satisfactory standard entails certain behaviors: the landlord is responsible for certain future actions to ensure that his property satisfies reasonable safety standards.

The prevention of harm is therefore of overriding importance when discussing legal responsibility: the underlying rationale of legally imposed negative duties is to prevent harm. It is tempting to infer a further similarity between social and moral responsibility, on the one hand, and legal responsibility, on the other: that if someone is legally liable for some offense, he must therefore also be morally responsible.

But take our landlord: suppose that he is not aware that there is some fault with his property and that, as a consequence, one of his tenants sustains an injury. Under the law, he may be liable on grounds of negligence, but not everyone would endorse the view that if the agent does not foresee, and thus does not intend, a certain outcome, he is morally responsible for it.

It cannot be assumed at the outset that an account of the scientist's moral responsibility would also cover his legal responsibility, but interesting questions certainly arise here. Science and the law are important societal institutions, and, as might be expected, grave matters crop up at their intersection. Forensic science, for example, has revolutionized crime detection. Further, recent scientific advances, especially in the biosciences—such as the possibility of human cloning—demand revisions of existing legislation. Suppose that a biologist is engaged in research that he sees could lead to faster and more accurate DNA fingerprinting, but he fails to tell anyone, publishes his research in an obscure journal, gets his grant and promotion, and rests content with life. Later it turns out that a gang of violent criminals would have been caught much earlier, before harming many innocent victims, had the new fingerprinting technique been available. Whatever is made of the scientist's responsibility here, it is clearly *not* a question of legal responsibility. Citizens may be required to report accidents, help the injured, and so forth, but their positive duties do not extend to actually developing new crime-fighting techniques. However, the scientist's *moral* responsibility might certainly be investigated. Perhaps this investigation can be conducted in terms of the minimum condition—the responsibility not to do harm— even though it appears as if the new fingerprinting technique would have prevented harm, seemingly more a positive than a negative duty.

Philosophy and Moral Responsibility

Philosophers have long been interested in moral responsibility.[12] Many accept that Aristotle wrote about the topic in the fourth century B.C.E., in the *Nicomachean Ethics*, so it is indeed a venerable philosophical issue.[13] Of course, not all aspects of the topic that are of interest to philosophers are relevant here. For example, the long-standing debate about determinism's compatibility with free will has implications for questions about responsibility, in that it would seem that one can only be responsible for something if one freely chose to do it. Compatibilitists, however, believe that free will—and thus responsibility—is in fact compatible with determinism. It would, of course, be pointless to undertake an examination of the moral responsibility of a particular group of people, like scientists, and then conclude with an endorsement of determinism and a declaration that responsibility is *incompatible* with determinism. No one in this case, not scientists or anyone else, would be responsible for anything. Is it necessary therefore to review all the current arguments against determinism or in favor of compatibilism before we can start thinking about science and responsibility? No: it can simply be assumed that, on the whole, agents are responsible for what they do; if this is not the case, then the whole range of our moral, social, and legal practices are a sham. Having made this assumption, however, I will briefly mention some current work on this "metaphysical" side of responsibility to demonstrate what assumptions are made here about the kinds of constraints that do and do not apply to scientists as agents.

The origin of much recent work on responsibility is a series of articles by Harry Frankfurt that argue that it is possible for an agent to be responsible for something even if he could not have acted otherwise. Suppose A decides to shoot B and goes ahead with his intention. However, C has planted a device in A's brain such that, had he decided at any stage not to shoot B, this device would have overridden his own volition and made him carry out his original intention. If we believe that an agent can only be responsible for an outcome if he could have acted otherwise—if there existed at least one "alternative possibility"—then this challenges us to think again. Such examples have at least certainly challenged many philosophers to think again and led to a considerable literature. One might dismiss these examples as silly and artificial, but that is to miss the point: they issue a challenge to long-standing assumptions about what must be the case in attributions of responsibility. John Martin Fischer and Mark Ravizza, who have devoted much time to responding to Frankfurt, acknowledge the force of such examples, discuss their implications for compatibilism, and conclude that agents can only be responsible for outcomes if they have "guidance control."[14]

When an agent lacks guidance control, according to Fischer and Ravizza, then he is excused from responsibility for the outcome at issue. Guidance control, in their account, describes what they call "freedom relevant or control" conditions for responsibility. The other kind of excusing condition Fischer and Ravizza discuss is termed "epistemic." They see both of these kinds of conditions as deriving from Aristotle, in the *Nicomachean Ethics*. To clarify, suppose an agent does something that leads to an outcome that, in my terminology, he did not, could not, and should not have known about; that is, he had no special responsibility to try to anticipate this particular outcome. In this case, it can be agreed that the agent bears no responsibility. By contrast, suppose the agent was well aware of what he was doing, and of what would result, but was under duress. In this case, he may also be excused, even though he knew exactly what he was doing. In the former scenario, there is an "epistemic excuse," while in the latter there is a failure of control. Looking at the matter from the "negative" perspective, then, seems useful to determine what needs to be true for there actually to be responsibility on the part of an agent for an outcome: if there are two types of excusing conditions for responsibility, then to give an account of responsibility is to determine when there are *no* excuses. My concern here is in particular with the responsibility of scientists for what they do and what outcomes follow from their research. It seems most unlikely that any of Fischer and Ravizza's control conditions are going to be relevant here because certain scientists fail to be in control of their actions along any "affective, volitional or executive" dimension, although one perhaps thinks here of Soviet or Iraqi scientists being forced to work for the state. Epistemic conditions, on the other hand, do seem to be pertinent.

Relevant here are issues to do with what scientists know in *two* respects. In the first place, the whole topic of science and responsibility revolves around the fact that it is what scientists *discover*, what they come to know, that affects others most dramatically. When Fischer and Ravizza discuss "epistemic conditions" for responsibility, this is *not* what they have in mind; rather, the central concern of such conditions is what the agent knows in relation to his actions and the outcomes following from them. In regard to science, then, the central concern is what scientists can and should know about what they discover in the course of their research. Knowledge and knowing are therefore, as it were, doubly important. This is of special interest here, because discovering new things by means of research is precisely what scientists do: it is their job, their work, what distinguishes them from others. The present investigation, then, takes as its point of departure the assumption that scientists are agents who, on the whole, satisfy the control conditions for moral responsibility.

Part 1

OUTCOMES AND RESPONSIBILITY

Outcomes of Scientific Research

IKE MANY OTHER PHILOSOPHERS, I BELIEVE THAT IT IS important to be quite clear on how a question is to be interpreted, or "read," before any attempt is made to answer it. It is necessary to understand how pure science can lead to applications, and to other outcomes, if we are to address questions about responsibility in connection with pure science. So the vital clarification here concerns the role of pure scientific research—that is, research less directly concerned with outcomes than applied research is. Pure research is related to outcomes via applied research, so if we are able to determine how the former leads to outcomes, we will also understand how the latter does so.

Two kinds of outcomes will be considered in this chapter: those that have to do with *technology*, such as products and processes—the central concern of this book—and those forthcoming from science considered as a body of *ideas*. Put simply and crudely, science can affect both our material welfare and how we think about things, and therefore science is responsible for both sorts of outcome. However, it is not the case that "technological outcomes" are solely the province of applied research, while pure research exclusively gives rise to outcomes from science as a body of ideas. To clarify the relations among the two kinds of outcomes and the two kinds of research, it is necessary in the first place to carefully draw the distinction between pure and applied research and then to see how research leads to outcomes.

Outcomes

Suppose the work of a particular scientist leads to some outcome. While this seems to be the normal course of events, one might still ask whether that scientist is responsible for that outcome. More information, however, is necessary if this question is to be answered or even taken seriously. At the least, we need to know what the outcome is and how it is related to the scientist's work—to say that his work "led" to the outcome is not precise enough. If a scientist, for example, does his research at a university, then there is a good chance that it is undertaken without any particular application in mind beyond publication, which makes his results known to the scientific community for further discussion.[1] He might also see publication as a step toward a grant or promotion. The proximate result of pure scientific research is thus the scholarly scientific paper, which I will call the intended or "proper" product of such research. With respect to this aspect of science, the question posed above is not hard to answer: the fact that a scientist is named as an author of a paper should suffice to establish his responsibility for publication.

But other kinds of outcomes stem from pure research as well. Science has widespread application as a basis for technology, and technology in turn can have equally broad effects. If a scientist is an *applied* scientist who consciously seeks to design or develop some product, then again it initially appears obvious that he is responsible for that outcome if he did some of the work leading up to it. But there is a complicating factor: unlike scientific papers, technologies, products, and so on cannot be brought into the world by one person, at least not anymore. So while the single-author paper still exists, the "single-author technology" does not. Further, all different "kinds" of people, so to speak, are responsible for such outcomes: scientists, engineers, entrepreneurs, industrialists, even the military and politicians. If a scientist is an employee of a corporation, for instance, it might even be said that he has *no* responsibility for the outcome under consideration; he just sells his labor to others, who use it for their own ends.[2] Thus, answering the question now becomes much less straightforward than in the earlier case.

If these two cases are "combined," the following situation results: The scientist is aiming to publish a paper, the "proper" product of his pure research project. He does so, and the publication makes a contribution to some technology or some product thereof. In other words, "outcome" is here understood in accordance with the second case, but the scientist remains in the context of pure research, as in the first case. Now, it is possible that the scientist realizes that his work might well have such an external outcome—he might, for instance, have accepted a grant from a company in exchange for agreeing to provide it with his results before publication—although that is not his specific goal. Alternatively, the application might be unexpected—a possibility that is not uncommon, as pure research often becomes applied over time. This third case, then, raises new considerations, over and above those that must be taken into account for the other two. For example, can someone be responsible for an outcome that was not his aim? And what about an outcome that he did not have in mind or imagine might be possible?

To answer such questions, a sensible first step would be to gather some information about the research *group* to which our scientist belongs. Not all scientists work in groups, but most do, and thus most research is a cooperative effort. This is important from the present standpoint if there is something distinctive about group or *collective* responsibility. Suppose several individuals are needed to produce a given outcome. Does their collective activity add anything over and above each person's effort, as regards their responsibility for the outcome? Two views exist on this question: one holds that collective responsibility merely reduces to individual responsibility, and one holds that it does not. Those who maintain the latter position normally distinguish among different kinds of groups and attribute a special kind of collective responsibility to those with sufficient organization, such as corporations. Here the issue becomes whether any such thing as genuine collective responsibility exists, and, if so, whether research groups display sufficient organization to be charged with it. Of the scenarios just considered, the first and the third have the same institutional setting, or so I will assume—namely, the university or research institute. The second case, by contrast, is set in some industrial system, in some company or corporation that, I will assume, has its own research facility. How different, then, are these settings?

The Research System

Ascertaining the characteristics of these settings is key, because if they are radically different, then they may give rise to two altogether unconnected notions of scientific responsibility: that of the academic scientist on the one hand, and that of the industrial scientist on the other. But pure and applied research are allied activities. Taken together, they constitute the scientific research system, or what J-J. Salomon simply calls the "research system." I will argue that what distinguishes pure and applied research is not in fact the "content" of the work: the work of pure scientists is not of a different kind compared to the work of applied scientists. What then does distinguish pure from applied research, given that they are indeed different? I do not think it is possible to draw this distinction by means of philosophical analysis; rather, such fields as science policy studies and the sociology of science are most germane here.[3]

I want to return to the idea that the proper product of pure scientific research is the scientific paper, particularly the question of why scientists publish papers.[4] Publication might be a kind of end in itself, or it could have some further purpose. Scientists could simply be interested in making and communicating discoveries, which seems a more noble goal than getting promotions, swinging grants, and building a research empire. But browsing the specialist journals to see what has been discovered lately, I believe, would typically leave the questioner profoundly unexcited, unconvinced that science has much of interest to communicate, especially if one looks through journals in the physical sciences. Scientific papers on the whole record minute details of systems created in the laboratory, often the values of variables. Such values can provide the key to startling applications (see chapter 2), but surely they hold little interest in and of themselves. How, then, might the sociology of science help elucidate the purpose of publication?

Several different approaches exist in this field, some of which go beyond the traditional division of labor that would see the sociologist's task as discovering the nature of the scientist's activities and the structure of the scientific community and explaining away mistaken beliefs. Some sociologists, including Bruno Latour, have addressed issues that were earlier the exclusive province of philosophers, provoking sharp territorial reactions in some quarters. Philosophers' objections aside, Latour's view of what pure researchers do and why they do it is relevant. Specifically, what Latour discovered during his famous sojourn at the Salk Institute is, simply, that scientists publish papers: "The production of papers is acknowledged by participants as the main objective of their activity" (Latour and Woolgar 1979, 71). Much other evidence exists in favor of this claim, which is undisputed in the sociology of science. When Latour remarks that scientists take publication to be their main objective, he could mean that it is an end in itself, or that it is a common aim of all scientists, or that it is something that they must do if they are to do anything else. On any of these understandings, publishing papers is at least a candidate for the *criterion* necessary for distinguishing pure scientists in terms of what they do, even if Latour's claim is not anything like a definition of science.[5]

It is not, however, true that applied scientists never publish anything, so the criterion must be articulated a little further. It might then be suggested that what differentiates the products of applied research is that they are not the intellectual *property* of their authors, as are the products of pure research, and, further, that they are intellectual *capital* and, as such, that access to them is restricted. On the other hand, the products of pure research are freely available: anyone can buy a journal, access Web sites, and so on. The results of applied research, by contrast, are normally restricted and held in-house. While this may be the case on the whole, however, applied research or technical journals do exist, as do some examples of applied research results being made available immediately and for free. For instance, a U.S. biotechnology company sequenced the rice genome in 2001 and declared that it would make available any useful genetically modified variety free to Third World countries (one hopes for more success here than was achieved by the Green Revolution). While the original "wild-type" sequencing work seems to be typically pure research, the modified version is typically applied.

That pure scientists normally publish papers and applied scientists normally do not is thus not a sufficient distinguishing criterion. So it is appropriate to turn to another field: science policy studies. Science policy studies are focused on government and industry plans for science, including governmental funding. One issue here concerns the appropriate mix of pure and applied research for fulfilling national objectives: as taxpayers' money is being used to support science, it is only fair that taxpayers eventually benefit from the research. It appears, then, that applied research should get the lion's share of available funds, but strong arguments have also been made in favor of significant funding for pure research (see Bush 1945 for a classic statement). To carry on this debate and to implement policies, the two kinds of research must first be distinguished. This is done not with direct reference to the product of the

research, but with reference to its purpose or aim. Thus, applied research, in the field of science policy studies, is research that aims at some.
application, while pure research is done *for its own sake* (ASTEC 1981, 3).
The question now becomes not what counts as a scientific paper, but
what counts as an application.

Applied science is *practical;* it often enables us to do things that we
could not do otherwise. Applied research is therefore also connected to
technology: in fact, applied research often gives rise to technology. To
say that pure science is done "for its own sake" is to draw a contrast with
this practical side of science. What is "applied" in applied research is
"science itself," its theories and methods. Pure research, on the other
hand—science done for its own sake—can also come to have applications later on. So again, there are not two distinct sorts of things, both
called science; rather, there are two kinds of scientific projects, one that
aims ultimately beyond science itself, to practical matters, and another
that does not. If the "context" of a scientific research project is understood as what gives rise to or defines its aims, then in this sense, context
will determine whether research is pure or applied. More could be said
about the research system itself, from the perspectives of science policy,
sociology of science, and other views, that could lead to an even greater
understanding of the system's elements and how these condition the
nature of research projects. Interesting though that might be, what is
essential here is to recognize that different types of research projects represent different kinds of aims.

The Realist View of Pure and Applied Research

Suppose that the specific aim of an applied research project is to
come up with a blueprint or design for a product or process. The project
may have several stages, with various tasks and problems to be solved.
When the design is achieved, in other words, the project moves on to
the development of a prototype, testing, and so on. The design, then,
eventually achieves some output or realizes some function—namely,
what the product or process is supposed to accomplish. How is this possible? How is it possible, to take a simple example, to design a working
clock or watch or chronometer? Is successful design the result of good
luck or trial and error? Clearly not, at least in the case of sophisticated
electronic or atomic clocks. A clock requires a reliable periodic system,
such as a pendulum driven by gravity or a spring, or a vibrating crystal,

or a radioactive element that decays at a constant rate. Clocks are possible because such systems exist, because we know about such systems, and because we are able to incorporate them into artifacts via design. But periodic systems are also studied "for their own sake." Radioactive decay, for instance, discovered at the beginning of the twentieth century, was investigated by Pierre and Marie Curie and by many others. But the radium studied by the Curies and the radium incorporated into an atomic clock are one and the same element, and the clock works as a consequence of the same "natural" properties of the element that the Curies investigated.

A design, then, makes use of the properties of natural things and the principles that describe these properties, which are the self-same things that are studied "for their own sake" in pure science. This is, in broad outline, the realist interpretation of science and technology.[6] This view, in the first place, explains the relationship between science and technology—how it is that science underpins technology. It also addresses the problem of the relevance of pure research to practical matters, because it holds that both pure and applied research make use of the same theories, ideas, and results. Thus, the maker of a grandfather clock uses the relation between the length and the period of the pendulum to design the mechanism—the clockwork—to fix how far the hands must move for each swing back and forth; it is the exact same relation studied, in another time, by Galileo. This, of course, is not a startling or radical conclusion: most will readily agree that science can be applied because artifacts, while not naturally occurring, are natural objects. As such, they conform to our theories: indeed, they must, because they are designed in light of these theories. It is possible, then, to conclude that there is no intrinsic difference between pure and applied research, in that the "content" of pure research is not different in nature or character from the "content" of applied research. While this conclusion clearly requires qualification, the view of science on which it rests might also be questioned: Is the realist account of science well supported? What are the alternatives?

The realist view of the relationship between science and technology is an extension of the realist account of science itself—of how science informs technology. Realism, of one stripe or another, has become the prevailing view in the philosophy of science, but this predominance in itself does not guarantee that it yields a good explanation of the relationship between science and technology. The core of all realist accounts of science, in other words, is still a realist *interpretation*, according to which scientific theories are literal statements about the natural world, in that their kind, property, and relation terms refer to corresponding items in the world and are true or false depending on what the world is like.[7] Realists, then, appeal to this interpretation to account for such things as experimental practice, explanatory and predictive roles, and the success of science.

Realism is compatible with several different scientific methodologies, but all acceptable methodologies must purport that theories are tested, or "applied" in some way, by means of experiment—experiment providing the means for scientists to confirm what theory says about the world. The fact that science is successful in this regard, with most predictions emerging in favor of the theory being tested, has a straightforward realist explanation: theories make predictions that are borne out in practice because theories describe the world, more or less accurately, and because experiment increases the store of information about the world, more or less reliably. This formulation is the so-called Ultimate Argument for realism.[8] This argument, first put forward in the early 1960s, was influential in eroding the (logical) empiricist view of science that held sway at the time. Part and parcel of the empiricist position was *instrumentalism*, according to which the characteristic terms of scientific theories do not refer literally to kind, properties, and relations but are shorthand for directly observable effects.

So, for instance, while realism takes "radium," "alpha particle," "gravity," and so on to refer to real things, instrumentalism denies the existence of such microscopic particles and forces. The instrumentalist understands "radium" as shorthand for talking about certain observable effects, such as those resulting when one uses particle counters and fluorescent screens in conjunction with radioactive substances. Theories in this view are "instruments" for making predictions, couched in the language of observation, and they are successful because they comprise descriptions of such observations. Both realists and instrumentalists would therefore predict that a Geiger counter will register if placed near a sample of radium, but only the realist could explain why it registers. The instrumentalist would instead perceive the "radium" as simply a compendium of observable effects, including effects on particle counters, so all the "explanans" could do is restate the explanandum. While the realist would appeal to the fact that radium emits charged particles that stimulate the counter to register, the instrumentalist can only observe that science succeeds when it employs good instruments but cannot explain why certain instruments are good.

The Ultimate Argument for realism (and the shortcomings of instrumentalism in this regard) is more pertinent here than any of the other arguments in favor of realism because it has an obvious extension to technology. Technology is successful, in the realist view, because the practical purposes for which it was devised are, on the whole, fulfilled—because it makes use of what we know about the world. Pendulums are reliable periodic systems because they are acted on by a constant gravitational force; radium can be used in an atomic clock because it emits alpha particles at a constant rate. The instrumentalist explanation of the success of technology, in contrast, is as unsatisfactory as the instrumentalist explanation of the success of science. "Radium" here is nothing but a shorthand description of observable effects, including the Geiger counter's clicking at a constant rate, which means that the instrumentalist has no basis on which to explain the constancy of this observable effect and hence why radium can be used in an atomic clock.[9]

Returning to my assertion that there is no intrinsic difference between pure and applied research, I do not mean that a particular piece of work could *always* appear either as a paper in a journal or as a classified technical report. For instance, suppose that a problem has already been solved for a given set of parameters (initial and boundary conditions), and the results published in a journal, but that another solution, for another set of parameters, is needed for an application, perhaps for "scaling up" an effect. An editor might tell the author submitting a paper addressing this application that it does not add to the scholarly literature on the subject, but not publishing the work on which some applied research is based would be only a contingent fact about the history of science.

There are also several examples of scientific research that was first done in an industrial setting but whose results clearly could have been, and in some instances eventually were, published in learned journals. One of the best-known examples is the discovery and subsequent use of the transistor by William Shockley and his coworkers in the Bell Laboratories in the 1950s. This discovery had an almost immediate application, but at the same time, it was important in the field of material science. Even better known are a series of discoveries associated with the making of the atomic bomb, in particular Enrico Fermi's realization of a self-sustaining nuclear chain reaction in 1942. This was simultaneously the first step in the manufacture of plutonium, the initiation of nuclear power, *and* confirmation of important theoretical work in nuclear physics. At another time, Fermi's work would have first been published in scholarly journals.[10] To clarify, the work of Shockley, Fermi, and others is classified as applied research because of the institutional setting or *context* in which it was done, not because of its "intrinsic" character. This context dictated that the research's aim was practical, that it was intended for some purpose beyond publication in a learned journal. It should be acknowledged here that some industrial research is classified as "basic" or "pure"—again, Shockley is an example—although recently the labels "strategic basic research" and "generic research" have become fashionable. Such research has no specific end in view and so differs from applied research, but it is conducted in areas that look promising from the point of view of future application and so differs from pure research in that its funding rationale is application.[11]

On the other hand, a paper on quantum cosmology written by Stephen Hawking would most likely not ever be reproduced in an industrial setting. Aside from this particular author's individual brilliance (and hence the unlikelihood of finding others like him), quantum cosmology is not a field that is likely to yield immediate (or any) applications.[12] So, just as some technical reports would not be suitable for publication in academic journals, some pure research would not be forthcoming from industrial laboratories. Indeed, highly theoretical research—such as quantum cosmology, the foundations of quantum and relativity theory, and so on—is not likely to be sponsored by those interested in applications. Nevertheless, such research *can* have application, as was famously demonstrated in the Manhattan Project, when Einstein's formula $E = mc^2$ was used to estimate the explosive power of a nuclear bomb and explain the source of its energy. This formula amounted to a prediction of the special theory of relativity in that it was a consequence of Einstein's use of Lorentz invariance. Einstein thought of this formula as a peculiarity and did not expect that it would ever be realized or even confirmed. Thus, although highly theoretical research is sometimes applied, this application is usually unanticipated or inadvertent and hence not something that can be planned.

If highly theoretical research does not typically lead to outcomes, or only does so well after publication—the Einstein formula was only confirmed some thirty-five years after special relativity was discovered—or only has applications that cannot be anticipated, then the issue of responsibility for outcomes would not appear to be a live one. It is worth asking here how common such research is, for if it is widespread, then pure research will not be of great relevance when it comes to outcomes, and hence the issue of responsibility for such outcomes will not really arise. In fact, however, highly theoretical research is not at all common, especially when considering the huge amount of scientific research undertaken worldwide. In Kuhnian language, most scientific research is puzzle-solving, work within a paradigm, whereas highly theoretical research would instead be directed toward formulating new paradigms, working on foundational problems within paradigms, addressing incompatibilities between paradigms, and so forth. Not many scientists are so engaged. Therefore, the question of the responsibility of pure researchers for outcomes is of more than merely marginal interest.

It will be necessary to return to the distinction between pure and applied research. But if the realist account of the relationship between science and technology is accurate, then we can at least generally see how pure science leads to outcomes—namely, it does so in the *same way* as does applied research. The difference, again, lies not in the research's intrinsic character but in its institutional setting, or whatever else determines a project's aims. Thus, if scientists working in industry, for the government, or for some other organization that aims to produce outcomes have different responsibilities than do pure scientists who work in universities or research institutes, then such differences will be a function and consequence of the institutional settings, not of the research's intrinsic character.

Pure Science as "Ideas"

I remarked earlier that the proper products of scientific research can often seem dull and uninteresting to the wider public. In the past, however, some scientific works—indeed, works full of numbers and calculations—were of profound interest and importance, and their influence has been felt far and wide: Copernicus's *De Revolutionibus Orbium Caelestum*, Kepler's *Astronomia Nova*, Galileo's *Dialogue on Two New Sciences* (Galileo published in the vernacular), and Newton's *Principia Mathematica Philosophia Naturalis* are examples from the Scientific Revolution. These books provided convincing evidence against the Greek worldview, which placed the earth at the center of the universe, and their authors, although devout Christians, thus seemed to challenge the authority of both the Bible and the Church.[13] It is clear that science as knowledge—as a body of ideas—has had a huge impact on our understanding of the world and our place in it. And of course, when we move beyond the Scientific Revolution to the late eighteenth and nineteenth centuries, we find geologists demonstrating that the earth is much older than previously believed, and Darwin bringing us to think of ourselves as having evolved naturally from animals, rather as than special divine creations.

What science does as a body of ideas is therefore perhaps of even greater significance than what it does as the foundation of technology—assuming that the comparison can be made in a meaningful way. If so, the notion of "outcome" must be broadened to include such things. Further, this broadening might serve to distinguish pure from applied science in a way not apparent when attention is directed exclusively toward technology; it may indeed reveal some "autonomous role" for the pure scientist with respect to outcomes. This impression is reinforced by the fact that it is not so much the process and reasoning that lead to such important discoveries but the discoveries themselves, detached from such details and expressed in simple terms, that have the greatest impact. Copernicus, for example, constructed a system of epicycles in which the earth moves around the sun (although the latter was not itself at rest) that was able to save the "quantitative phenomena," but it was the conclusion of his work, the heliocentric hypothesis, that carried the greatest force. Similarly, while Kepler's works are highly technical, the inclusion of three simple expressions that describe the motion of the planets widened its impact. What is important about pure science as a body of ideas therefore seems to differ from what is important about science as a basis for technology. Thus, beyond broadening the concept of outcome, taking account of science as a body of ideas might also lead to a reconsideration of the decision to assimilate the relation between pure scientific research and outcomes to that between applied research and outcomes.

However, while it would be a mistake to underestimate the importance of the work of such scientists as Copernicus, Galileo, and Darwin—to deny that responsibility for science as a body of ideas is as important as responsibility for science as the foundation for technology—the claims made in the previous paragraph overstate the case for the "autonomy" of pure research with respect to outcomes. First of all, does this aspect of pure science really distinguish it from applied science? Notice here that it is perfectly *possible* for an applied research project to produce novel and important ideas. It is also suggested above that the *conclusion* of research has the greatest impact here—that the earth goes around the sun, that the earth is many millions of years old, that we are descended from animals—rather than the painstaking reasoning supporting such propositions. But the same is of course true of the products of science-based technology: we simply want to use these products, not to understand the designs on which they are based or the physical principles in virtue of which they work. While some people might want to understand how, say, a computer works, or even build one, such knowledge is clearly not necessary to use a computer, nor is it the manufacturer's aim. Thus, the products of science-based technology and propositions rooted in science as a body of ideas are alike in that both are *outcomes* of science and can be used or grasped without understanding the underlying theory. By so broadening the concept of an outcome, certain conclusions or "propositions" are acknowledged as analogous to the products of technology in that both kinds of outcome stand in a *similar* relation to pure science.

The issue of the *relative* importance of the two kinds of outcomes becomes relevant here, but I believe in fact that science as a body of ideas is at the present time relatively *unimportant*, at least as regards the physical sciences, compared to science as the foundation for technology. One explanation for this situation is hinted at above—namely, that pure research in the physical sciences is aimed at uncovering minutiae; the paradigms under which it is conducted are themselves technical and as such difficult to understand. But Copernicus's epicycles were also hard to understand, so this cannot be the whole story. However, when propositions from modern physical science are "detached"—counterparts to "the earth goes round the sun"—the resulting statements are more likely to confound than to illuminate. For instance, it is said that quantum mechanics implies, among other things, that the world is "indefinite" until experienced by an "observer"; that while there is no action at a distance, there is "passion at a distance"; and that there exist two radically different equations of motion for measurement and non-measurement processes. Difficult books have been written on these matters, and popularizers of science have struggled to explain them, but their very reconditeness ensures that they will not have much of an impact outside the community of specialists.[14]

If this judgment about the physical sciences is accurate—and more would need to be said to back it up properly—the situation seems rather different in the biomedical sciences. Since the discovery of the structure of DNA, steady progress has been made toward uncovering the human genome, which is now essentially complete. This project seems to be a good example of strategic basic research, in that the rationale for all the resources that have been invested in it is the promise of future applications, although their precise form is not yet known. Advances are nonetheless anticipated in such areas as understanding the genetic basis of more diseases. Concurrently, however, these developments as a body of ideas could also have societal implications. The category of outcomes that was earlier characterized as significant propositions implied by science as a body of ideas is therefore not after all an empty one, and so it seems that it must not be overlooked. On the other hand, some argue that these outcomes can indeed be set aside when it comes to questions about the *responsibility* of the scientist. While this argument cannot be adequately supported, it is still worth considering, since it allows us to probe yet another perspective on the topic of scientists' responsibility for outcomes—the idea that science is a "mixed blessing."

Mixed Blessing?

The argument for science as a "mixed blessing" runs as follows: Science, as pure research, aims to discover the truth about the world, whether in cosmology, quantum physics, or genetics. Discovering the truth is *always* a good thing. Therefore, if we are asking questions about scientists' responsibility for outcomes because we are concerned about these outcomes—their potential to be used for harm, and so on—then *this* category of outcomes should not lead to concern, as it contains only true propositions. Three premises are assumed here. As to the first, since I accept the realist account of science, I am content with this description of the aim of pure research. The other two premises, however, are open to objection, especially the second, which holds that discovering the truth is always a good thing. The third premise is that we need only concern ourselves with the topic of the scientist's responsibility if we are worried about what scientists do.

It might be readily agreed that discovering or stating the truth, or trying to do so, is positive, if the alternative is fabrication or falsification *and* if our attention is restricted to the community of pure researchers. That is to say, it is surely better to publish findings that are correct rather than incorrect, for several reasons. Accurate findings are more probably based on careful and diligent experimentation, as opposed to careless and sloppy work, and the former have been recognized as virtues since at least the seventeenth century.[15] Moreover, correct findings provide a reliable basis for others who wish to build on original research, while incorrect findings mislead others and waste time. Finally, accurate research is independently verifiable by others, which safeguards the reputations of those doing the original work. So, when it is asserted that publishing the truth is always a good thing, and that no harm can come from it, one or more of these (or similar) reasons are, I believe, at base. But what is unwarranted is the claim that publishing the truth always secures good outcomes: this is most certainly false.[16] Even if the horrid experiments performed on human subjects during World War 2, at Auschwitz and Ping Fang, had been impeccably conducted, this would have weighed nothing in balance against the harm that was done to unwilling and innocent people.

It is not enough to reply that it is not the discovery of results but their publication that is wrong here. In order to produce results, it is necessary to embark on a specific research program, so the *intention* to discover certain things is in place at the start. It is not fanciful to suppose that in such a research environment, all such projects would be centrally approved and monitored. In any case, the idea that discovery is good in and of itself, independent of anything else—even publication—is at best a pun and at worst senseless. "Good," as I understand the word, refers to a state of affairs in which moral subjects are on the whole happy, have their interests looked after, and so on. "Good," then, is in this sense an evaluation of a state of affairs with reference to moral subjects and how things go for them. There can thus be no "good" that is abstracted from issues that affect moral subjects. The truth of this proposition, I think, explains the disgust we feel when we read about present-day experiments that cause pain and suffering, such as the animal experiments documented by Peter Singer (1993, 65–68). The only conceivable way that such experiments can be justified is if they produce some greater good for people or for other animals—good that outweighs the pain they cause. The suggestion that it is good in and of itself to discover, say, the circumstances that will bring an ape to kill its offspring is grotesque.[17]

Propositions derived from science as a body of ideas can be conceived of as a "mixed blessing" in two ways. First, different groups of people with different cultures, backgrounds, and traditions can have their most cherished beliefs confirmed or challenged by science—witness, for example, the implications of Darwinism for creationists and deists. Second, scientific propositions can give rise to different social and political policies and measures, such as eugenics and genetic counseling. It is this second sense that, I think, is more troublesome with regard to the scientist's responsibilities. If creationists are deluded, then it may be better to let them remain so, but not at the price of depriving others of the truth. But if scientific findings are going to support repressive policies, then the scientist is faced with a choice between suppressing what he believes to be true and contributing to the persecution of a minority. This representation of science as a mixed blessing becomes even more obvious in relation to the first category of outcomes, those of science-based technology.

Examples of such technology that can be considered "good things" are plentiful—for instance, our understanding of infectious diseases and the therapies and practices based on that understanding. Thus, Robert Koch's discovery of the bacterium responsible for tuberculosis was a great boon, as it led to health-care measures and eventually to drugs to fight the disease. On the other hand, some technological outcomes amount to methods for destroying life, not saving it, above all weapons of mass destruction, such as atomic and thermonuclear bombs. I classify these outcomes as "bad" and believe that we would be better off without them. However, the claim that science is a mixed blessing because it leads to both good and bad outcomes should not be understood to imply that some outcomes are *undisputedly* good and others are *undisputedly* bad. This would presuppose that we are in possession of a perfect value system that enables us to unerringly make such judgments. In practice, competing systems of values are informed by different ideas about what is right, and these can be expected to lead to conflicting judgments about which outcomes are good and which are bad.

If science were an unalloyed good, then discerning the nature of the scientist's responsibility would be relatively straightforward, and the scientist could simply press on with his work. Policy issues would remain, but these would be of technical interest only. Conversely, if science were thoroughly bad, the issue would be similarly clear: the scientist should stop work. However, the position contrary to both scenarios, that science is a mixed blessing, implies that scientists must acknowledge the issue of responsibility, and this is no longer straightforward.

Earlier I suggested that the question of whether a scientist is responsible for an outcome can be interpreted in two different ways. First, the question concerns how scientists *produce* outcomes, what conditions must be in place before it can be said that a scientist is responsible for an outcome. Second, the question concerns the responsibilities of the scientist, what he should do in relation to his work and what he should not do. Do these two interpretations divide the question neatly in two, leaving behind two distinct and separate topics? Or is there perhaps a more subtle connection to be made between these "backward-looking" and "forward-looking" aspects of responsibility? Some philosophers, such as Kurt Baier and most consequentialists, maintain that there is not much point in talking about responsibility unless we have an eye toward what will happen in the future. But I think that we cannot sufficiently address responsibility without taking both "directions" into account.

The Manhattan Project

THE MANHATTAN PROJECT IS FAMILIAR TO MOST PEOPLE, in outline at least, because of its impact. The bombs it produced ended the most recent world war and ushered in the "atomic age," marked by the arms race and the attendant fear of nuclear catastrophe. Not only was the atomic bomb the most terrifying weapon ever seen, but it was from its inception associated with science. Indeed, more than radar, the VI and V2 rockets, or any other science-devised weapon of World War 2, the atomic bomb was seen as a quintessential product of science. It was twentieth-century science that had made the bomb possible, and it was scientists who had drawn the attention of the British and U.S. governments to the possibility of such a weapon and hence of the necessity, given the war, of determining whether it could be realized. Further, the development of the bomb dropped on Nagasaki, known as Fat Man, supports the account of pure research that argues that research's aims, not its content, determine its status.[1] In this case, the research itself was focused on such matters as the properties of the elements uranium and plutonium, which revealed important principles about the nucleus. It is easy to imagine such work being carried out in a university rather than at the weapons laboratory at Los Alamos, as much preliminary prewar work on atomic and nuclear physics was academic. The research done at Los Alamos was seemingly a natural continuation of the work that had come before.

The Manhattan Project has a special place in the evolution of the awareness of scientists' responsibilities. Robert Oppenheimer, the director at Los Alamos, is famous for having remarked, in the aftermath of the war, that physics had known sin. I am not so much interested in whether or not using the bombs was right or wrong, but in how the bombs' development provides a useful case study for investigating scientists' responsibility for outcomes.[2] Oppenheimer's admission of sin is, of course, an admission of responsibility. It has, however, been claimed that science itself nonetheless remains neutral—here a possible "good use" of the physics of nuclear fission is the production of electricity. It will become clear, however, that this "argument from neutrality" is but another failed attempt to insulate the scientist from responsibility.

Science in a Changed Context

The context in which scientists work has changed since the seventeenth century, in particular the complex process that now leads from pure scientific research to the production of artifacts, processes, technology, and so on. Today a great deal of scientific research is conducted by government agencies and industry, either directly in government or industrial laboratories or via grants to academic scientists, with the aim of producing outcomes. This in itself is significant for those scientists engaged solely in pure research. Remember that what distinguishes pure from applied research is not primarily the work's character or "content," but rather where and why it is carried out. This distinction is based on the realist account of the relationship between science and technology, which explains that the "proper product" of pure research, a scientific paper, can provide the means for some broader outcome. For example, a publication from a university laboratory might be read by an alert member of an industrial R&D team. What is important is that *all* scientists now know this, including pure, academic, university-based scientists: all scientists are aware that their work could have some application in the future.[3] We can therefore say that the overall context of scientific research has changed, even for pure scientists.[4]

While it would be incorrect to see the harnessing of science to outcomes as anything but a slow and gradual process, taking place over centuries, the *realization* that the overall context of science has changed has been much more dramatic and sudden, taking place after August 1945, in the wake of Hiroshima and Nagasaki. And this realization was not confined to scientists: World War 2 is widely said to mark a "watershed" in the relations between science and government (Brooks 1968, 2) and to have inaugurated the "war-born relationship" between the two

(Greenberg 1999, 68). The governments of the United States and the USSR in particular invested huge amounts of money in science, especially physics, immediately after the war. The United States wanted to ensure that it could maintain or increase the capability that had led to atomic weapons, while ten days after Hiroshima, Stalin similarly charged the People's Commissar for Munitions and his deputies: "A single demand to you, comrades, provide us with atomic weapons in the shortest possible time" (Rhodes 1995, 179). Commissions, national laboratories, and other government organizations, such as the Atomic Energy Commission in the United States, the Leningrad Physicochemical Institute in the USSR, and the Atomic Energy Authority in the UK, were established with this purpose in mind. In the United States, millions of dollars were also granted to universities to promote basic research in physics (see Hewlett and Anderson 1969, chapter 8; Leslie 1993).

A great deal of evidence thus supports the proposition that the use of nuclear weapons changed the relationship between science and government. But Hiroshima and Nagasaki also represented a shift across *all* forms of scientific research, not just government-sponsored research, and a shift in the relationship not just between science and government, but between science and society as a whole. Much evidence favors this claim as well: support for science from industry and other sectors rose steeply after World War 2, as did public awareness and understanding. I believe, then, that Hiroshima and Nagasaki changed the ways in which scientists can be held responsible for outcomes, even pure scientists who do not intend their work to do anything but produce scientific papers (cf. Callahan 1976, 3). Of course, scientists cannot be responsible for science-based outcomes if there are in fact no such outcomes: there was, as it were, a quantitative increase in scientists' responsibilities after World War 2 because science had been applied on a much greater scale than ever before, leading to more, and more varied, outcomes.

This claim—that the responsibilities of scientists, including pure scientists, shifted in the wake of the war because of changes in the overall context of science—will be crucial for my later argument that pure scientists are inherently responsible for more than producing scientific papers. To anticipate: suppose it is established that scientist S intends only to produce a particular paper but that his findings are used in connection with the outcome X, assumed to be a bad thing. Before the overall context of science changed, S could have claimed that he was unaware that scientific research could lead to outcomes and that hence he could not have been expected to take such matters into account when publishing his paper. Since World War 2, however, *all* scientists know that their research could lead to outcomes, regardless of whether that is their intention: ignorance of the general proposition is no excuse. Now, while the argument from neutrality acknowledges the changed context of science—while it admits that scientists are generally aware that pure research has outcomes—it still seeks to insulate the scientist from responsibility for these outcomes. The argument from neutrality will be addressed before my account of responsibility is advanced further, but it is first necessary to examine more closely the events that changed the context of science.[5]

Nuclear Weapons and Nuclear Research

There are two kinds of nuclear weapons: weapons that make use of *fission* reactions, liberating energy via nuclear reactions, and those that make use of *fusion* reactions. The latter presuppose the former, in that a "fission trigger" is needed to make a fusion bomb go off. The Manhattan Project built three fission bombs—one Little Boy bomb made with uranium-235 and two Fat Man bombs made with plutonium-239—but some speculated even then, notably Edward Teller, about the "super" or thermonuclear bomb. After the USSR tested a fission weapon in 1949, the United States decided to go ahead with the "super" bomb, with Teller playing a leading role. While the focus here is only on those bombs that exploited nuclear fission, it should be stressed here that the manufacture of these "small" bombs was the first step in the development of the terrifying arsenals that exist today, containing weapons that could produce destruction on a scale that is almost beyond imagination.

Broadly, a nuclear weapon works by means of a self-sustaining divergent chain reaction in an assembly of fissile material, such as uranium-235 or plutonium-239. A chain reaction comprises a sequence of reactions —or rather, a sequence of generations of reactions—in which each reaction causes, or generates, the next. For example, suppose a uranium nucleus fissions into two (or more) fragments and releases in the process two neutrons (see figure 1). Neutrons cause fission reactions when they are absorbed into a nucleus and form an unstable combination of nuclear particles; fission results when this "compound" nucleus breaks apart. For this to occur, a neutron must hit the "target nucleus" and be absorbed, rather than bouncing off or being captured in a way that does not lead to fission (e.g., neutron activation or isotope formation).[6] Suppose, in the present example, that the two released neutrons do indeed cause two fission reactions, which in turn yield four neutrons, which cause four more fission reactions, and so on. Each generation of reactions has twice as many members as the one preceding it; hence the reaction "diverges" by a factor of two in each new generation. When the number of generations reaches about eighty for either uranium-235 or plutonium-239, energy equivalent to that caused by detonating thousands of tons of TNT is released.

This results because each fission reaction releases energy in the form of the kinetic energy of the fission products, including the neutrons,

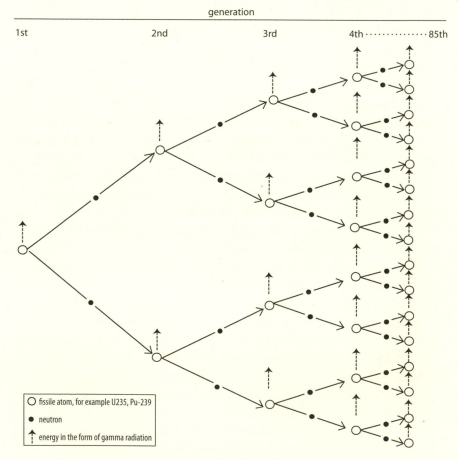

Figure 1: Divergent Chain

and radiation. While each individual reaction liberates only a small amount of energy ($\approx 10^{-13}$ joules), there are many, many billions of reactions ($\approx 2^{80} \approx 10^{24}$), adding up to a great deal of energy ($\approx 10^{11}$ joules). Because the reactions in question are nuclear, any concomitant rearrangement of electrons and subsequent release of chemical energy is vanishingly small (the characteristic energy of a nuclear "bond" is a million times that of a chemical bond). In fact, the energy's source is the so-called mass defect of the fissioned nucleus: a nucleus's mass is very slightly less than the sum of the masses of its individual protons and neutrons. For instance, if one adds the masses of 92 protons and 143 neutrons, the total will be slightly greater than the mass of a uranium-235 nucleus. Some mass has been given up—an amount $m = E/c^2$, given by the Einstein formula—to bind the protons together and overcome their mutual electrostatic repulsion. Both neutrons and protons are attracted by the short-range strong interaction, but extra neutrons are needed to overcome the protons' electrostatic repulsion. As one moves down the periodic table of elements, one finds progressively more protons in the nucleus and so more individual proton-proton electrostatic interactions.[7] This means that extra neutrons are needed: adding one proton to a nucleus requires more than one extra neutron. Heavy elements, such as uranium, therefore tend to fission, with some isotopes fissioning more readily than others because all the extra neutrons make them bulky and unstable. However, the resulting fragments, or fission products, are isotopes of lighter elements, such as barium or krypton. Initially, these isotopes have excess neutrons that are then released, usually "promptly." This explains both why fission reactions yield neutrons and why they release energy—energy that previously acted as the binding energy needed to overcome the extra proton-proton interactions in the heavy nucleus.

All of this information about fission was widely known in the physics community by the beginning of 1940. The mass-energy formula had been known since 1905, when it "fell out" as a consequence of Einstein's use of the Lorentz transformations in the formulation of special relativity.[8] Until pressed into service as an explanation of fission, this relation was regarded as a strange theoretical curiosity. The neutron had been discovered in England in 1932, and fission had certainly been observed—although not identified as such—by Fermi in Rome in 1935. Fission was then confirmed in Berlin in 1938 by Otto Hahn and Fritz Strassman, with help from Lise Meitner and Otto Frisch, and Niels Bohr then explained how and why it is possible (Rhodes 1986, 282–88). From this point, several laboratories, in the United States, England, France, and Germany, were working on fission reactions and trying to obtain information about the decay of various elements and isotopes, how many neutrons are released, what their kinetic energies are, the cross-sections for fission versus scattering, and so on. In other words, scientists working in nuclear physics were trying to discover certain crucial nuclear parameters.

Were they doing so to see whether nuclear weapons were possible—in other words, doing applied research? Until the British "Tube Alloys" project was set up in 1940, there was no government-sponsored research into nuclear weapons. However, some scientists were nonetheless certainly concerned about the possibility of nuclear weapons, with Leo Szilard most often mentioned in this regard. Richard Rhodes credits Szilard with the idea for the atomic bomb, because Szilard speculated about chain reactions in uranium in the early 1930s. Certainly Szilard's role was vital in the early years of atomic research: he wrote to Frederic Joliot-Curie in France in 1939, asking him not to publish his experimental results on neutron multiplication using heavy water as a moderator; moved to the United States to conduct nuclear research at Columbia; encouraged Eugene Wigner to persuade Einstein to write his famous letter to Roosevelt, and so forth.[9] Thus, if the intentions of such scientists as Szilard regarding nuclear research determine the character of their work as pure or applied, then some were indeed engaged in applied research before Tube Alloys.

Two examples of scientific research done to advance the development of nuclear weapons are notable here—the first in England, before formal government-sponsored research; the second in the United States, with government support but before the Manhattan Project. I accordingly classify this research as applied, although in another time, either project could have just as easily been termed pure. Both were vital in demonstrating that nuclear weapons were not only possible in theory but also feasible in practice. This distinction is pertinent because by 1940, many scientists were aware of nuclear physics' potential to deliver a new kind of weapon of exceptional power, but this potential was only *theoretical*. There was, in other words, a possible mechanism (the chain reaction) and a possible source of energy (the mass defect), but there was no information about whether a chain reaction was achievable in practice and, if it was, whether the resulting bang would be big enough (or too big) or whether it was possible to obtain enough of the right fissile material.

The parameters mentioned above were crucial. For instance, if the fission cross-sections of all fissile materials were very small relative to the scattering cross-sections of all types of reactions, then very few events of neutrons hitting targets would result in fission, a scattered neutron losing too much of its energy to cause fission or taking too long to do so. If too much energy were released per fission, then the critical masses of the element for all geometries—the mass needed to sustain a divergent chain reaction—would be too small for a big bang to result. If the kinetic energy of the fissioned neutron were too small and its mean free path too great, there would also be too small a bang, again because there would be too few generations. If the rate of spontaneous fission were too great, then assembling a bomb might not be possible at all. For example, the "obvious" way to make an atomic bomb is to fire one hemispherical subcritical piece of fissile material at another such piece in a "gun barrel," so that the combined pieces are supercritical (above critical mass) (see figure 2). Spontaneous fission might initiate the chain reaction too soon and prevent the assembly from staying together long enough. All of these parameters are contingent from the point of view of theory and therefore had to be determined by experiment—or guessed.

In early 1940, two German émigré scientists, Otto Frisch and Rudolf Peierls, wrote a remarkable paper—known as the Frisch-Peierls Memorandum—in which they did indeed fix some of these parameters, such as the critical mass of a sphere of uranium-235.[10] They did this by using estimates (guesses) of the cross-sections—estimates that turned out to be very nearly correct. This led to a critical mass for uranium-235 in the

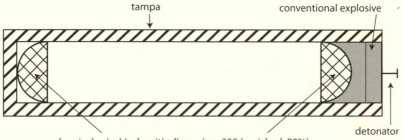

Figure 2: Gun Barrel (Little Boy) Design

order of ten kilograms. Frisch and Peierls further predicted that a device containing this much fissile material would produce a yield in the order of kilotons of TNT, which again proved to be right. While much of this was speculation, not experimental determination, it nevertheless showed that the "right numbers" would indeed suffice to produce a potent weapon. This result galvanized the British government, which set up Tube Alloys. The Frisch-Peierls Memorandum was also sent to the United States, where it served as an important signpost along the road to Hiroshima and Nagasaki. It is worth mentioning here that Frisch and Peierls, like Szilard, were worried that the Nazis might develop an atomic bomb. One of the two was Jewish, the other had a Jewish wife, and both had left Germany for England in the 1930s. Aware of how aggressive the Nazis were, they wanted to use their scientific abilities to help the Allies, and they thus drew attention to what they thought was the *practical* possibility of developing the bomb.[11] At the time, Peierls was a professor of physics at Birmingham University, but Frisch had no post.[12] In fact, they wrote their memorandum at home, in their spare time.

Another essential step in the realization of the bomb was the provision of the explosive substance—the fissile material in which the chain reaction was to be produced. If it is granted that Frisch and Peierls had demonstrated that an atomic bomb was a practical possibility—given that their guessed-at values were near-enough right—it still does not follow that a bomb could indeed be made. It was first necessary to obtain sufficient fissile material, and this might not have been possible. For instance, the isotope uranium-235 is only 0.7 percent naturally occurring, and separating it from the more abundant uranium-238 might have been prohibitively impractical (too expensive, too time-consuming). These days, the favored fissile material is an isotope of plutonium, which is made in a nuclear reactor and is in fact a by-product of its operation, occurring when the isotope uranium-238 "captures" a neutron and then transmutes into plutonium-239 via beta-decay.[13]

The first reactor was built by Enrico Fermi in a squash court on the grounds of the University of Chicago in December 1942. Fermi used a configuration of specially made graphite bricks, machined uranium plugs that could be inserted within channels in the bricks, and cadmium-coated control rods. This was a major project, and it needed government support in wartime, so the U.S. government paid for Fermi's graphite. The reactor's principle was as follows: the fissile isotope uranium-235 spontaneously emits neutrons that are slowed by the graphite moderator to a velocity needed to fission other uranium-235 atoms, with the cadmium available to absorb the neutrons if the reaction looked as if it were becoming too vigorous.[14] Plutonium is a by-product of fission in the sense that a neutron is not "usually" captured by uranium-238 in a power reactor (the sum of the scattering and fission cross-sections for slow neutrons being greater that the absorption cross-section), but a weapons reactor can be configured to maximize plutonium production by creating conditions that maximize neutron capture. Fermi's assembly was built up layer by layer and continually tested to measure the neutron flux, but his reactor "went critical" just at the point he predicted it would. Fermi's pioneering work established the basics of reactor design and provided the model for the plutonium-producing reactors that were built in Washington State in 1943.

These two examples—Frisch-Peierls and Fermi—further support the claim that it is not research's "content" that determines its status, whether pure or applied. The Frisch-Peierls Memorandum can stand as a brilliant piece of speculation by two theorists about the implications of best estimates of certain important nuclear parameters—as a set of predictions of what these values are and what they mean. One could even, albeit with difficulty, think of the Manhattan Project as an experimental program designed to test these predictions. All this would thus be pure research: science aimed at determining some fundamental properties and values and thus verifying a prediction of relativity theory ($E = mc^2$). Similarly, Fermi's realization of the chain reaction could similarly be viewed as experimental confirmation of the prediction, made by Szilard and many others, that such a mechanism can exist. All this too is the business of pure science, according to any methodology: formulating a theory and hypothesis and then testing that hypothesis through experiment to see if it is true. It just so happened in this case, however, that circumstances dictated that this research, in both cases, was applied —aimed at nuclear weapons, not at determining the fundamental properties of the nucleus "for their own sake."

Implosion

Richard Hewlett and Oscar Anderson observe that "one of the first decisions at Los Alamos was what emphasis to give the various methods of assembly" (1962, 245). Implosion is one way of assembling a super-critical mass—that is, of bringing together two or more subcritical pieces of fissionable material or of changing the geometry of one subcritical piece so that the result is supercritical. The gun-barrel design was the first method of assembly investigated by the Manhattan Project—and used at Hiroshima—while implosion was the second. The prevailing view at the project's beginning was that the "obvious" gun-barrel design would be used for both uranium-235 and plutonium-239. At this early stage, in the spring of 1943, the idea of implosion was being championed by the physicist Seth Neddermeyer, attached to the ordnance division.[15] But Neddermeyer was not able to convince others of its efficacy, especially not William Parsons, the head of the division. Neddermeyer therefore undertook some experimental work largely on his own initiative, and somewhat out of the mainstream, during the summer of 1943.

However, all of the research divisions at Los Alamos conducted work on implosion, especially after 1944, when it became clear that predetonation problems would prevent the gun-barrel design from being used with plutonium.[16] (Predetonation occurs when the subcritical elements are not assembled quickly enough, and the nuclear reaction begins too soon; this prevents completion of the process, and the reaction "fizzles out." Implosion is typically more than one hundred times faster than gun-barrel assembly and hence is an effective way of dealing with predetonation.) Within each division at Los Alamos, specific groups were devoted to different aspects of implosion, with progress and developments reported in regular colloquia attended by the entire staff. Thus, research on implosion is also an example of group research—moreover, of group research involving groups within groups.

Fat Man was ultimately designed as a plutonium sphere of about twenty-two kilograms with a hollow center packed with polonium and beryllium, which, when mixed, give out a high flux of neutrons to initiate the nuclear reaction (see figure 3). This hollow center is in a subcritical state. For it to reach a supercritical state, it must be imploded, so that it retains, as nearly as possible, its spherical shape but is no longer hollow. This implosion allows the neutrons that would have been emitted from the inner surface of the sphere before compression to cause fission. The idea here is the same as it is in the gun-barrel method, when neutrons emitted from the two flat surfaces of each of the hemispheres of uranium-235 cause fission when the hemispheres are brought together. In both cases, these extra "opportunities" for fission effect the transformation from subcritical to supercritical mass. However, if it were not possible to squeeze the hollow sphere of plutonium in such a way that the implosion is sufficiently symmetrical and regular, the result would not be a solid sphere of plutonium, destined to exist for a tiny fraction of a second, but an object of some other geometry, with too much surface area to constitute a critical assembly. An implosion bomb therefore comprises two parts: a shock-wave generator made up of high explosives suitably arranged and fused; and implosion hardware of a plutonium sphere, a neutron generator, and any other inert material used to tamp the system or reflect the neutrons.

Accordingly, the implosion design might not work for two reasons. First, any shock wave traveling from the outer edge of a sphere to its center sufficiently quickly (in the order of microseconds) might not be smooth enough to ensure symmetrical collapse of the system, making an implosion bomb for plutonium impossible for *physical* reasons. That is, the physical characteristics of implosive shock waves might be such that as they converge, they become too turbulent. Second, a sufficiently quick shock wave might be impossible to realize because of limits on conventional explosives, fusing, and so on, making the bomb impossible for *practical* reasons. Neddermeyer's experiments were aimed at uncovering some preliminary data along both these lines of inquiry.

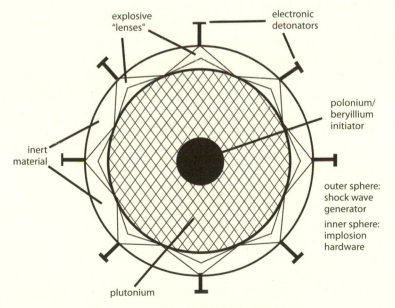

Figure 3: Implosion (Fat Man) Design

However, Neddermeyer could not use plutonium, because none was available in 1943, and he could not use very large amounts of TNT to generate shock waves, because he had to be able to examine the results of his tests, and some of his experimental objects had to be left to examine. But Neddermeyer found an ally when the mathematician and theoretical physicist John von Neumann, who had been studying shock waves from the theoretical perspective at Princeton, visited Los Alamos in the summer of 1943 (Hawkins 1946, 139).[17] Von Neumann suggested that they try to develop an idea put forward by the English physicist James Tuck, which proposed that the shock-wave generator might be developed by means of "explosive lenses."

To grasp this idea, first picture what happens when a single drop of water falls into a still pond: ripples spread outward and, if the pond is big enough, keep on going and getting bigger. The shape of the moving wavefront is therefore *convex:* at any point on the traveling wave, its neighbors arc backward. The same is true in three dimensions, although now it becomes harder to picture: if a depth charge goes off under water, a three-dimensional spherical shock wave moves outward from the detonation. The problem in constructing a shock-wave generator was *reversing* this process, making a collapsing or *concave* wave in three dimensions, a kind of shrinking spherical disturbance strong enough to implode a sphere of plutonium. Tuck's idea, then, was to focus a shock wave using explosive lenses. This was eventually done by using explosives that burned at different rates shaped into cones. The inner cone was made of the slowest-burning explosive known at the time (substance B), embedded in an outer cone of the fastest-burning explosive known (substance A). Firing the lens from the tip meant that the convex wave caused by the burning of A would be slowed by the time it reached B; provided the lens geometry was correct, the result would be a concave wave focused on the center of the sphere (see figure 4). With an array of such lenses correctly placed over the surface of the sphere, and with the correct timing of detonations, the individually concave waves would join up at the surface of the sphere to produce the required symmetrical squeeze of the plutonium.[18]

This clever design demanded many small experimental test firings, and a final major test, before it could be shown to work. But it required theoretical work as well: determining the geometry of the lenses, the speed of the shock wave, how the wave would behave as the implosion process continued, and so on. The theory in question is that of hydro-

dynamics, which deals with stresses, strains, and energy transfers in continuous media. All of this was complicated, requiring the solution of
partial differential equations and the estimation of key parameters. For
instance, if the wave became highly distorted near the center, then the
pressure at different points on the same surface would be different,
meaning that the whole assembly would distort. Such information
would preclude the design. The problem itself is typically one that today
would be routinely solved by numerical means, with computers making
estimates of the integrals (expressed as difference equations) to almost
any desired accuracy. In 1943, however, such techniques were not available, and the equations had to be solved "by hand" until some IBM cal-
culators arrived at Los Alamos in 1944. A succession of theorists made
key contributions here: von Neumann; Peierls; Richard Tolman; Stan
Ulam, a Polish mathematician and protégé of von Neumann who later
solved the assembly problem for thermonuclear weapons with Edward
Teller; and several others.[19] This, as noted earlier, was group research,

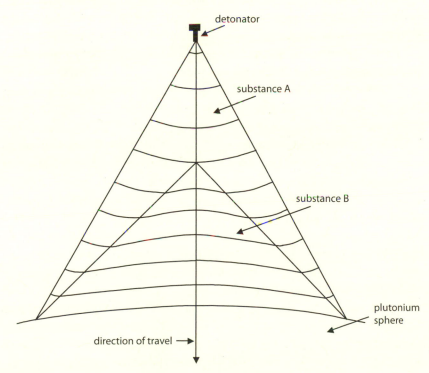

Figure 4: "Explosive Lens"

with ideas being discussed at regular colloquia. However, Peierls's contribution should be singled out here for special mention because Peierls suggested a new analytical approach to solving the integrals (Hewlett and Anderson 1962, 249).[20]

It turned out, as history has witnessed, that it is indeed possible to implode a hollow sphere of plutonium and thereby achieve a supercritical mass. This outcome had been predicted by the calculations of the "implosion group," which suggested that converging shock waves could retain their (concave) symmetry long enough to regularly compress the hardware (Hawkins 1946, 76). The ordnance division at Los Alamos was thereafter reorganized to concentrate on developing new testing techniques to obtain data that would inform the specific design contemplated, with George Kistiakowsky appointed as deputy director as a foil to Parsons (Hawkins 1946, 126). Thus, from the beginning of 1944, work at Los Alamos proceeded in two directions, one dictated by gun-barrel assembly and the other by implosion. The former course was steady and smooth, while the latter was difficult; indeed, right up to the end, uncertainty about whether implosion would work at all made necessary the Trinity test Alamogordo. However, it proved much easier to obtain plutonium-239 from reactors based on Fermi's original experiments than it was to separate uranium-235, so enough material was available for a test. The other Fat Man bomb and the Little Boy bomb were then handed over to the military, and the scientists were then no longer in the picture. The decision to use the atomic bombs was ultimately made by President Harry Truman, the last direct orders issued by the captains of the two B-29 bombers, Colonel Paul Tibbets and Major Charles Sweeney, who flew their planes to Hiroshima and Nagasaki, respectively. But many other military, civilian, and scientific personnel gave advice on matters ranging from target selection to the question as of whether the Japanese would give in.

I have described this episode in some detail in part to show that even in a program devoted so single-mindedly to one outcome—the production of an atomic bomb—the work done is not somehow "intrinsically applied." Von Neumann, for example, could make useful suggestions about implosion because he had been working on shock waves at Princeton. Peierls had been asked to think about hydrodynamics before he came to Los Alamos, while Ulam, on the other hand, only began to work on the problems when he was actually at the weapons laboratory. It is therefore the *context* of work that determines whether it is applied, directed toward an outcome, in this case the weaponization of plutonium. If the work had instead been done "for its own sake," out of curiosity, then it would have been pure. Indeed, the problem of solving the equations with the particular parameters associated with inverting a convex wave could well have been intriguing enough for a pure scientist to tackle it. It is by no means implausible to think of von Neumann or Peierls or Ulam, or any of the other theoreticians, sitting down to work on this problem at leisure, at their respective universities, in peace time. Thus, while the Manhattan Project was special in view of what it produced and how it was conducted, it was nonetheless typical of the way that science is used in the production of artifacts.

But does this mean that scientific research, and science itself, is "neutral" and that any responsibility for outcomes does not therefore fall on the scientist? Perhaps the fact that the content of the research does not determine its character as pure or applied can be used to argue *against* the idea that scientists have responsibility for outcomes: the scientist simply does his work, whether in a university or a military laboratory, and others use it and thus take responsibility for those uses. Such a claim cannot be fully assessed until we know under what conditions it is appropriate to assign responsibility for outcomes, until we have an *account* of responsibility—in this sense a prima facie case against attributing responsibility. On its face, however, this claim seems implausible: why should one kind of contribution to an outcome, that made by science, be excused from responsibility? A great many things had to be done by a great many people before Nagasaki was annihilated. Surely some of those people must accept responsibility for that act. Why should one particular group be exempt? The onus is on those who make this claim to prove it.

Science and Neutrality

There remains, however, an argument for neutrality that must be taken seriously, which takes its starting point from the fact that science is neutral until it is applied via technology. This argument begins with the observation that technology can have good or bad uses—for instance, atomic bombs can be dropped on Japan and kill thousands of innocents or be employed as a deterrent and save just as many. A scientist who deliberately undertakes research that will bring about some technology therefore cannot be held responsible, because how the technology will be used is not up to him. President Truman, Colonel Tibbets, and other military and political leaders were responsible for Hiroshima and Nagasaki, not Neddermeyer or Fermi or Peierls, or any of the other scientists—at least not in their capacity *as* scientists. This argument depends on two premises: that technology is itself "neutral" and that scientists who provide the results needed to develop technologies do not know whether they will be used for good or ill. This second premise is vital, for if the scientist has reason to believe that the technology will be used for ill and has no reason to believe that the "bad" use will be outweighed at some stage by a "good" one, then the supposed neutrality of the technology will not shield the scientist from responsibility. The second premise surely cannot be established, for to do so would be to demonstrate that no scientist ever has any idea how his research is going to be used; there is thus already reason to reject the argument as unsound. Moreover, the first premise needs to be clarified, for the meaning of the claim that technology is neutral is not yet clear.[21]

Technology, or rather *a* technology, can be understood here as knowledge of a technique—a way of doing something. Suppose, in keeping with our example, that this "something" is the production of some artifact. An artifact, by definition, has a use or function; artifacts are produced for a purpose. The neutrality thesis requires that artifacts actually have several purposes, which are in some kind of moral equilibrium. The suggestion already canvassed is that atomic bombs can be dropped, which is bad because it invariably kills innocent people, or they can be used as deterrents, which is good because it prevents wars. Suppose we concede that nuclear deterrence, which involves the threat of the use of force, can be justified (not everyone's view) and so agree that atomic bombs can have a "good use." At what point, however, can we stop finding uses? This argument requires that each technological product has at least two uses in order for there to be a "state of moral equilibrium," but what counts as a use?

I would argue that an artifact has (at least) one *primary* purpose, for which it was designed and made, and various *secondary* and *derivative* purposes. Thus, an atomic bomb is designed and made to explode in a dramatic and destructive manner: that is what it does when it is used. Deterrence is a "derivative purpose" in the sense that it depends on the primary purpose: one cannot threaten a nuclear attack if one's atomic bombs will not go off. But the converse is not true. The use of an atomic bomb as an explosive device does not entail that it can be used as a deterrent: if, for example, no more nuclear weapons were built after

Nagasaki, they could never have been used as deterrents. Hence the primary purpose does not entail the derivative purpose. Secondary purposes are fortuitous; they are, as it were, post hoc spin-offs.[22] The position that I wish to maintain, as against the neutrality thesis, is that artifacts are "value-laden" as a consequence of their primary purpose. This does not mean that the value in question is necessarily "expressed" when the technology is implemented and the artifact made, but it does mean that the technology embodies the value—whatever this might amount to in actual practice.

To the objection that this typology of purposes is overly simple, or that it does not apply to every artifact and technology, or that it cannot stand on the basis of just one instance, I would reply that only one counterexample is necessary to refute the neutrality thesis as a general claim. Moreover, if it turns out that some technologies are such that their primary purpose is too general or vague for anything like a value to enter into moral deliberations, then it might be conceded that in such a case a scientist devising the technology's underpinning could not be held responsible for any of its uses. A jet engine, for example, appears to be a much more likely neutral-artifact candidate than does a bomb. What a jet engine actually does is suck air in at the front and blow it out at the back. If a jet engine is attached to a B-52 bomber, its use might be taken as "bad," but if it is used to improve the efficiency of a mobile medical service, this use would seem "good." If the primary purpose of the jet engine is swifter, more economical travel, then any other uses would, in the typology suggested here, be derivative—perhaps its use in drag-car racing would be a secondary. Swifter, more economical travel is, however, evidently something that is valued, and perhaps it can be valued in and of itself, without reference to just what it is that is traveling more swiftly and economically. Indeed, it seems that if the notion of *the* primary purpose is to apply in this case, this view must be adopted. Perhaps, on the other hand, the typology of purposes does not apply here, and value can only be attached to bombers flying more swiftly or doctors being transported more economically.

What this means is that technologies and artifacts are more variegated than allowed above, which in turn means that the issue of values and neutrality is complicated. This complexity, however, does not vindicate the neutrality thesis. Note also that the second premise of the argument—that the scientist does not know what a technology will be used for—has not yet been addressed. If a materials scientist working on heat-resistant light alloys receives a grant from the Defense Department to investigate how they might be relevant to jet engines, he would not immediately think of how his work might help the mobile doctor. Again, the research's context will often suggest, or even determine, which of an artifact's secondary or derivative purposes are going to be realized. These secondary purposes can even override the primary purpose. Thus, the Pakistani engineers who designed the bombs tested in 1998 surely realized that they were to function as deterrents to India, without actually being used. Without the derivative purpose, there would have been no reason to make the bombs.

This suggests that, unlike a technology's primary purpose, its derivative purpose can only be determined from the context in which it is to be implemented (see chapter 9). "Context" here does not refer exclusively to the research setting, but to the historical or political setting.[23] For example, the Cold War was a historical epoch when nuclear weapons were used for the derivative purpose of deterrence. Before 1949—before "Stalin's comrades" had obeyed Stalin's command to make a bomb—there could have been no nuclear deterrence, because no country besides the United States had nuclear weapons. However, the primary purpose of a nuclear weapon, or of a jet engine, can be seen simply as what it does, free of all such contextual factors. In this regard, the primary purpose of a technology or an artifact is analogous to the content of a piece of pure research, which is just what the research "says." Thus, a set of equations and parameters for a converging shock wave just describes a certain physical process, regardless of its realization or the purpose for which it will be used. This analogy is what we would expect from the realist interpretation of science.

The neutrality thesis therefore fails to "immunize" science from moral concerns, because both of the premises on which it relies can be successfully challenged. This argument does not, however, establish my alternative position as a *general* account of technology. While the typology of purposes seems to work well enough for bombs, it is not so plausible when it comes to "generic" technologies such as jet engines, or microelectronic components, or process technologies. In these instances, the neutrality thesis seems more plausible. However, it is not yet necessary to move into an extended discussion of the nature of technology; the demonstration that the neutrality thesis cannot provide an accurate overall account of technology and "value" is sufficient at this point.

On Responsibility

UESTIONS ABOUT RESPONSIBILITY ARE TYPICALLY ASKED *after* the event. A historian looking back at the Manhattan Project, for example, might find that it is necessary to read the original reports and papers to sort out who did what. But one can also imagine Robert Oppenheimer, at one of the early technical reviews, asking who was responsible for technical work on implosion, who was responsible for testing gun-barrel designs, and so forth. Oppenheimer, in this case, would not have been looking *back* but *forward*, asking who was responsible for certain assignments. Thus, *two* different notions of responsibility apply here, depending on the temporal frame of reference, which, not surprisingly, are labeled *backward-looking* and *forward-looking* responsibility (Baier 1987, 103).[1]

Two Concepts of Responsibility

What connection, if any, exists between these two kinds of responsibility? Perhaps Rudolf Peierls could only have been responsible for implosion design in the backward-looking sense if he had earlier been responsible in the forward-looking sense. And if so, perhaps there is really only one kind of responsibility, which has forward- and backward-looking aspects, depending on the frame of reference. Thus, to ask whether Peierls was responsible in the backward-looking sense would be to presuppose that he was responsible in the forward-looking sense: the issue would be whether he had succeeded in carrying out his assignments. This is not, however, how the two kinds of responsibility are

51

always understood. In particular, statements about backward-looking responsibility for acts do not entail statements about forward-looking responsibility, unless we identify forward-looking responsibility with (something like) the overall standards by which any moral agent is supposed to abide. But until omissions come into the picture, and until it is clear just how judgments of responsibility presuppose moral standards, backward-looking responsibility, for the purposes of analysis, can be thought of as something separate from forward-looking responsibility.

Whether any definite sort of forward-looking responsibility is associated with science is debatable. Saying that Peierls was responsible for conducting research into implosion seems to mean simply that this was his job, what he was supposed to do. If he did it, well and good; if not, then he let the side down, disappointed his employer, and failed to earn his wage. There does not *appear* to be any very weighty matter here concerning responsibility and the scientist. But this is not the whole story: the question remains of whether Peierls discharged his responsibility *as a scientist* when he worked on implosion. This way of understanding forward-looking responsibility is different from that canvassed above. The suggestion here is that some sort of *role-responsibility* is associated with being a scientist, and the related question is whether doing war research is incompatible with that role. Here we touch on issues that arise in connection with the professional ethics of science, when ethics is taken to have a scope that comprises more than just what goes on in the scientific community. It has been argued that there is no such thing as an "external" professional ethics of science because, unlike lawyers and doctors, scientists have no special or particular clientele. Uncovering some constituency also seems necessary if there is to be such a thing as the "role" of the scientist, but this does not exhaust the possibility of there being some special forward-looking responsibility of the scientist qua scientist.

Before setting aside questions about the responsibility of the Manhattan Project scientists, it is worth raising again the big question of responsibility for the deaths at Nagasaki. Does this particular question embody some broader law or principle, such that being responsible for the deaths at Nagasaki is to have (one assumes) violated that law or principle? There are certainly a number of candidates for such a principle, especially since most of the deaths were of civilians. For example, the Just War tradition, stretching back at least to St Augustine, states the principles of *jus in bello*, which proscribe the killing of noncombatants

(Fisher 1985, 16). The responsibility of Enrico Fermi, Peierls, and others for the deaths at Nagasaki could thus be understood in terms of the Just War Theory: they were responsible in so far as they violated *jus in bello*. Alternatively, international laws against killing civilians, such as Geneva Protocol I, forbid making civilians "objects of attack" (Finnis, Boyle, and Grisez 1987, 101). One might claim, on reflection (the Geneva Protocol dates from 1977), that Fermi and his associates were responsible for the civilian deaths in that they violated the Geneva Convention. One might further appeal to some general principle of ethics, such as the Kantian prohibition on killing innocents, or one might simply appeal to a "common morality" that prohibits all forms of harming. In this case, the scientists were indeed responsible, having killed innocents. The idea in each case is that Fermi, Peierls, and the others fell below some standard, whether set by Just War tradition, law, or morality.

There appear to be two problems with this way of conceiving backward-looking responsibility. First, an individual's responsibility for something cannot *only* be a matter of standards and norms. If Fermi or Peierls failed to live up to a standard, then they must have done (or not done) something that amounted to them not satisfying the standard. To violate the Just War tradition is to have done *something* contrary to that tradition. If the distinction between facts and values can be evoked here, then some fact of the matter must be involved, as well as some value. This seems obvious enough. Second, if responsibility is understood in this way, it will be rendered a relative, or determinable, idea, in that it will always be necessary to make explicit the standard invoked. Thus, it could be argued that because the Geneva Protocol was not in place in 1945, it is unfair to assign responsibility to a Manhattan scientist for having failed to live up to it. The Just War tradition and the Kantian prohibition on killing innocents, however, were presumably in place. Which of these principles, then, applies? One, both, or some other principle altogether? It is possible that Fermi was responsible relative to one, but not to another. Such considerations would certainly complicate the picture, introducing a form of *relativism* into judgments of responsibility—the bane of philosophers. Fortunately, the situation is not so bleak.

Agent-Responsibility and Thing-Responsibility

If P's responsibility for X is a matter of certain facts or states of affairs, then it will be necessary to determine whether the facts are such that P is indeed responsible for X. This will certainly be how things stand if P is not a person but some "act of God." Thus, if the issue is whether a tidal wave or a volcanic eruption destroyed a village, it will be necessary to see which of them did the damage—ash and lava or seawater? Once this has been decided, then responsibility will be clear. Kurt Baier refers to this sort of responsibility as "thing-responsibility" and distinguishes it from "agent-responsibility" (1987, 102). Determinations of thing-responsibility are thus determinations about the facts of the matter and indeed will (nearly always) revolve around whether the "thing" caused X.[2] Agent-responsibility is different, at least regarding the *sorts* of facts that are relevant. Thus, simply being the cause of X is not normally regarded as sufficient for being assigned agent-responsibility—it is if one accepts so-called *strict liability*, but that viewpoint does not have many adherents these days. Normally, P will need to have deliberately acted to bring about X or deliberately refrained from preventing X in order to be said to be responsible for X. There are considerable differences of opinion in the literature on what this responsibility amounts to and how to spell it out. However, it seems that the issues in any case still center on the facts, although now they are facts about the agent's actions, omissions, intentions, and so on—facts that determine whether the acts and omissions *belong* to the agent.

Agents—and I assume here that humans are the only agents—can be blamed or praised for what they do.[3] One could blame the volcano for destroying the village—or even praise the fine weather for the good harvest—but it won't do any good: the volcano won't change its ways, make reparations, or spend time in jail. Blaming and praising, in the normal course of events, only make sense in relation to those who have the capacity to look ahead, make plans, do things rationally and deliberately, and change their ways. (The doctrine of strict liability takes none of this into account and thereby reduces agents to things, which is why it is largely disregarded as a mechanism for ascribing responsibility.) But does this mean that, in addition to considering certain facts about what P did in connection with X, we also need to see how praise and blame attach in order to determine whether P is responsible for X? That is to say, is there more to the difference between agent- and thing-responsibility than the extra facts of the matter? Is there also some praising or blaming to be determined? For instance, if P is responsible for X, does this mean that P is actually praised or blamed by someone?

If this were the case, then matters would certainly be more complicated, because working out what praise and blame amount to might not be easy. For instance, if one is blameworthy when one has done the wrong thing, then the investigation might need to address what constitutes wrong action. But what is wrong from one perspective may not be wrong, or may even be right, from another.[4] These perspectives could be moral, informed by different normative theories; or legal; or more broadly social. Thus, if X is wrong from the point of view of T_1 but is "indifferent"—neither right nor wrong—from T_2's, then whether P is responsible for X will depend on which point of view is adopted: if X is indifferent, then under this hypothesis, P is not responsible for it. If responsibility were thus relative, then we would be faced with the choice of which of the various determinate perspectives to adopt. But it is not obvious that such a choice arises in connection with the *concept* of responsibility, as opposed to making judgments about right and wrong, praise and blame, in connection with the things for which the agent is responsible.

The following simple example shows that P's responsibility for X does not *entail* that P is praiseworthy or blameworthy. Suppose P shoots Q, and P's shooting Q is not in any way a praiseworthy act: P did not thereby prevent a disaster at great cost to himself; he merely acted in self-defense. His action, then, was not praiseworthy, but neither is he to be blamed. Self-defense is (I assume) "justifiable homicide," and therefore P has a *justification* for what he did. A justification, unlike an excuse, is an *admission* of responsibility but a *denial* of blame.[5] So it can be quickly established that responsibility can exist without blame or praise. However, if justification is, as it were, interposed between blame and the responsible agent in such a case, and if it is necessary to deflect blame from the agent, then being responsible does appear to "open up" the agent to blame. Justification can then be thought of as an answer or account that the agent gives. Thus, while P's responsibility for X does not (in such cases) entail that P is therefore to blame for X, it does imply that P must give a suitable account of himself if he wants to avoid blame. In this way, the impression that responsibility implies blame can be explained.

Justifications and excuses are not usually associated with praise, only with blame, for presumably we are happy to accept praise but would rather not be blamed. Everything to do with praise, then, could be simply set aside by restricting the concept of responsibility to those actions and outcomes that can attract blame, focusing exclusively on some notion of "blame-responsibility." I do not think that we can confidently assert whether "our" concept of responsibility has a dimension of praise or whether it does not. Experts are divided on this question, but Jay Wallace believes there is an overall consensus, as least in regard to moral responsibility: "But praise does not seem to have the central, defining role that blame and moral sanction have in our practice of assigning moral responsibility" (1996, 61). So, in Wallace's view, it appears that there is a dimension of praise, but that it is not "central," which seems a sensible assessment of the way the concept is used. Moreover, in such a project as the present one, which seeks to *apply* the idea of responsibility, it is preferable to allow that scientists can be praised as well as blamed when they are responsible. It is therefore necessary to investigate praise and see what, if anything, justification has to do with it.

Suppose it were possible to classify all instances of doing or bringing about X, or of omitting to do or bring about X, as good, bad, or indifferent, setting aside all the practical difficulties that this would involve (e.g., choosing between T_1 and T_2). Restricting responsibility to "blame-responsibility," as suggested above, would mean that responsibility would only be assigned for instances that fall into the class of bad things. For things falling into the other two classes, "P is responsible for X" would always be false or not applicable. On the other hand, allowing for a dimension of praise would make the class of good things relevant to responsibility. So suppose that X is good and P is responsible for X; it then seems that P is, ipso facto, worthy of praise. But perhaps P, a very honest person, says that he did not actually *intend* to bring X about—perhaps he did not even know that he would cause X to happen. I think it unlikely that P would be praised for X if he did not intend it, but it is much less clear whether he would *also* be held not responsible for X.

For instance, consider the case of the common effects X and Y of the cause Z, and let P intend to bring about Y via Z, but not X. If X is a bad thing, some—myself among them—would want to say that P is indeed responsible for X even though he did not intend it, and that he therefore needs some justification to avoid blame (typically that the bad X is outweighed by the good Y). Now change the example to make Y "indifferent"—some unimportant matter that concerns only P—and X something good. If P wants credit for X, is it sufficient for him to argue that he was responsible for X, or does he have to establish something more? My view here—one that I think is widely held—is that praise requires more on the part of the agent than does blame—that the agent must "do more" to deserve praise. It seems, then, that while being responsible is *sufficient* for (opening up the agent to) blame, it is only *necessary* for praise. In this regard, praise and blame are different. Suppose, again, that P is responsible for X; then there are two moves that he can make, depending on whether X is good or bad. If good, he might try to establish credit for it, but if bad, he might try to justify his actions. I shall suppose that praise is like blame in *this* respect, for if it were necessary for P to "justify" himself as being worthy of praise for X, then there would be a kind of symmetry between praise and blame: in both instances, there is more for P to do, once it is established that he is responsible.

This leaves the class of those things that are neither good nor bad, those to which we are "indifferent." We would expect to find here trivial matters, mundane and unimportant, things brought about every day in the normal course of events. If P is only responsible for important matters, matters for which he can be blamed or praised, then again it will be necessary to decide what these are, for the contrast now is not between things that are good and things that are bad, but between both of these classes and the class of "indifferent" things. The relativism question thus surfaces again. But perhaps too much is being made of relativism here, and perhaps, on closer examination, relativism may turn out to be not nearly so troublesome as it is elsewhere in philosophy. As an illustration, consider the following story about legal liability: The speed limit by a school near my house has been lowered from fifty to forty kilometers per hour, a fact unknown to me because I have been living interstate. After a long journey home, I drive by at forty-five kilometers per hour, believing that I am obeying the law, but in fact I am legally liable for breaking it. Last year, driving at this speed would have been indifferent—one of those trivial matters that concern no one; now it is an offense for which I can be blamed. The difference has nothing to do with the act itself, with the physical movements that I and my car make; rather, the difference comes from a change in the law that warrants the description, or redescription, of the action as "breaking the law." In one sense, then—that of the physical movements that make up the acts— what I did last year and what I do now are more or less the same; in another sense, because of the change in the way the acts are evaluated, they are now quite different. But discerning the similarity and difference here seems simple. So, at any given time, the class of types of action supposed to be good or bad is determined by a set of accepted standards. This class's membership may change with any change in standards, and this in turn will make differences in ascriptions of responsibility.

The basic characterization might therefore be slightly reformulated:

agents are morally responsible for their actions and omissions that are
worthy of blame or praise. And this suggests how to move forward: *first*
fix the class of actions or omissions that "belong" to the agent, which
are "his," and *then* decide which of them are worthy of praise or blame.
If the focus of attention is on action X rather than agent P, we might
reverse the order and first see whether the action is blame- or praiseworthy and then determine whose action it is. All this presupposes that
there are principles, norms, laws, and so on—what I will collectively call
standards—available for evaluating actions. Without standards, it seems
we are committed to saying that the agent is responsible either for all his
actions and omissions or for none of them. This is surely wrong: agents
are only responsible for those actions that somehow matter. Or, to make
the same point differently, agents are only responsible for those actions
for which they can be *held* responsible. It is possible to draw the distinction between being responsible for X and being held responsible for X
in different ways, or even to deny that there is any such distinction. I
say that P is held responsible for X if he is actually called on to respond
to the fact that he has done, or omitted to do, X. It is quite possible that
P "gets away" with X, like every perpetrator of an unsolved crime, and
hence it is a mistake to conflate "P is responsible for X" with "P is held
responsible for X." However, if it makes no sense to hold P responsible
for X, then presumably X is not one of those actions or omissions that
matter to us.

Relativism concerning moral responsibility would mean that judging
whether P is responsible for X would depend on which of two or more
incompatible moral standards is adopted. Some moral philosophers do
not believe that there are incompatible moral standards; they believe in a
set of timeless duties, such as "thou shalt not kill" and "always keep your
promises." Thus, any action that can be described as killing or promise-
breaking is such that someone can be blamed, wherever and whenever the
action occurred. Others would not be so confident in the existence of such
a set of standards. In this case, it might be said that whether an action of
type X is blameworthy depends on further factors, perhaps on historical and contingent circumstances that determine whether that action
increases aggregate welfare (see chapter 8, which addresses ethics proper).
But this does *not* mean that different concepts of responsibility are associated with different traditions of ethics: it means, rather, that judgments
about which actions and omissions are worthy of further investigation—

discovering who they belong to and what they are—will depend on which standards are chosen, as will ascriptions of responsibility. This kind of relativity should not cause undue concern, although if different ideas of responsibility were associated with each system of moral standards, then, as noted above, our task would be much harder.

That we can, for the purpose of analysis, separate the conditions under which X belongs to P and the standards by which X is evaluated also allows different judgments of responsibility along social, legal, and moral dimensions. Earlier, the notion was mooted that social and legal responsibility for X, at least for the scientist, might be moral responsibility in disguise, although it was acknowledged that this point needed further discussion. Now it is clear just how such a reduction might not work, specifically if distinct standards of moral, social, and legal responsibility lead to different judgments. There is no doubt that a historical account of this question would find that sometimes actions that are taken to be in accordance with socially sanctioned standards conflict with minimum moral prohibitions against harm. In such a case, any apparent inconsistency regarding where responsibility lies could be easily resolved. A society that accepts slavery and torture, for instance, is a bad society; the "socially responsible action" of torturing slaves is easy to criticize. There may, however, be more subtle tensions between social and moral responsibility, which will be examined later.

Backward- and Forward-Looking Responsibility Revisited

Thus far, X has been interpreted as an outcome, something the agent has caused or omitted to prevent or do. The difference between agent- and thing-responsibility is that the former is bound up with the special capacities of people, opening the door to evaluation of the agent's actions and omissions. However, agent-responsibility is not exhausted by responsibility for outcomes, for things that the agent has done: X can be something besides an outcome, besides something that has already occurred. To use one of H. L. A. Hart's famous examples, suppose X is "the ship" and P is "the captain of the ship"; then the relevant relation is not one of causing or acting or omitting to act in some specific way. Rather, in relation to the ship, P is Captain P and has "specific duties" attached to his role, duties that comprise his "role-responsibility" (Hart 1968, 212). He has, so to speak, a specific duty of care. Role-responsibility, as noted earlier, is a kind of forward-looking responsibility. Its relationship with backward-looking responsibility will now be examined in more detail.

To say that the captain of a ship has role-responsibility is to identify specific standards of behavior that derive from his role as captain. This constitutes forward-looking responsibility because, as long as P is acting as captain, he must continue to do certain things. For instance, he must continue to look after his passengers and crew as he has done in the past. Here the connection between forward- and backward-looking responsibility is clear: the sorts of outcomes, and so on, that count as instances of backward-looking responsibility "comprise" forward-looking-responsibility. P is captain of the ship, and he thus assumed his role-responsibility when it set out on a voyage last summer. When the ship returned to port in the autumn, all of the particular things Captain P had done to look after passengers, crew, and so forth "shifted," in a sense, becoming responsibilities in the backward-looking sense; he had thus discharged his role-responsibility, which had set him the task of doing just those things in the first place. Had he not, then whatever else might be said of him, he would have been guilty of not discharging his role-responsibility. Suppose he somehow failed to look after his passengers properly. Suppose too that the chief engineer also neglected to look after the passengers in some way. The captain and the chief engineer failed to do the same thing—namely, properly attend to the passengers' welfare—but only the captain can be blamed, assuming that the captain's responsibilities do not devolve to the chief engineer when the former is neglectful via some formal chain of command.

Instances of neglect and negligence are omissions: certain actions that should have been done were not. The roles of "passenger" and "captain" serve to fix *both* that there was an omission *and* who is responsible for it. Suppose that the captain failed to look after his passengers by not attending to weather reports and hence not avoiding rough seas. The experienced crew did not suffer, but many passengers were seasick. Had no passengers been on board, then "not looking after the passengers" would not have been instantiated. There were passengers, however, and the captain is responsible for not looking after them. It is less clear whether this type of culpable neglect can be fixed when there is *no* specific role-responsibility. If there were no role-responsibility associated with scientists, for example, then scientists could not be responsible for any acts of negligence—and perhaps not for any omissions. On the other hand, if there are grounds for attributions of responsibility other than explicit or formal role-responsibilities, then scientists thus might still be responsible, along with other moral agents. These are important issues that will later be addressed in more detail. For the moment, the relationship between forward- and backward-looking responsibility must be further clarified.

When we hold P responsible for X in the backward-looking sense, we apply essentially the *same* moral standards that we expected to inform P's forward-looking responsibilities. That is, before P did (or omitted to do) X, certain forward-looking responsibilities determined the standards that he was supposed to observe in respect to actions (or omissions) of type X. Later, after P has done (or has omitted to do) X, then he is responsible for X in view of those self-same standards. Taking the simplest case, if X can be described as "doing harm," then at some time in the past, when doing X, P did not abide by the injunction not to do harm. His forward-looking responsibilities as a moral agent should at least be guided by this standard, whatever role-responsibilities he might have. He is *therefore* responsible in the backward-looking sense *because* he did something harmful. The two concepts of responsibility are thus (obviously) distinguished by the fact that moral agents go about their business in a world that has a past and a future. The same moral standards (pace the remarks at the end of the previous section) therefore have different functions with respect to the concept of responsibility: to supply the rationale for ascriptions of responsibility for past actions and to guide future action. Moreover, these standards apply to what P *should* do, perhaps because he has some specific role or other forward-looking responsibility.

All this seems straightforward. Not so straightforward, as suggested earlier, is what these standards are and what justifies our holding them. Nevertheless, assuming that such standards exist—that all moral agents act against a background of a prevailing morality—then forward-looking responsibility and backward-looking responsibility are symmetrical. What role-responsibility does is supplement these commonly held standards. "Supplementing" might mean "overriding," according to some moral theories, as when the duty "thou shalt not kill" is suspended for a soldier fighting in a Just War, or it may mean emphasizing specific duties, as with the ship's captain. How these extra demands will influence judgments of backward-looking responsibility depends on the role in question. Again, the importance of deciding whether a role-responsibility is associated with the scientist is obvious here, for the scientist may have extra responsibilities, over and above those of the ordinary moral agent, which will in turn inform our ascriptions of backward-looking responsibility. The particular task of fixing the conditions under which certain actions and omissions belong to the agent will be taken up later (see part 2). This is a question, first of all, of determining the facts of the matter. In other words, I believe that the conditions under which X belongs to P, and the evaluation of X by some standard, can be distinguished here for the purposes of analysis.

The Consequentialist "Reduction" of Responsibility

Two possible objections can be raised to the "methodological proposal" just made—objections to the effect that the two kinds of responsibility cannot be separated in the way suggested above. The first objection is that the distinction between discovering "the facts of matter"—for example, in relation to backward-looking responsibility—and invoking standards in connection with forward-looking responsibility does not stand up because it presupposes an unacceptably sharp distinction between facts and values. Now, when making decisions, people discover which options are available via facts, while they discover which they prefer via values. Those who deny the fact-value distinction rarely deny this sort of functional division, rather holding that values are like facts in that they are objective or that facts are like values in that they are not secure and unchallengeable. In neither case, however, does there seem to be any substantial objection to the present proposal. Standards, after all, are not the same as values, although they might (well) be taken to express values that recommend certain ways of behaving. In sorting out a particular occurrence of backward-looking responsibility, it hardly seems likely that we would keep running up against standards when we were seeking out the facts of the matter. Perhaps it should be kept in mind that these facts are not as secure or firm as might be thought, and that they thus resemble values in that regard, but it does not follow that anything like normative theory must intrude into such an investigation. This objection, then, does not amount to much at all.

The second objection, the consequentialist denial of the existence of any nonnormative concept of responsibility, is more pressing. To evaluate it, I begin again with Baier, who claims that a close connection between the two forms of responsibility becomes apparent when the rationale for ascriptions of backward-looking responsibility is examined. For thing-responsibility, we look to the cause of the occurrence in order to forestall its happening again if it is a bad outcome and, presumably, to realize its happening again if it is good. For agent-responsibility, we again look to the cause, for similar reasons, but here the agent can be held responsible, and this may entail blame and punishment or praise. This is so, Baier says, because normal humans are moral agents (1987, 103). Suppose, then, that we never bother with agents' backward-looking responsibility without keeping an eye on their forward-looking responsibility—that our aim is always to modify or reinforce agents' behavior and responsibilities.[6] These responsibilities will, as above, cover certain actions, conduct that is supposed to measure up to given standards. Thus, in Baier's view, we would only investigate an incident of negligence toward passengers if this would have an impact on the future responsibilities of captain and crew. To do so, we must already have an idea about what these responsibilities are and about how the captain's actions failed to satisfy them; we must thus be aware of the standards for the role. This argument, which resembles the consequentialist position on responsibility, would in fact be reduced to this position if a consequentialist were investigating role-responsibilities and other forms of agent-responsibility.[7] It is this version of the argument that must be addressed here.

In a well-known essay on utilitarianism, Jack Smart wrote, "Whose was *the* responsibility (for losing the battle)? The act-utilitarian will, quite consistently, reply that the notion of the responsibility is a piece of metaphysical nonsense and should be replaced by 'Whom would it be useful to blame?'" (Smart and Williams 1973, 54). This has been taken to mean that Smart and, in his view, all other act-utilitarians (and, I will assume, all other consequentialists) believe that the idea of assigning *the* responsibility for anything whatsoever is metaphysical nonsense (Van den Beld 2000, 2).[8] On the other hand, Smart could mean that in the sort of case he is discussing—namely, a case in which many persons play a role in a grand event, such as a battle—it is nonsense to talk about *the* responsibility. In any case, Smart's exposition of utilitarianism explains and applies Henry Sidgwick's distinction between the utility of an action, which makes it right or wrong, and the utility of praising or blaming the agent. Praising and blaming are actions as well and so, from the utilitarian perspective, must be assessed in terms of how they promote happiness, welfare, or whatever is the prevailing conception of the good. Thus, not only does it sometimes make sense to praise a wrong action and blame someone for doing the right thing, but it is sometimes right to praise wrong action and wrong to praise someone for doing the right thing. Under the utilitarian gaze, every action is assessable in terms of its impact on the realization of the good, *including* those actions that attribute responsibility. The consistent utilitarian must therefore attribute responsibility in such a way that his actions in so doing promote the good. If it would be right to praise or blame Q for doing X, even though P did it, then Q should be held responsible for X—maximizing good consequences—as it is otherwise not possible to praise or blame Q.

For Baier, the rationale for attributions of backward-looking responsibility is that these have an impact on forward-looking responsibility. The utilitarian apparently goes further and actually assimilates the former to what typically ensues when someone is actually *held* responsible—namely, the praise or blame they receive for what has been done. Even excuses and justifications are not accepted by the utilitarian, unless these promote good outcomes. That the utilitarian does "go further" than Baier is evident. Suppose it is said, in response to Baier, that a historian might be interested in determining who and what was responsible for some episode in the distant past—say for the French defeat at the battle of Borodino. Tolstoy's view was that all kinds of small, unplanned, and contingent circumstances added up to cause the French defeat. The historian who adopts Tolstoy's outlook might wish to catalog as many of these as he can. But this investigation will not change anyone's forward-looking responsibility—or if it does affect some young officer at the staff college who reads the account, then that is quite by chance. It makes perfectly good sense for the historian to work this way, to decide which actions belong to which actor in the battle, without any regard for standards or conduct. Judgments about whether this unit of horse artillery *should* have gone here or there are possible, as are judgments about whether the Old Guard *did their duty*, but the inquiry does not have to delve into such matters: it can simply detail which people and which units were responsible for the ebb and flow of the fight.[9]

Whatever Baier claims about the normal rationale for our interest in backward-looking responsibility, it is entirely possible to have such an interest without regard for what lies in the future, as the example shows. The "normal rationale" is therefore not such as to impose *logical* constraints on what is done with the backward-looking variety of responsibility, such that it is impossible to deal with it without invoking normative considerations. For example, our interest in responsibility and the scientist might take us some distance from the normal rationale, as it did the historian, and be such that it is appropriate, in the first place, to focus exclusively on the backward-looking kind of responsibility. However, this response does seem to not answer the utilitarian. From the utilitarian's standpoint, it might be supposed, the historian should be looking to his audience—perhaps in the staff college—and so reconstruct the battle of Borodino in such a way as to promote the best outcome for his readers. The captain of horse artillery, for example, should be castigated for making the wrong decision about where to move his guns and blamed for contributing to the loss of ground if this provides a salutary lesson for future field commanders, regardless of whether his decision really was wrong, whether he should be blamed for it, whether it led to loss of ground, and so on. For the utilitarian, it is not that such judgments "normally" enter into attributions of backward-looking responsibility; they always do.

Here, the familiar point that utilitarianism is simply too demanding if it requires us to constantly have an eye to maximizing consequences could be reaffirmed, and a preference for nonconsequentialism stated. But it is preferable not to have to make decisions about which normative theory, and hence which standards, to adopt at the very outset of the investigation. The previous section proposed a separation of issues to do with responsibility, with concerns about backward-looking responsibility remaining neutral with respect to standards. To dismiss one of the main theories of ethics so early would be to admit defeat. The same is true for any suggested retreat to the minority position, rule-utilitarianism, which could be taken to entail the view that it is better, on the whole, to hold responsible those who actually are responsible, because it provides a reliable rule of thumb for deciding which actions lead to the best consequences. Not only is this a lesser variant of the theory, but preferring it leads to the kind of question-begging that should be avoided. But does consequentialism actually imply that there really is *no* independent conception of backward-looking responsibility and that *all* responsibility is to be conflated with holding responsible? If so, then the attempted reduction begins to look like a *reductio*.

Suppose that a utilitarian historian, inspired by reading Smart, decides, for whatever reason, that it would be best if he could convince his readership that General Junot was to blame for the defeat at Borodino.

He does his best to make his case but eventually gives up because he finds there is no way to get around the fact that Junot was in Spain at the time, fighting Wellington. In what ways do *truth*, *evidence*, and the *facts* of the matter constrain the utilitarian? The historian might take the extreme line of the propagandist and decide to rewrite history to the degree that he thinks he can "get away with it," maintaining that he is making the past useful. If he does not get away with it, then his stories will not be accepted, and his utilitarian project will fail. So, if he claims that Junot lost the battle of Borodino by his impetuous use of the horse artillery, and everyone knows Junot was on the Peninsula, then no one will accept his account and learn from his brilliant use of the degenerate general's life as an object lesson. But while the historian's motivation in deciding what he can get away with is utilitarian, his reasoning and methods must be those of the professional historian—looking at the facts, evidence, and so on—for they will determine what he can "get away with."

The same surely holds for all other attributions of responsibility. There is no point, from the utilitarian perspective, in holding someone responsible for doing something if they clearly could not have done it. Act-utilitarians, such as Smart, usually accept that, on the whole, applications of such rules as "always tell the truth" and "keep your promises" coincide with the act-utilitarian calculation of best consequences. But act-utilitarians do not "worship rules," and hence where there is conflict, the act-utilitarian drops the rule. But this does not mean that the act-utilitarian thinks the rule is meaningless or interprets it in some strange way. Anyone familiar with Smart's philosophy of science knows that Smart has a robust realist conception of what it means for a statement to be true and therefore has a sensible view of what it means to tell the truth. As an act-utilitarian, however, he might (very reluctantly, I suspect) recommend that the truth not be told in certain circumstances. He would not do so, however, if his utilitarian calculation showed that it did not maximize probable benefit because of the magnitude of the "disutility" associated with revealing the truth. But again, in making such a calculation, a utilitarian like Smart would not adopt some special utilitarian conception of the truth.[10] Precisely the same is the case for responsibility. On the whole, the "responsibility rule" ("hold those responsible who are responsible") yields the best consequences, and this *presupposes* a nonnormative conception of backward-looking responsibility, for if "responsible" is already conflated with "hold responsible," then the rule cannot be applied.

Finally, it may be possible to combine a pragmatic theory of truth, and of responsibility, with an act-utilitarian outlook to form a composite system in which what it is for something to be true *is* that it maximizes happiness, welfare, or whatever is the preferred idea of the good. The rules that the act-utilitarian uses in making day-to-day judgments about what to do would then be differently interpreted from what was just suggested: there would be no "neutral conception" of responsibility. But whatever the merits of such a system, it would be unacceptable to such realists as myself and Smart—unacceptable not because of any utilitarian outlook, but because of the pragmatic theory of truth. If there is a supposition here, then, it is in favor of realism. However, this was already in place before this discussion of forward-looking and backward-looking responsibility ensued: a realist account of science and technology, in outline at least, had already been accepted. The decision to reject the kind of pragmatism just mooted, whatever its merits, is entirely consistent with what has gone before. We are, therefore, able to overcome the most stubborn objection to separating the question of backward-looking responsibility from matters involving standards. Nevertheless, we may remain suspicious of consequentialism, in all its forms.

To conclude, if it is true that Peierls was responsible for the implosion design, then certain facts about what he did or did not do are in place. Peierls was not a "thing," and hence to deem him responsible is to claim more than just that he caused the implosion design; it is to say that he is open to praise and blame for what he did. In this case, there must have been something praise- or blameworthy about his work's outcome, because of the part it played in the Manhattan Project, ensuring that Fat Man was available for testing in July 1945 and for use in August. Whether what Peierls did was worthy of praise or blame depends, if one takes the consequentialist perspective, on how one ranks the state of affairs of many thousands of dead civilians at Nagasaki against other more or less likely possibilities. This ranking will be subject to some standard allowing judgment of which states of affairs are better or worse and, in that respect, which embody some conception of the good.

Peierls could have been responsible for the implosion design in the backward-looking sense even if he had no relevant forward-looking responsibility, granted that the latter continues to be understood as some special obligation that Peierls had, perhaps in fulfilling the role of scientist. Again, whether there is such a thing as the scientist's role-responsibility has not yet been decided, but all that is needed to decide whether Peierls was responsible for the implosion design is *some* accepted standard by which to evaluate that outcome. The practical problems of agreeing on and applying such standards should not, of course, be underestimated, as the "conflicting judgments of history" about Nagasaki show. Concomitantly, there are conflicting judgments about the precise nature of the responsibility of Peierls and of others engaged in the Manhattan Project, but this does not mean that the idea of moral responsibility is infected by some pernicious relativism. Such contradictory judgments are a result of conflicting standards: some might see Nagasaki as a courageous act, while others would judge it as evil, and Peierls's work might be similarly evaluated. In this sense, responsibility is relative. But whether the work Peierls did really belongs to Peierls does not depend on any standard or value; if it did, that would amount to an unacceptable form of relativism.

Keeping in mind a summary of the main considerations addressed here, we might set out the conditions under which an agent P is responsible for an outcome X. In doing so, we first determine what it is for X to be "P's outcome." That is, we first work out what it is for an action or omission to "belong" to P. If this is possible, then we should be able to associate a class {X} of outcomes with P—a class of actions and omissions that belong to him. One might think of this class as all the outcomes that are P's in his life, or within a more restricted timeframe, or whatever is the focus of attention. The idea then is to next appeal to suitable standards—again, whatever these are—to evaluate what P is responsible for. This approach would divide our inquiry neatly into two parts: a "factual" part for the determination of {X} and then a normative part that evaluates and divides {X} into subclasses.[11] It is to be expected that these would amount to rather different tasks, with matters bearing on the forward-looking aspect of responsibility confined to the second. To look ahead, I think it is possible to proceed in this way, but I believe it will still force undue limitations on the scope of backward-looking responsibility: unless some appeal is made to what P should have done (or omitted to do), or what he should have been aware of, the class {X} will be more restricted than it should be.

Part 2

LOOKING BACK

Actions, Consequences, and Omissions

"WIDE VIEW" OF RESPONSIBILITY, AS THE LABEL
suggests, means one that allows the scientist to be held responsible for
more of his actions and more of his work's consequences, as well as
some omissions, than do some of the available alternative positions—in
other words, more of the outcomes of the class {X} (identified at the end
of the previous chapter) rather than fewer of them. I will maintain that
scientists can even be responsible for outcomes of their work that they
do not foresee.[1] This position is thus in sharp contrast to the "narrow
view"—or *standard view*, as I shall call it—which sees all agents as only
responsible for what they intend.

How do we decide between these alternatives? The wider view provides a broader framework—in my opinion the broadest available—for
engaging the scientist with the outcomes of his work.[2] But this in itself
will not suffice to support this wider account: just because it is clear that
a particular viewpoint would be helpful does not mean that it can be
taken up without further thought and argument. Indeed, a general
philosophical question may be raised here concerning the relationship
between persons and their actions (or omissions), which determines
which of these they are morally responsible for, and why. These are significant issues. One virtue of the standard view is that it yields a straightforward reading: people are responsible for what they *intend* to do,
nothing more. As agents, people reflect on what they can do and make
choices informed by the values and preferences they hold; these issue in

intended actions. People are therefore responsible for these actions alone. But I think this "straight rule of moral responsibility," in John Mackie's words, can be bent sufficiently to incorporate both foreseen and some unforeseen actions.[3]

Some other matters must be addressed, however, before we can move on to examine the standard view in greater detail, matters concerning the range of possible actions that it makes sense to say the scientist performed and the range of possible omissions that it makes sense to say he could have performed (the members of {X}). These are the things that he *could* be responsible for. As regards actions, making this determination might seem straightforward: When someone does something, doesn't he just *do* that thing? What could be more obvious than that? Certainly being able to identify actions with bodily movements occurring at a given time and place (e.g., me moving my fingers over this keyboard) would render such judgments neat and tidy: movements have outcomes, and these may then be screened off as the actions' *consequences*. But Joel Feinberg proposes that at least some of these consequences may be identified with actions performed by the agent. It is easy to see how this can be done with the fingers-on-the-keys example, for, unlikely as it may be, I can be said to be writing a best-selling philosophical treatise, and that it is best-selling is something decided after (long after) the event of my moving my fingers over the keys.[4] The reason I want to do things this way, rather than just talk about actions and their consequences, is that it turns out that this works better in terms of assessing the standard view and canvassing the alternatives. In particular, I want to suggest that a scientist who claims to just be doing pure research—this being his intention—can also be seen as doing applied work. I begin, then, with an example that demonstrates why we might be inclined to accept the wide view of responsibility.

A Cautionary Tale

In the spring of 1939, just a few months before the outbreak of World War 2, the French scientist Frederic Joliot-Curie and his coworkers in Paris, at one of three important centers for nuclear research (the others being in New York and Berlin), prepared to publish their results on neutron multiplication in an assembly of heavy water (heavy water "moderates" or slows down the neutrons liberated by natural uranium and changes the rate of fission). Neutron multiplication is the measure of how many neutrons are liberated on average by each nuclear-fission event in an assembly. If neutron multiplication is greater than 1, then a divergent chain reaction may be possible, and a large value would appear to make this increasingly likely. Joliot recorded a value of 3.5, which he published. This value was wrong, Joliot having made several mistakes and miscalculations, but this was certainly the kind of wrong result that would encourage others to repeat his work and carry on with their own along similar lines. Moreover, Joliot wrote that if enough uranium were immersed in a suitable moderator, "the fission chain will perpetuate itself and break up only after reaching the walls limiting the medium. Our experimental results show that this condition will most probably be satisfied" (Rhodes 1986, 296).

Leo Szilard, then living and working in New York, along with Enrico Fermi and other important émigré scientists, had managed to institute a moratorium on publishing the work that was being done on nuclear physics at Columbia. Fermi and others had reluctantly agreed with Szilard, who wrote to Joliot asking him to join the moratorium.[5] The reason Szilard did so, and the reason he agitated for and worked on the atomic bomb project in the United States, was that he was worried about the Nazis getting their own atomic weapon, and any data on neutron multiplication (especially good data) would be useful for a bomb project. However, Joliot refused to join the moratorium, claiming that he was not working on anything to do with weaponry or war and that, in investigating the properties of the uranium atom, he was simply doing pure science. He was quite right: if his *intention* was to do pure research, then that is what he did, even if identical work, done in the context of a weapons program, would have been applied. Notice that in saying that it was his intention to do pure research, Joliot was giving Szilard his *reason* for what he did—namely that he was interested in discovering the properties of uranium "for their own sake." He published his paper in *Nature* in April.[6]

Both Richard Rhodes and Paul Lawrence Rose report that Joliot's research in fact inspired the British atomic bomb project, as Joliot was "an authoritative figure," and that his project eventually led to the Frisch-Peierls Memorandum. So maybe it was crucial after all for Fat Man's and Little Boy's availability in July 1945. However, Joliot's research did not, apparently, inspire German nuclear scientists to greater efforts to build an atomic bomb. Nevertheless, I think that further questions can be asked about Joliot. For instance, was it irresponsible or reckless of him to publish, given the political situation at the time? If we focus just on the Germans, then I think this question would be answered in the affirmative if it is judged that his data would actually have helped German scientists in their quest for a bomb or if there was reason at the time to believe that it would help them. In this regard, Szilard believed that there was indeed such reason. For Szilard, it was too risky to publish anything that might help the Germans. Because it turned out that the Germans in fact had no idea how to make a bomb, such questions have little historical import: Joliot's data did not motivate the Germans. But let us suppose, for the sake of a good story, that Werner Heisenberg and Otto Hahn and the other German scientists interested in nuclear physics read Joliot's paper, and it inspired them to a greater research effort. That situation is not at all far-fetched—Joliot's research did, after all, inspire the British. Was Joliot thus *responsible* for aiding the German bomb project?

Assume that Joliot's work did in fact aid the German bomb project, but grant that providing such aid was not his intention when he published his data. There then appear to be two further alternatives: either he had grounds for believing that this would be a consequence of his decision to publish, albeit an unintended one, and he published anyway, or he did not have such grounds. One assumes that Joliot had good reason to suppose that his paper would be read with interest by colleagues in nuclear physics. It would be strange if he did not suppose this, as he was an experienced physicist who had interacted with many others in the past, including Heisenberg and Hahn, and who knew the purpose of publication—after all, he is on record as having said that he was investigating the properties of the uranium atom "for their own sake," and such research is always communicated to others via publication and letter. Did he have reason to think that his research would aid the Germans in their bomb project? Joliot, like Szilard, must have been aware of the volatile political situation in Europe and the dangers posed by the Nazis. But did he think that nuclear physics could provide the basis for a terrible weapon? This is the central issue.

If Joliot did think that his work might help German scientists (or anyone else) develop an atomic bomb, even though this was not his intention, and if, given our story, it did help them, then there seems to be a strong case for saying that he *was* responsible for aiding the German scientists. One might put it this way: in this case, it *looks as if* what he did was wrong and *as if* he were to blame for doing it. But if he was not responsible, then he cannot be blamed, as an agent can only be blamed for those outcomes he is responsible for. Helping the Nazis (or anyone else) develop an atomic bomb would have been a terrible thing to do, and this might well make us all the more ready to blame Joliot for doing it. But if it were clear that no one is ever responsible for what they foresee but do not intend, then it would *also* be clear that Joliot would not be to blame. The terribleness of the example is such as to bring home to us, graphically, that it is *by no means clear* that people are only responsible for what they intend. In other words, it is by no means clear that what I call the standard view of responsibility—that agents are responsible for all and only their intended actions—is correct. One could go even further and say that Joliot was to blame for aiding the German bomb project, even if he did not think that his work might help the German scientists, or maybe even if he did not think his work would help them *and* he was unaware of the prevailing political situation. That is, we might affirm that Joliot was responsible under the second of the two alternatives. It seems, in other words, that this example might also illustrate the second of the two alternatives detailed earlier and thus support the wide view of responsibility.

It is quite possible, however, that Joliot was not as "worldly" or imaginative a person as Szilard. He might not have considered the possibility that his research might provide the basis for a terrible weapon. The situation today, sixty-five years later, is quite different, the Manhattan Project and many other armaments programs having set a precedent for weapons development. And Joliot might not have noted the political situation. This second suggestion leads to the supposition that Joliot was *ignorant* of the effects that his research would, or might, bring about. If one holds the standard view and denies that foreseen but unintended actions bring with them responsibility, then one will (of course) also deny that anyone can be responsible for something of which they are ignorant. And even if it is acknowledged that there can be responsibility for foreseen but unintended actions, it can still be maintained that ignorance always excuses. (Aristotle's view was that actions done out of ignorance are involuntary, and therefore the agent is not responsible for them.)

But we are at liberty to reject both of these positions. Suppose we accept that agents can be responsible for what they foresee, not only what they intend, and suppose further that we routinely expect people to be aware of the consequences of certain of their actions. For example, we expect people to be aware of what might happen if they drive too fast or drive when they are intoxicated. If someone fails to be look ahead to the consequences of his actions and thereby causes harm to some others, there is a case for holding him responsible for this harm, even though he neither intended nor foresaw it, provided that the circumstances are of the kind in which we expect people to take due care: he *should have* foreseen that harm would occur, and that is why we blame him. Should Joliot have foreseen that his work would aid the Nazis' atomic bomb project?

It was, perhaps, not true in 1939 that scientists were expected to try to look ahead and see where their research might lead. Szilard was able to do so, but this might have been because he was unusually prescient. In spite of this, the terribleness of the example might influence our decision to blame Joliot, because we expect extra care to be taken when a truly disastrous outcome might eventuate, even though the risk is slight. It is true, I think, that we do expect people to take extra care in such cases, but it is not clear that Joliot could be held to that expectation as regards his 1939 work in nuclear physics. The situation may well be different today, in part (reverting to what actually happened) because of Joliot's example: his work could have easily aided a German atomic bomb project. Earlier, I maintained that science has changed since 1945 and that scientists now work in a "changed context" (see chapter 1). This means that scientists cannot now deny that their work has at least the potential to affect others in dramatic ways: we expect them to know this. That is, we expect them to know that science can affect our lives, even when the researchers' intention is simply to do pure research and discover things "for their own sakes."

Actions and Consequences

Now suppose (returning to make-believe) that on being asked why he had been so rash as to make his results available to Heisenberg, Hahn, and the other German scientists, Joliot announced that any help he might have given them was merely a consequence of what he had done. Aiding the German scientists, in other words, was not something he had done, not an action of his, but only a *consequence* of his actions in doing pure research. We may well be less than convinced by the efficacy of this response as an excuse, for why should someone not be held responsible for the consequences of his actions? Perhaps Joliot's response here affirms the standard view, with the reason one gives for one's action being identified with the intention that informed the action, all else being relegated to consequences for which one is therefore not responsible. But more generally, it may seem that our actions' consequences are less in our control than our actions, hence making it harder to pin down responsibility. It is clear that agents should not be held responsible for remote consequences of their actions—consequences that they could not, under any circumstances, have been expected to know about. However, what exactly might these be? For instance, I agree with Szilard here: Joliot should not have published because he might have aided a German atomic bomb project, but not because he might have aided production of the "super" or thermonuclear bomb that the Americans developed after 1949—there is no way that Joliot could have anticipated the super.

The range of application of the idea of action might thus be expanded. Joliot moved about his lab, manipulated his apparatus, recorded his data, and wrote up his paper—all actions of his hands, mind, and body that can be summarized as "doing research into the properties of uranium." This is how we describe what people do: we don't just describe how they shift themselves about ("At 10:15, Joliot moved his left hand"). But in this case, we might also say that Joliot was helping the Germans, granted that the paper he wrote did in fact help them. It is possible, although we know it is not true, that Joliot actually intended to help them and that this is why he did his experiments. That is to say, Joliot, when asked, might have replied that he was a Nazi sympathizer, and that he did his work in an attempt to aid the Nazi cause. In this case, it seems we could say that "aiding the German bomb project" was something Joliot also actually did. If the description "aiding the German bomb project" fits when his action was intended, why should it not also fit when his action was *not* intended? In general, if it is possible to see what individuals do at given times and places "under several descriptions," the limits to the range of actions that can actually be attributed to them need to be determined. Responsibility is not yet at issue here, only the *candidate* actions for which responsibility might be assigned. My eventual answer will be that the limits on action coincide with the limits on responsibility, but to reach the point at which several different actions can be attributed to an agent as a result of one and same set of bodily

movements, I must first explore further how actions and their consequences are normally understood.

The difference between an action and a consequence can be understood simply: an action is what a person does, and a consequence is an
event or state of affairs that follows. This does not in itself serve to
unambiguously separate actions from consequences, because actions
are also events constituted by movements of the agent's body. But the
intuition is that the consequence takes place (an event) or persists (a
state of affairs) after the action is over. Yet another example will illustrate this difference, showing that it does *not* capture the way we habitually talk about what people do; this will suffice to justify employing
what Feinberg calls the "accordion effect" when attributing actions to
agents. The example: Crazy Horse (CH) shoots Standing Bear (SB) with
a bow and arrow at long range: CH fires his arrow, and a few seconds
later SB is hit. The fact that CH has completed the range of bodily
movements in question—fitting the arrow in the bow, drawing back
the string, aiming, and letting go—does not mean that SB's being hit
must be seen and described merely as a consequence of what CH did.
What CH *did* was to shoot his enemy, SB; SB's being hit was not a consequence of something else that CH did that was the main focus of his
intentions. At least this is what we would normally say. If we were particularly interested in CH's bowmanship, then we might describe how
he fitted the arrow, pulled back the string, and so on. Thus, how we
describe what an agent does may well reflect our interests. But the point
of this example is to demonstrate that we are not constrained to describe what the agent does as coterminus in space and time with the
events made up by his bodily movements. CH was doing nothing at all
at the instant when SB was hit, yet what he did would normally be
described as "shooting Standing Bear."

An objection to this position will help us to understand it better.
Consider Joliot again. I have suggested that it might be said of him, inter
alia, that he was finding out some interesting properties of uranium, getting data to publish a paper, and aiding the German atomic bomb project. And all these things were what he did in his lab in Paris. To simplify
things, suppose what he did took place on just one morning. These
actions may only be correctly *attributed* to him after the event, at some
later time when what he did that morning is over. To clarify, suppose
that after Joliot collected the data that morning, he received the

telegram from Szilard and decided not to publish after all. Of course, having made that decision, he would not have aided the Germans. There is thus a sense in which later actions depend on earlier ones, although this is not *causal* dependence. Joliot's action of collecting data did not cause him to also publish a paper: we are talking about one and the same set of bodily movements but describing them in different ways.[7] Rather, certain *other* things had to happen later before "publishing a paper" could be a correct description of what Joliot did that morning. Joliot had to type his manuscript and send it off to the journal, the editor had to approve it, the typesetter had to set the type, and the printer had to print it—none of which affected his collecting the data. Moreover, the journal had to be delivered to Berlin, Munich, Göttingen, and so on; read and understood by Heisenberg, Hahn, and others; and then acted upon, if Joliot could also be said to have aided the Germans. There are therefore *other* causal factors, besides the things that Joliot did in his lab, that need to be in place before these "consequences" of what he did in the lab could come to be.

This might well also have been the case when Crazy Horse shot Standing Bear. If the wind was blowing so that CH had to allow for it and not aim directly at SB, then wind is a causal factor, necessary for the arrow to hit its target and hence for it to be true that what CH did was "shoot Standing Bear."[8] Thus, certain other causal factors, besides those initiated by the agent's bodily movements, are in place even in an example of an action that, I claim, would routinely be described with reference to an event that takes place *after* these movements are over— namely SB's being shot. In terms of what it takes for events and states of affairs to take place, the bodily movements in question are rarely *sufficient* but are always *necessary*.[9] And so the fact that the things that the agent does with his arms, hands, and so on are not usually sufficient to bring about the events that are referred to in descriptions of what he has done holds true in most if not all of the ways in which we characterize the agent's actions. Therefore, the objection to incorporating later consequences into the description of what the agent does cannot be sustained. I think that we can agree with Feinberg when he writes that "this well-known feature of our language, whereby a man's action can be described as narrowly or as broadly [by incorporating consequences] as we please, I propose to call the 'accordion effect,' because an act, like the folding musical instrument, can be squeezed down to a minimum or else stretched out" (1965, 146).[10] I will thus follow Feinberg in calling what we have been doing the accordion effect, or "playing the accordion."

Playing the Accordion

Are there any limits to playing the accordion? These are really matters of convention and hence should be chosen to suit our purposes. For instance, consider Isaac Newton in the years before 1687, when he published his great treatise on classical mechanics, which contained his discovery of the inverse square law of gravitation. One application of this law is in the determination of how fast such an object as Fat Man will fall from a plane in a given amount of time. Such information was important for the bombardier aboard Bock's Car, the plane that Major Sweeney flew to Nagasaki. So, we could entertain the following description of Newton's work: "Newton was providing the basis for calibrating the bomsight used on Bock's Car over Nagasaki." But to say that this is what Newton was doing is to invite the response that he could not possibly have known this would result, and so why bother to describe it as something he did? Notice that the absurdity rests not so much on the fact that Newton could not have *intended* this but on the fact that he could not have *known* about it. If we wanted to make the point that the work of such scientists as Newton can have applications far in the future that they cannot know about at the time, we might say something like, "Unbeknownst to him, Newton was providing the basis for . . . ". Thus, the accordion can be stretched pretty far, if such qualification is included. But this qualification immediately excuses the scientist from any responsibility for the outcome. I suggest that the accordion be played only to the point at which the actions attributed to the agent are such that he can be responsible for them, as that is the most suitable convention here.

I will now set out more precisely what I think is a useful way to fix the actions that can be attributed to an agent. Suppose first that an event or a state of affairs is the product of the actions of one or more agents, in the sense that what they did was necessary for that outcome. The event of dropping Fat Man on Nagasaki is one such outcome that was the result of many actions by many agents, from the scientists who did the research, to the politicians who made the decision, to the airman who carried out his orders. Each of these agents was necessary: had

Rudolf Peierls not done his work on the implosion technique that weaponized plutonium, had the members of the Chemistry Division not devised the explosive "lenses" that made the technique realizable, had Major Sweeney not flown the plane—*and if no one else had done these things either*—there would have been no Nagasaki. Each of the things that every individual did played a *causal role*, and when someone enacts a causal role with reference to X, they are *causally responsible* for X. A causal role with respect to a given outcome is thus something without which the outcome would not have eventuated, and it does not have to be uniquely associated with a particular agent. Major Sweeney himself did not have to fly Bock's Car to Nagasaki; his backup, Captain Swartz, could have performed this role. And one assumes that someone else could also, at least in principle, have done what Peierls did. In all such cases, one can say that "P contributed to Nagasaki because he did X," where X refers to the causal role.

X is constituted by something that P did by moving his hands, speaking, writing, and so on—namely, by the kind of bodily movements listed earlier. These movements will be described in terms of the actions needed to fulfill the causal role with respect to the outcome in question, when this outcome is the focus of attention. P can only have contributed to Nagasaki if there was some X by means of which he did so. For such a complex undertaking as the bombing of Nagasaki, there will be causal roles such that the agent who undertook those roles could not have been aware of the outcome. I just mentioned Newton in this regard; earlier I noted Einstein's 1905 discovery of $E = mc^2$, which explains where the energy liberated in an atomic explosion comes from. Both of these scientists made Nagasaki possible in view of something they did, but we do not, for the reasons already given, want to describe what they did as "contributing to Nagasaki" or "providing some of the physics necessary for making an atomic bomb" without some excusing qualification. So if X refers to a causal role needed for some outcome O, then let us only allow P's doing X to be described as (something like) "contributing to O" if P should have foreseen that this would be the case. As suggested earlier, I will take this to be the limit of what an agent can be responsible for as far as he acts. The rest, one might say, is a matter of background or received knowledge.

There is another way to view action X: when P does X, X may well be necessary for all manner of future events and states of affairs in addition to O. For example, Peierls's work on implosion did not just make

Nagasaki possible but was also the basis for all the fission triggers used in thermonuclear weapons. While this development was independent of Nagasaki, Nagasaki itself led to all manner of other things, such as the Japanese surrender, the occupation of Japan by the U.S. military, changes to the balance of power in Asia, and so on. We could then ask whether, in virtue of this work on implosion, Peierls could be said to have "contributed to thermonuclear weaponry," "contributed to the Japanese surrender," and so on when he was doing his work on implosion in the Theoretical Division at Los Alamos in 1944. Our answer, according to the suggested criterion, will depend on whether he could have been expected to know these things. Most likely he could not. Thus, when P does X, we may be able to consider this action as contributing to a range of future occurrences, many of which will require other agents to have done certain things as well; hence X can stand as a causal role with respect to a range of future events and states of affairs. Again, whether or not it is appropriate to say that P contributed to these will, according to our criterion, depend on whether or not he should have foreseen these outcomes. However, one can be responsible for more than what one actually does.

Actions, Causes, and Omissions

Suppose P passes a colleague slumped over in a fume cupboard and does nothing to help. The colleague dies, but P did not cause his colleague's death. To adapt the terminology of the last section, there is no X such that P did X and X was necessary for P's colleague's death. However, even though P did not do anything to cause the death of his colleague, he would still be held responsible, if not for his colleague's dying then at least for not assisting him to live. In other words, it appears clear that the concept of responsibility covers not only what we do but also what we *omit* to do. At this stage, I am not interested in deciding just how to assign blame to those who omit to do something, as compared with those who act. For instance, most people would see P's killing his colleague as far worse than P's omitting to prevent him from dying, but such a comparison may not be correct for all instances of omitting. I will, however, set this issue aside here to focus instead on the range of those things that an agent can be said to have omitted to do. And here again, as with actions, I want to do so in such a way that it makes sense to ask whether the agent could have been responsible for what he did not do. I will assume that examples of the kind just given are enough to convince us that there can be responsibility for omissions. Note that this topic is important for science, at least because there are many more projects that scientists could undertake than, in practice, they are able to undertake. Scientists, in other words, make choices. Are they then responsible for what they choose not to do?

Two issues must be discussed in regard to omissions. The first concerns just what an omission is: when does P omit to do X, as opposed to being unable to do X or not being the one who should do X? The second concerns what sort of omissions there are. This question is rather easier to answer. The omission in the death of P's colleague was an instance of "omit to prevent." The object or "content" of the omission, so to speak, was an undesirable state of affairs, namely P's colleague being dead in the fume cupboard. Therefore, what P omitted was to prevent this undesirable state of affairs from being realized. In order to prevent his colleague from dying, P would, of course, have had to do something: drag her out of the fume cupboard, give her CPR, call an ambulance, and so on. So we can say that P omitted to prevent his colleague's death *because* he failed to do these things. Instances of "omit to prevent" are such that an event happens or a state of affairs obtains that is judged undesirable—there can, of course, be debate and disagreement over these judgments—and agent P had the opportunity to prevent this taking place but did not do so. On the other hand, the object or content of instances of "omit to do" are desirable events or states of affairs that do not happen or obtain because no one "does" them.

If we think of "omit to prevent" and "omit to do" as *relations* between agent P and certain events, then we can express these using counterfactual conditionals and in terms of the ideas of causal process and causal interaction. This provides a formal account of omissions. Thus, for "omit to prevent" we have:

(Op) P stands in the relation "omit to prevent" to X if X occurred, event p did not, and there is a process x such that (1) x caused X; (2) if p had occurred, it would have prevented X by interacting with x; and (3) P could have brought p about.

This looks a little more elaborate than may be thought necessary, as it refers to processes as well as events, but as we will see, this allows a better account of omissions than would be possible if we were restricted to talking about events. Thus, by a (causal) process, I mean a spatio-continuous transmission of information or mass/energy or structure.[11] Here, we are not interested in the notion of causal process so much, for instance, for its adequacy as a theory of scientific explanation, but rather for the way it can inform our views on how causal relations are relevant to omissions (and actions). However, some connections between the topics of explanation and responsibility can be exploited, and it is worth taking a moment to consider these before returning to discuss (Op).

For instance, suppose we want to know what causes a certain natural occurrence—this could be a complex event, such as a volcanic eruption, or something simpler, such as the fission of a plutonium nucleus. A plutonium nucleus fissions because it has been struck by a neutron that gave up its kinetic energy to the nucleus, rendering the latter unstable and thereby making it split apart. The neutron traveling toward the nucleus is a causal process that transmits "structure" in the form of kinetic energy, some of which is given up on interaction. In providing the explanation, it is necessary to show that the neutron has enough energy to fission the plutonium nucleus, and that will entail citing various laws and principles that describe its structure and stability. It is also possible to trace the history of the neutron back to a previous fission event or to the action of a neutron initiator, depending on how complete an explanation is required. The processes that figure in a (correct) causal explanation are therefore what are *causally responsible* for the occurrence. Again, depending on the focus of attention, the neutron, the neutron hitting the plutonium nucleus, the previous fission event, and so on are variously causally responsible for the plutonium nucleus fissioning. Thus, the connection between explanation and responsibility here is that the items causally responsible for the occurrence appear in the explanation of the occurrence. But relevant laws will also be cited in an explanation, together with supporting calculations and initial conditions, so an explanation could also be thought of as a *justified* attribution of causal responsibility. Can we think of an agent's actions, in the sense of what he causes and omits to cause, in the same sort of way?

As shown earlier, the production of the Fat Man bomb and its being dropped on Nagasaki can be thought of as outcomes of the performance of a class of causal roles, each of which stands for a necessary condition. On the basis of the causal process theory, the performance of each role can be represented as the transmitting of a causal process, all adding up to a causal pattern or nexus in which the occurrence is the outcome (cf.

Salmon 1984, 275). This will be a complicated pattern, stretching back in time. Let's look at Peierls and his solution of the hydrodynamic problem for converging shockwaves, which we can refer to as C. This contribution might be viewed along the following lines: Peierls, given the problem to solve when he arrived at Los Alamos, went to work with the Theoretical Division. His solution was then written up, along with the relevant equations and calculations, and presented at one of the weekly colloquia. It was discussed, revised, and then submitted as a classified technical report and stored in the archives. A causal explanation for how Peierls solved the equation would focus on what went on in his brain and would hence be a matter for neurophysiology and other specialist disciplines. At this time, an account of a creative act of this nature cannot be given in terms of the underlying brain processes, although it is hoped that one day sufficient understanding may be brought to bear on such problems.[12] There is, however, evidence to the effect that such acts are the products of brain processes in which various chemical and physical signals mediate the operation of neuronal structures, and as such these appear to be causal processes. If we are simply interested in who was causally responsible for solving the problem, then the answer is clear: it was Peierls; these were his brain processes.

Once the solution had been written down, the document that Peierls had produced itself became a causal process that, literally, transmits information. By "information," Wesley Salmon, who first clarified this notion of "causal process," had in mind the technical sense of information as negative entropy: the amount of information that a signal carries can be expressed as negative entropy, and its capacity to carry that information is a function of its physical constitution. Peierls's report carries information in the more literal sense, as an item of knowledge; this could, one supposes, be given a value on the negative-entropy scale and thus be shown to accord with Salmon's description of causal processes as carrying information. The report could literally *transmit* the information that it carries in several ways. The bomb designers could have sat down with the report and used it to work out a blueprint—perhaps C provided the exact dimensions for the plutonium "pit" and the apex angles of the explosive lenses. If this were the case, then C would be embodied in any Fat Man bomb manufactured on that blueprint; here, there is a sense in which C would be "inside" each bomb. It is more likely, however, that C gave the green light for further research into implosion, inspiring Hans Bethe, Seth Neddermeyer, and others to continue with more theoretical and experimental work. In this case, the causal process C would, as it were, come to its conclusion in the conference rooms of Los Alamos, but its effect would be to initiate further processes that eventually converged on Nagasaki. This allows us to formulate a definition of causal responsibility:

(Cr) P stands in the relation of causal responsibility to X if (1) X and p occur, (2) p is necessary for the occurrence of X, and (3) P brings about p.

With this understanding of causal process, we can return to (Op), with a simple illustration using the fission example. A plutonium atom fissions—event X—because a neutron hits it, enters its nucleus, and causes sufficient instability for it to fission—process x. P stands to X in (Op) because he is able to interfere with x, for instance, by adding a neutron absorber, such as beryllium, to the assembly—event p. P could not add a neutron absorber to the assembly if he were not in the lab, or if he did not know what a neutron absorber is, or if he could not recognize one. Suppose P were the lab manager, with no understanding of the physics, and suppose that plutonium fission would ruin the current experiment. In this case, were P to omit to add a neutron absorber, then he could not be held responsible, and hence could not be blamed, for ruining the experiment. We can so investigate putative individual instances of (Op) and decide whether they conform, but on the whole it is difficult to give an informative *general* account of the difference between someone omitting to prevent something and someone simply failing to prevent it. However, when we focus on a particular example with all the details at hand, matters seem much more straightforward: the lab manager, along with many other nonexperts, fails to prevent the fission event but cannot be held responsible for it; the failure of the scientist running the experiment to prevent the fission event, however, is a different matter and seems like an omission.

The problem of giving a general account of the conditions under which (Op) is satisfied is itself part of a more general problem of supporting counterfactual conditionals. (Op) is a counterfactual in the sense that it is about what the agent did not do but states that he could have done the thing in question—namely, bring about event p. When counterfactuals refer to natural occurrences, it is sometimes possible to support them with reference to laws of nature, although this only works if these laws are understood as relations of natural necessity. To claim, for example, that any body held suspended above the surface of the earth would fall if released is supported by the law of gravitation. Nothing comparable can be appealed to in order to support (Op). But I think this is not really a problem if it is accepted that each such case needs to be addressed on its own merits. And we know that if P is to bring about p, which serves to prevent X, by interacting with x, then he must have access to whatever it takes to do p, he must be aware that p will prevent X, and he must realize that X is an undesirable state of affairs. If any one of these three elements of (Op) is absent, then I would claim *both* that the case would not count as an omission on P's part *and* that he was not responsible for omitting to prevent X.

It can be agreed that anyone who qualifies as a moral agent, in view of their age and mental capacity, should try to prevent someone's death if this poses little or no risk to themselves. If the subject under threat is a mass murderer or dangerous in some other way, then philosophers will begin to argue as to whether letting the subject die is justified; the case is similar regarding not treating terminally ill patients. The experiment example is different because it requires special expertise, which marks a difference between the lab manager and the supervising scientist: the former does not know how to prevent the fission event and so cannot be said to have omitted to do so. Further, suppose P and Q both know how to add the moderator, but it is P's experiment, or P's turn to monitor the system and make sure no fission events take place. If the event then does take place, and the experiment is ruined, we would say that it was P, not Q, who omitted to prevent it from taking place. Moreover, the fact that X is an undesirable event or state of affairs implies that when we say P omitted to prevent it, we do not merely mean that P omitted to prevent what he could have prevented but that he omitted to prevent what he *should* have prevented. Our interest here is with moral responsibility: we want to treat omissions like actions and hold agents accountable for not doing what they should have done, as well as for doing what they should not have done. In this regard, however, it seems that when it comes to omissions, certain agents, such as the supervising scientist, have *special* responsibilities.

The idea of special responsibility is already a familiar one, having come up earlier in regard to role-responsibilities and professional ethics, professionals and other specialists using their expert knowledge to offer some service to clients who lack that knowledge. Professional ethics, in particular, focuses on ensuring that professionals, whose knowledge puts them in positions of power, do not misuse their expertise. Professionals therefore have what we have called *forward-looking responsibilities.* Others with special expertise or knowledge who might not be classified as professionals may also be said to have such responsibilities.[13] For instance, if P pulls his colleague from the fume cupboard and calls for help, and if among those available only Q is trained in CPR, then Q has the responsibility to administer that form of assistance, given that CPR is what is called for. If no one then assists the colleague, only Q can be said to have omitted to do so; the others merely failed to offer aid. Again, this is how I distinguish failing to do something from omitting to do it: only certain agents, in my view, can be said to have omitted to do certain things, because only they are able to do those things. However, the very idea of an omission presupposes a framework of expectations that are derived from what are really forward-looking responsibilities, except that they are not usually referred to in this way for normal moral agents. So while we expect people to offer help to others in dire straits, where there is little risk to themselves and where they are the only ones on hand to help, we do not normally say that this expectation is explicitly based on their having certain "forward-looking responsibilities." The latter term is reserved for those with special expertise.

Following, then, is the counterfactual for "omit to do":

(Od) P stands in the relation "omit to do" to X if X does not occur and none of p_1, p_2, and so on occur; and if (1) X would have occurred had any of p_1, p_2, and so on occurred; and (2) P could have brought about at least one of p_1, p_2, and so on.

The assumption here is that X may be caused in more than one way—namely, via p_1, p_2, and so on. We apply (Od) to give omissions in circumstances in which X is a desirable state of affairs, and P knows this. Moreover, depending on just what X is, it may be that P has some special responsibility in connection with X, and that is why P, as opposed to Q, is the one charged with the omission to do X. The main question raised by omissions here is whether any such special responsibilities attach to scientists qua scientists that are such that both (Op) and (Od) apply. I think that this will likely be true for applied science, but, as usual, this is more straightforward than pure science.

I have tried to identify and limit what an agent does when he initiates certain movements of his body and what he omits to do when he does not make certain movements, arguing that it is possible to attribute to the agent actions that refer to certain events and states of affairs that take place later in time. The limits I place on such attributions are a function of what the agent is in a position to know about. I gave a similar account of the limits on what an agent can be said to have omitted, the notion of forward-looking responsibility becoming relevant here. Further, I proposed that the cautionary tale of Joliot, whose research fortunately failed to inspire the German nuclear scientists, might make us more sympathetic to a wider account of the conditions for (backward-looking) moral responsibility than is available in the standard view.

All three of these conditions can be brought together under the umbrella of *control:*

(Con) P has control of X if P stands to X in either Cr, Op, or Od.

If someone P is to be morally responsible for something X, then P must either have acted in some way that is relevant to X coming about—"doing X," for instance—or have omitted to do or to prevent X. These are the only available alternatives, and they can be expressed together by saying that P has *control* of X. This does not, of course, suffice for P to be morally responsible for X. For one thing, control is only necessary for P having "done X." Further, for this action to "belong" to P, he must have been in a position to know that he was doing X. And were he indeed in that position but with an excuse for doing X, he still would not be responsible for X. Nevertheless, (Con) is a useful way to express the causal content of the idea of moral responsibility: it selects the class {X}.

CHAPTER 5

Intention and Responsibility

THE STANDARD VIEW OF RESPONSIBILITY PROVIDES an *excuse* (a blanket excuse) for the scientist who does pure research. As long as he does not intend that his work has a certain outcome—or, to "play the accordion," as long as he does not intend what he does to be described with reference to that outcome—then he will not be responsible for that outcome even if he foresees it.[1] It is, for instance, enough for the scientist to say that he was undertaking a research project for the sake of science itself and that this was why he published his work—one is inclined to call this "the Joliot excuse." Further, the standard view engenders an attitude such that scientists will not be interested in or concerned with the wider applications of their work: if they are not responsible for what they foresee but do not intend, they will thus be disinterested in any unintended applications and hence will not try, or be disposed, to look ahead and assess what these might be. Similarly, things can be said about applied research. Applied research can be "dual capable," with one application transferable to one or more other fields.[2] If the intention is just to provide the basis for one such application, then any others that are foreseen but not intended will therefore not bestow any responsibility on the scientist. As to the future, the standard view will not support a demand that the scientist look ahead to where his work might lead before he begins a research project; his forward-looking responsibilities will only concern what he intends to do.

Earlier examples have already suggested that the standard view is not acceptable, but this was based on intuitive responses, not on any systematic examination of the relationship between intention and moral responsibility. Such an examination might show that these intuitive responses are at fault, but I don't believe this is the case. Further, the best arguments that can be given in support of the standard view still fail to rule out the conclusions drawn in the Joliot example. My strategy here will be to canvass the version of the standard view that I think is best, the work of R. J. Wallace, leaving aside other versions such as those of Aristotle and John Mackie, although they too have their merits.[3] I will focus on what Wallace sees as the relationship between intention and moral responsibility: why is it that agents are only supposed to be responsible for what they intend to do? Wallace provides an answer to this question, one that we need to be clear about, but one, I will argue, that also provides a basis for moving on to the wide view of responsibility that I favor. I think Wallace's answer is *sufficient* for the standard view, in the sense that it lets us see why agents are responsible for what they intend, but it is not *necessary*, in the sense that it allows for agents to be responsible for more than they intend.

While Wallace does not affirm or make explicit what he means by "intentions" at the outset, I think intentions can be understood on at least two levels. First, intentions can be stated as reasons for actions. In the formula "I did it because r," r stands for the intention of the agent, which he afterward gives as the reason for why he did what he did. This seems straightforward, and Wallace is content with it. On a second level, however, some analysis of the sort of thing that can both be a reason for action *and* play a role in the actual mental antecedents of acting might be provided. One such analysis of intentions both as causes for acting and reasons for actions—the one I will adopt here—is the "received account," as I will call it, of Donald Davidson and Alvin Goldman.[4] This account helps to clarify just what it is for an agent to foresee but not intend an outcome, and it also clarifies the notion that agents can be responsible for what they foresee. This analysis will lead to what I call the "modified standard view," something of a halfway house between the standard view and the wide view that I wish to establish.

Strawson and Wallace on the Standard View

Our overall understanding of responsibility is based on a *relation* between an agent P and an action "doing X" (or an outcome X), such that P is open to praise or blame in regard to X. This is the *accountability* notion of responsibility: P needs to account for having done (or caused) X by making some "response" that, if unsatisfactory, *means that he is blameworthy* (mutatis mutandis for praise). In a widely discussed article, "Freedom and Resentment" (1962), Peter Strawson put forward what has come to be called the "reactive attitudes" approach to moral responsibility, to explain or interpret what it is to call an agent to account (Wallace 1996, 51). Here, the relevance of the reactive attitudes approach is that it commits Strawson, and others who hold it, to the standard view. Or at least that is R. J. Wallace's position.[5] Wallace thinks that Strawson's account of *excusing* provides an argument for the standard view, in that it provides reasons for tying responsible action to intentional action: if an action's being unintended always excuses the agent, then the standard account is correct. But why do Strawson and Wallace believe this to be the case and hence hold the standard view?

The core of the reactive attitudes approach is that we—that is, moral agents—have a framework of *expectations* in connection with the conduct of our fellows. When these expectations are disappointed, then a negative *emotional* response is appropriate (indignation, disappointment, disapprobation, etc.). To hold someone to account as a morally responsible agent is therefore to hold him to certain expectations—for example, to keep his promises. If someone fails to live up to these expectations, then we should feel (have every right to feel) indignant, annoyed, upset, and so forth, and to display these feelings. Further, it seems clear to me that we also have such feelings about *ourselves*—that we feel we have let ourselves down, failed to live up to the expectations we have for ourselves.[6] Moreover, a person can feel this way about himself even if no one else knows what he has done, and no one else reacts negatively to his actions. Evidently, only *moral* agents are subject to such an emotional response, because only moral agents have moral obligations; other purposive creatures, such as little children and cats, do not. Agents are subject to reactive attitudes because they have the capacity to understand moral obligations and should conduct themselves in accordance with those obligations.

This last point is held in common with most moral philosophers: agents are supposed to limit their behavior in accordance with moral principles. Distinctive about the reactive attitudes approach, however, is the way in which it understands what happens when an agent fails to limit his behavior in the right way. It may be noted that this approach also suggests a reason for agents to behave morally—namely, to avoid being an object of their fellows' disgust. The reactive attitudes approach therefore yields a simple, straightforward way of understanding what it is to hold a person responsible, and it locates the actions and so on that attract responsibility in a social context.[7] I think this is an enlightening contribution to our understanding of moral responsibility. However, it already seems clear that someone could fail to live up to our expectations of him as a moral agent by his foreseen but unintended actions or even by actions that he was not aware he was doing. Does Wallace have any argument that should persuade us otherwise?

Turning to intended action, if excuses defeat the charge that someone is morally responsible for doing X, then, Wallace tells us, this "suggests that doing X intentionally is a condition of blameworthiness for X. . . . But why does blameworthiness require intention in this way? Strawson's proposal is that unintentional X-ing is not really a moral wrong in the first place, because the demands to which we hold people are regulated not just by bodily movements but also the qualities of the will expressed" (1996, 119). If we hold people responsible for their actions, and if actions are bodily movements viewed in a certain way, under some appropriate description, then we hold Joliot responsible not just for walking around his lab that morning in Paris and manipulating bits of apparatus: we hold him responsible for aiding the German scientists. But in some cases, bodily movements themselves appear to be enough. If Crazy Horse had strangled Standing Bear, then what he did with his hands would be enough to hold him worthy of blame. There are, then, some examples that do not support Wallace's position. Nevertheless, we can agree with Wallace that we do not *usually* hold people responsible for just their bodily movements. However, whether it is correct, helpful, or informative to say that "qualities of will" are also necessary to turn bodily movements into actions remains to be seen, as does the notion that "qualities of will" only refers to or covers intentions.

Having stated Strawson's proposal, Wallace looks for reasons to support it, eventually explaining what he means by "qualities of the will" in terms of choice: "The stance of holding someone to blame is connected with a special class of moral *obligations* that one accepts; qualities of the will are therefore important only insofar as they bear on the question of whether such moral obligations have been violated. But for this purpose, the qualities of the will that seem to matter would seem primarily to be an agent's *choices.* Only if an action expresses a choice of some sort can we say that a moral obligation has been violated" (Wallace 1996,

128). For this to be relevant to Strawson's proposal, choosing must result in intention, or else Wallace would be suggesting some new approach to the whole issue, in terms of choice rather than intention. Choices are often, although not always, the result of deliberation and practical reasoning, and once made they can issue in the intention to do certain things.[8] The relevance of this seems to be that an agent's intentional actions signify the choices he makes, and these in turn stem from certain qualities of will, presumably those that inform the process of deliberation. These qualities of will are closely bound up with the agent's character and personality, about which we have certain expectations.[9] When these expectations are not met because the agent has chosen to violate some moral obligation, then he is the object of our resentment, indignation, and so on. Intention, then, for Wallace amounts to something like a *criterion* that warrants the application of the concept of responsibility because it reveals the agent's choices. It is these choices, however, and how they are made, that really determine what the agent is responsible for. Someone under duress may make a choice that results in an intention to perform some act that harms another person, but coercion often excuses. It is thus *not just* the fact that the agent chooses and intends to harm that determines whether or not we hold him responsible. Presumably, under duress, the agent's qualities of will dissolve, and he is in another's control, which means he has an excuse.

If someone is to be blamed, and hence be responsible, only when he has chosen to violate some moral obligation, then does this mean that agents are not responsible for what they actually do but only for their choices? If I choose to do harm and then do harm, am I only responsible for choosing, not for the actual harm? Perhaps this is a question that would only interest a philosopher. But we have seen that actions, or intended actions, express the agent's intentions, which reflect the choices the agent makes via deliberation on the basis of moral obligations, present needs and wants, and so on. Yet it would be strange if a serious attempt to express the conditions under which an agent is morally responsible concluded that an agent is not responsible for his actions. Wallace sometimes gives the impression that actions play, at most, a kind of auxiliary role as far as responsibility is concerned: "Consider the obligation of nonmaleficence, for instance: this is not simply an obligation not to make bodily movements that harm other people. Rather it is an obligation not to act in ways that *express* the choice to harm other people. . . . Accordingly, the primary target of moral assessment in terms of this obligation is not bodily movement *per se*, nor is it the emotion and desires we are subject to; rather, it is the *quality* of choice expressed in what we do" (Wallace 1996, 128; my emphasis). But this impression, I think, stems from a too-close identification of actions with bodily movements. Although it is occasionally true that bodily movements essentially constitute acting—Crazy Horse strangling Standing Bear—that is not normally the case. We can then again agree with Wallace that *actions* are the focus of our assessments of moral responsibility, not "bodily movement *per se*," with the qualification that these actions are uncoerced.

Recall that the limits to the actions that an agent performs at a given time, when he moves his body thus, can be characterized in two ways: as being coterminous with the things for which he could be held responsible and coterminous with what he should have been aware he was doing. Wallace has provided a way to establish a connection between these two characterizations. The quality of choice displayed in what the agent does is a function of what he wants to do and of how he sees what he wants to do as affecting others, and hence moral obligations should (at least) prevent him from gratuitous harming. It should be clear by now, because I keep repeating it, that I think there is even more to moral responsibility than what informs the agent's actual choosing: I think people are responsible for what they *should know* they are doing. The question, once more, for the standard view is why intentions should be crucial. Why not include those actions that the agent knows he does but does not intend, those "foreseen but unintended actions" I have talked so much about? There is, I suggest, *nothing whatsoever* in Wallace's account that provides us with any reason to think that intentions are crucial. Given that P decides to do X, and X harms someone, P has, by what he has done, expressed the choice to do harm. Hence, he is subject to our moral assessment, and if he cannot justify himself, or provide some grounds for being excused, he must bear the brunt of our reactive attitudes. For P to say that while he foresaw that X would harm others, this is not why he did X, will not suffice as an excuse, neither in real life nor in philosophy. We began with this intuition, and nothing we have seen in Wallace should incline us to drop it. Moreover, when we come to examine the technical work on intention, nothing there will make us revise this intuition either.

Intention and the "Modified Standard View"

To come to some final considered judgment about the standard view, we must ask just what it is to act intentionally. There is, as might be expected, a good deal of disagreement over the nature of intention, but in order to finally dispose of the standard view, it is only necessary to make some general observations about intentional action, and here there is agreement. For example, it is on the whole accepted that intentions have both a cognitive and a "conative" aspect, and as such they differ from purely cognitive states like belief, on the one hand, and from purely conative states like wishes and desires, on the other. (Hence there are *no* "unsought" intended actions.) Whether intentions are sui generis, whether they are reducible to beliefs plus desires, or whether they are reducible to some other mental state are all matters of debate and disagreement. The "desire-belief" model—the second of the three alternatives just mentioned—did attract considerable support because of the work of Donald Davidson and Alvin Goldman, but it has been subject to some criticism in recent years. Nevertheless, this model will serve present purposes, because it illustrates the two agreed-on aspects of intention.

P can believe all sorts of things, including that he will do X, without ever doing anything. Beliefs are propositional attitudes that are such that the believer accepts the proposition as true. But holding something to be true is not the sort of thing that "gets" the believer to actually do anything. Even if P believes he will do X, and so thinks that "I will do X" is true, he still needs something else to "get him going." On the other hand, P might have a whole array of things that he wants or wants to do, which form his desires. But one can desire things that are forever out of reach or desire two or more things that are impossible to achieve together. To desire to do X therefore provides P with the impetus to do X, but in the absence of beliefs about X being a viable option that P can actually accomplish, desiring X will not result in P doing X. This, roughly speaking, is how the story goes on the desire-belief model: to do X intentionally is to desire to do X and to believe that one will do X. According to the causal theory of action, the desire-belief combination constitutes the mental event M that *causes* P to do X. And according to Davidson's version of this theory, M is also the *reason* why P does X. It is easier to see how M could be the reason why P does X: if P believes he will do X, then desiring X is a reason for him to do X. Just how beliefs and desires cause an agent to act would seem to be a matter for advanced neurological science, not a topic for philosophical analysis. However, if P desires to do X after he has deliberated about the alternative possibilities in light of everything that informs this process, including, it can be assumed, certain general moral obligations, then his *reason* for doing X signifies the way he engages in this process. The desire-belief model of intention, coupled with the causal theory of action, therefore provides an account of what makes agents act that has at least some initial plausibility.

This account tells us that if an agent acts, as opposed to making some involuntary bodily jerk or twitch, then he must have intended to do *something*. Consider Joliot again. He moves about his lab on that morning in early 1939. By various means, asking him, for instance, we find out that he wants to find out the neutron-multiplication factor for a given arrangement of uranium with a heavy-water moderator. This was his intention: he gives it as the reason for what he was doing that morning, and, as causal theorists, we suppose it was the causal antecedent of his activities. What then of the purported action "aiding the German scientists"? Suppose Joliot believed this was true, so it was one of his propositional attitudes, but he did not desire to do it, and hence it was not causally effective in getting him to act. But one assumes that it could have been the thing that got him to do what he did that morning, had he desired it. Instead of M_R, the intention to do research, the causal antecedent could have been M_A, the intention to aid the Germans. In either case, he would have done the exact same thing.

But whereas Joliot intended to do pure research, Peierls and Fermi, in our example, intended to do applied research. Peierls knew that he had solved an interesting theoretical problem about implosion, but his intention—what got him to do the calculations he performed in 1944 at Los Alamos—was his desire to weaponize plutonium. Fermi wanted to develop a way to provide plutonium for the Manhattan Project, and that is why he built his reactor in Chicago in 1942, but he was also aware that a critical assembly would confirm much of the work he and others had done on nuclear physics for the past ten years. The desire to solve an interesting theoretical problem about implosion was not the reason why Peierls did what he did, and neither was the desire to confirm nuclear theory causally efficacious for Fermi, but there is an obvious sense in which both agents could have formed these intentions.

There is therefore nothing mysterious about our saying that Joliot,

Peierls, or Fermi can be seen as having done several quite distinct actions when they performed a given range of bodily movements, if we ascribe to them the attitudes of belief that could stand as the belief component of the corresponding intention. But for any of them to have acted on the occasions in question, they must have desired to do *something*, and that desire, in conjunction with the appropriate belief, was the spur to action. In fact, we now have an explanation for why a range of actions can be effected by the same bodily movements—an explanation that refers, this time, not to the "external" but to the "internal" aspect of action. Thus far, we can maintain that the range of actions that can be associated with given bodily movements is a function of those beliefs that the agent has about what he is doing—before we spoke about awareness, but now our technical account of intention warrants reference to belief. Wallace's "qualities of will" pertain to the mechanism whereby the agent decides, in light of what he believes, what to do, and that means coming to form the desire to do the thing that is expressed by what the agent does. They pertain to this mechanism because the actions that the agent performs, given all this about what he believes and desires, display how his behavior conforms to the moral obligations that we expect people to live by. In a sense, then, I think that Wallace is pointing to the distinctively moral part of moral agency when he talks about qualities of will. In other words, I think our digression into some of the technicalities of action theory helps clarify Wallace's position. It does not save the standard view, but it does allow us to present it in modified form.

If Joliot works on an interesting piece of pure research into the fission properties of uranium and publishes his results, even though he believes that this could aid the German scientists in their quest for an atomic bomb, then we can *infer* that his desire to discover these properties and publish them outweighs any "negative desire" he has in regard to aiding the German scientists—provided (as usual) that his decision making was rational and that he was under no coercion. So, even if he would rather not have aided the German scientists, his desire to solve the interesting research problem was stronger and overrode his misgivings. This suggests a general approach: when an action is seen by an agent under two or more descriptions, one of which the agent desires and at least one of which he would rather not do, then his competing desires give rise to a *preference* in favor of the action he most desires, when he does in fact perform that action. Joliot prefers to solve the interesting problem and make known to the scientific world, including the German scientists, the fission properties of uranium, rather than to do neither, because his desire in favor of the former is stronger than his desire against the latter. In this way, *all* the descriptions of the actions that bodily movements fall under can be brought together within the scope of Joliot's intentions. What Joliot intends is "solving an interesting problem and publishing its outcome, in spite of its aiding the German scientists," not just "solving an interesting problem."[10]

It can be objected here that intentions are not like this: they do not have a conditional form (something like), "I want to do X in spite of Y," but rather the "outright" form, "I want to do X." Perhaps there is room for argument here, given the contested nature of intention, in favor of intentions as conditional, but it is really not necessary here to make that commitment.[11] Instead of the agent's intentions being seen as constituted by a preference ranking, the preference can be located as a factor in the agent's deliberations, which then issue in the outright intention to do X. Whatever is the right way to express this detail, the point remains that we can infer (often if not always, as there is always the possibility of coercion) what an agent *prefers* from what he does, just as we can make inferences about his choices and qualities of will. And just as an agent's intentions, choices, qualities of will, and so on "belong" to him, so do his preferences. His preferences tell us how he orders possible states of affairs from most to least desirable, and if he prefers bad to good outcomes, then this provides more scope for the display of reactive attitudes. I will call this the *modified standard view:* the view that an agent's intentional actions support inferences about what he prefers, leaving open the question of whether this is because the intentions themselves have the conditional form or because the preferences came into play at an earlier stage, when the intentions were formed.

An agent can only be responsible for an action if he actually performs the action. This necessary truth might explain some of the appeal of the modified standard view, because people do not act on their beliefs alone, or on their desires alone, and so their responsibility is a consequence of what it is that does get them to act, namely their intentions. Allowing foreseen outcomes to figure in a preference ranking appears to allow such outcomes to be brought within this general picture. Responsibility, on the modified standard view, now attaches to all the actions (bodily movement under all the descriptions in question) that the agent foresees, because all of them are now undertaken intentionally. But it is still not enough to cover all the possibilities. Consider the cold-hearted scientist, as we might call him, who disregards entirely certain outcomes of his work. To use an example from Peter Singer, consider a scientist who deprives rats of food and water to see how they behave under conditions of extreme stress (1993, 55). Suppose the situation is *not* such that the scientist prefers to find out what happens and have the animals suffer, but rather that their suffering does not even enter into his decision to do the experiment. When asked if he thought that this was too high a price to pay for his data, he replies that the only price he paid was the cost of the rats, and that no cost to the rats themselves entered into his choice of research topic—just as Josef Mengele did not consider the cost to his human experimental subjects. It follows that, in this example, the inference licensed by the modified standard view is unsound, because the rats' suffering does not figure in the scientist's preference ranking. The modified standard view, then, does not ground a *complete* account of moral responsibility.

One way to defend the modified standard view against this charge—that it yields an incomplete account of science and moral responsibility—is to deny that the cold-hearted scientist is responsible for the animals' suffering. While we despise him as a scientist and deplore his limited capacity to make decisions, that is all—we do not hold him responsible for his actions. But it is far from clear that this is correct. Why can we not hold him responsible for his actions *and* despise him? This is not, as it may appear, a special example of limited relevance. Recall the "blanket excuse" sanctioned by the standard view—that a scientist undertaking a pure research project could be freed of any responsibility for outcomes, foreseen or not, by saying that he did not intend them to come about. A scientist can similarly maintain that he did not *take into account* the outcomes that he foresaw—they did not enter into his deliberations—and this gives him another "blanket excuse." The cold-hearted scientist is thus a subspecies of a larger variety.

Finally, yet another kind of case also suggests that the modified standard view is too narrow. Suppose now that the scientist forgets to look after his animals, or perhaps he does not realize that they need to be looked after in certain ways, and the animals suffer as a result. There is no suggestion that this neglect is either deliberate or knowing; the scientist is simply neglectful. When neglect causes harm, and where the agent "should have known better," we have an example of *negligence*. By definition, negligence implies that something has been overlooked or unknown that should have been attended to or known. If it is possible to be morally responsible for outcomes that come about as a consequence of negligence, then this is not covered by the modified standard view. The "disinterested scientist" and the "ignorant scientist" therefore represent two important challenges to the modified standard view.

The Cold-Hearted and the Disinterested Scientist

The disinterested scientist fails to take into account certain actions that he performs; that is, there are descriptions of what he does that he disregards when he considers what to do. The cold-hearted scientist (a genus of the species) who experiments on rats, observing their behavior as they starve, and submits his results to the *Journal of Rat Behavior* is different from the scientist who does take account of the rats' suffering but thinks it is worth it for him to publish.[12] In this second example, the scientist *admits* responsibility, or at least we can attribute responsibility to him on the modified standard view, but thinks he is justified. This scientist is *also* different from one who believes his work will have some other benefit, perhaps a way to control hungry rats in cities in the developing world. Here again the scientist accepts responsibility, but he now seems to have a stronger justification—and he also differs from the scientist who believes that such animals as rats don't suffer and hence that he cannot be doing anything wrong. Were the scientist in question working in the seventeenth century, under the thrall of Descartes, this might be an excuse, but today it is hardly believable. The question is whether the scientist is actually responsible for the rats' suffering, given that it does not figure in his reasons for action, and if so, why he is responsible. An alternative view is that he is responsible for his "character"—for being a cold-hearted person—but not for his actions.

If, however, the correct judgment here is that the scientist is callous, cold-hearted, and cruel, then his responsibility for making the rats suffer cannot be denied. What else could be the *basis* for the judgment? If he is cold-hearted, then this must be because of the *way* he does what he does. Hence he must be *responsible* for what he does. It is not correct to say that we criticize him for being cold-hearted and at the same time excuse him from responsibility for causing the animals distress. Compare this to the scientist who takes the animals' suffering into account but does the experiment anyway; we could say that this scientist preferred to cause pain rather than to forego his results. We might still conclude that he was cruel, but at least he did take the animals' suffering into account. In the first case, then, we criticize both what the scientist did *and* the way he made his decision, while in the second we only criticize what he did. Therefore, what is wrong with the conclusion—that we criticize the scientist's character and blame him for being cold-hearted but at the same time excuse him from responsibility for causing suffering—is that the excuse undercuts the criticism. If the scientist is never responsible for all the manifestations of his coldheartedness, how can he be said to be cold-hearted?

We hold the cold-hearted scientist responsible for what he did and blame him for it because we believe he should not have done what he did. We think that he should have considered the animals' capacity for suffering and then not proceeded with his experiment. When we find out that he did not even take the animals' suffering into consideration, we conclude that he does not make his choices on the proper basis: he fails to entertain relevant moral principles, such as that it is wrong to cause pain to sentient creatures. We can then agree that his action falls under the description "knowingly causes harm." If this were done intentionally, then we would blame him *and* judge him to be a sadist. If it were not done intentionally, but if the harm done was balanced against his greater desire to obtain data, then, as above, we would blame him *and* judge him exploitive of others for his own ends. If, finally, the animals' suffering did not enter into his deliberations at all, we would blame him *and* conclude that he lacks a properly developed moral sense. In all three cases, however, the scientist is responsible for the harm he causes.

The cold-hearted scientist therefore stands outside the reach of the modified standard view. The outcome of disinterested action need not necessarily be cruel, but it can be assumed that it is in some sense blameworthy when it contravenes some moral principle. The disinterested scientist cannot escape blame because his decision procedure is deemed defective, because he fails to take account of actions that fall under such descriptions as "causes harm." Notice that in the *absence* of the judgment that the disinterested scientist's decision procedure is defective, there would be a gap in the argument, which, again, is as follows: The disinterested scientist causes harm but does not view his action under this description. There is therefore something wrong with the way he makes decisions, because moral agents take account of actions that cause harm. But the premise is only evidence for the conclusion if the disinterested scientist is responsible for the harm he causes. In other words, if the decision-making procedure of the scientist were not defective, then it would be necessary to find some *other* way to establish the link between what he does and his choices, deliberation, and so on, on which moral principles bear directly.

Here the "spirit" of Wallace's explanation of the nature of moral responsibility has been retained: it is allowed that the "wills" expressed by the scientist-types are open to moral criticism in other ways, besides in terms of their intentional actions. It is not so much the "qualities" of will that are at issue in these examples, where "qualities" is understood to refer to the ways in which the agent acts with regard to the moral subjects he takes notice of and the moral obligations he recognizes with respect to these subjects. Rather, the issue is whom he takes into account and why. Not to take animals' suffering into account at all, or not to be aware that animals must be considered, seem to be moral disorders of a different or perhaps higher nature compared to regarding their suffering as an acceptable price to pay for publication. If the latter displays the wrong kind of quality of will, the former represents some defect of the will itself. It might well be that we feel more resentment and disgust toward the cold-hearted and the disinterested scientists than we do toward the casually cruel scientist who uses his animals for his own ends without regard for their welfare. But matters about degrees of blaming are not really of concern at this point. Our interest is in the conditions for responsibility; what happens next—once responsibility has been established—is so far of secondary concern.[13]

Ignorance and Responsibility

N O ONE, SURELY, CAN BE BLAMED AND HENCE RESPONSI-
ble for something that he did not know about or was not aware of, *unless*
that fact or state of affairs was something that he should have known
about. The expression "ignorance is no excuse" is reserved for such
instances. As demonstrated, the modified standard view is unable to
deal with ignorance because the conclusions that it licenses are based on
the subject's actual preferences and so on, and hence if the subject is not
aware that "doing X" is a possible action of his, it will not appear in his
list of preferences. But do we really need to worry about the ignorant scientist? Can we not, so to speak, leave him in peace? I think not: for one
thing, we want a complete account of the scientist's backward-looking
responsibility, so we need to know whether he can be responsible for
things he is not aware of. This leads to important practical ramifications.

Consider Joliot again, and suppose he is so engrossed in his work
that he is entirely unaware of the political situation of 1939. In his 1945
trial for aiding the enemy, he states that he was unaware of the political
situation, that he did not read Szilard's telegram, and moreover that
many others were similarly unaware of the state of the world in 1939.
The questions here are whether *as a scientist* Joliot should have been
aware of the political situation and the role his research might play and,
more generally, whether scientists have any such special responsibilities.
If Joliot was not obliged to keep abreast of events outside his laboratory—events that his work could affect—then there would be no case
against him. Without this special (forward-looking) obligation, he has
no (backward-looking) responsibility and so is not to blame.[1] While it

might have been difficult to make the case against Joliot in 1945, in real life, I think matters are different today as regards the scientist's obligations, precisely because the example of the Manhattan Project means that ignorance is no longer an excuse.

Ignorance as Morally Wrong

Being ignorant of something can (obviously) be contrasted with knowing about it. A person knows something, according to the usual account, when he believes it and has good grounds for believing it. I assume that the defining characteristic of being ignorant of something is when a person does not believe something, whether or not he has good grounds for belief, or whether or not he is at all aware of its possibility (cf. Zimmermann 1988, 75). We are not directly interested here in beliefs about statements being true or false, although such items are relevant, but in actions, and we already have a framework in place for addressing actions.[2] So with regard to doing X, P will be ignorant of his doing X simply if he does not believe that he does X when in fact he does do so. In this sense, Newton was ignorant of the fact that in publishing the law of universal gravitation, he was providing the basic formula for calculating the forces on Fat Man over Nagasaki. We know this because we can trace the origin of this expression back to Newton and assign to him this causal role with respect to that mission. However, in the earlier discussion of the possible actions that could be attributed to the agent by playing the accordion, the convention adopted was to restrict these actions to those that the agent could have been aware of or known about. Clearly, Newton could not have known that he was providing the basic formula for calculating the forces on Fat Man, and hence the convention rules this out as an action of Newton's. The construction "Unbeknownst to him, Newton was . . ." was earlier suggested as a way of expressing the fact that an agent has played a certain causal role; this construction will have all the substitution instances of "Although he was ignorant of the fact, Newton . . .". Here, such expressions as the latter will be used only where information about what an agent is doing is accessible to the agent, and the former will be used to signify that the agent has an excuse.

In some contexts, to talk about ignorance is to imply some sort of failure or that some mistake has been made. Because we want to avoid this connotation for Newton, we will resist talking about Newton being ignorant of his providing the basis for the Fat Man calculations. The issue becomes less clear, however, when we turn to Joliot. Assuming that Joliot was unaware that publishing his results on neutron multiplication would aid the Germans, is this possible outcome something that he should indeed have appreciated, and if so, was his not doing so some sort of failure on his part? It was certainly *possible* for him to have appreciated this, as Leo Szilard did so while he brooded on the other side of the Atlantic. To come to a decision on this question, it would be necessary to do some detailed historical research into what information was available to Joliot about the state of German science and its relation with the military and into Joliot's attitude toward the use of scientific research for warfare, and so on. But the key question arises here if it is assumed that Joliot could indeed have realized that he ran a real risk of aiding the Germans and then consider whether this is something he *should* have realised. Was his not knowing some sort of failure on his part? And if it was, was he *responsible* for this failure and hence for aiding the Germans?

If Joliot had aided the Germans intentionally, or if he had foreseen that he would aid the Germans when he did what he preferred to do—namely, publish his paper—then we can hold him responsible for aiding the Germans. This has already been established. Now the suggestion is that *if* he was responsible for failing to realize that he had aided the Germans, *then* he can also be held responsible for having done so. If Joliot is not responsible for failing to realize what he has done, he cannot be held responsible. To think otherwise would mean that Newton could be responsible for helping to guide Fat Man to its target. Two different things need to be established here: in general, if P does X without knowing that he has done so, then he can only be responsible for X *if* he is also responsible for not knowing that he did X.[3] What needs to be established first is whether being responsible for his ignorance of X means that P *can* be responsible for X and, if so, whether and under what conditions P is responsible for his ignorance. If P is responsible for not knowing that he has done X, then he can be called to account and asked to respond so as to try to prevent our reactive attitudes coming into play. This is the practical side of what it means to be responsible. The concern here is whether being responsible for one thing opens P up to being responsible for another, and this is a rather more theoretical issue, concerning a putative relation between responsibilities for different yet connected matters. It is worth pointing out that we may well react differently to P if he did X intentionally, did X unintentionally but with foresight, or did X in ignorance, provided that the case has been made about responsibility for ignorance; the present discussion, however, is not (yet) about how we should react—about degrees of blaming—but about the prior issue of responsibility.

If P is in some given state s and then proceeds to do X, which he would not have done if not in that state, and if he is responsible for being in state s, then it does *not* follow that he must *always* be responsible for doing X.[4] Attribution of responsibility for doing X depends on just what state s is and how P has entered into it. Aristotle famously discussed a person who gets drunk and then commits some wrong. His discussion, complicated from our point of view by the fact that he is talking about voluntary rather than responsible action, is taken to imply that the agent is responsible *both* for getting drunk *and* (therefore) for what he does while drunk (Aristotle 2000, xx). However, if the agent had no idea how drink would affect him—if he is a first-time drunk—I would dissent: he is responsible for getting himself drunk in that he knowingly and willingly drank too much but not for what he then did. This conclusion is open to the objection that if P was in any way aware of what too much drink might do to him, having perhaps observed others in the same state, then he may still be held responsible for X. On the other side of the coin, if P believes he can only do X if he gets himself into state s, whatever that is, and then goes ahead with this plan, he will certainly be held responsible for doing X. The upshot of these considerations is this: the extent to which P is genuinely ignorant of what will happen to him in state s, as regards his tendency to do X, will be the extent to which he will not be held responsible for doing X, even if he is responsible for getting himself into state s, given of course that being in state s itself would otherwise excuse P from blame for X.[5]

It is clear that what is crucial about s excusing P in regard to his doing X is that he did not realize that he would do X when he got himself into s. And this is true regardless of what s is: whether it is some psychological state (drunkenness, hypnosis, or drug-induced), such a condition as indebtedness to the mafia, or something else that P has taken on voluntarily. In other words, provided that P was *genuinely* ignorant of the fact that he would do X when in s, then he is excused, even though he is responsible for getting himself into s, again with the proviso that being in s excuses.[6] But the very point at issue is whether P can be responsible for X when he *is* responsible for not knowing that he does X. We do not yet know how P can be responsible for being ignorant of the fact that he would do X—this is the argument's next step—but suppose he is. Now we have the following scene: while in state s, P does X, which he would not do otherwise; he is ignorant of the fact that he would do X in s, but he is *responsible* for being ignorant of that fact.[7] Now P's previous excuse—that he was ignorant of the fact that he would do X—no longer has any purchase, because he is responsible for his ignorance, and if he is responsible for his ignorance, it cannot be cited as an excuse. The situation is now just the same as if P knew he would not normally do X but also that he *would* do X in s, and then P got himself into s. We are not really interested in state s, whatever it might be, but just in what follows for P being ignorant that he does, or will do, X. The same conclusion therefore holds when we consider instances of "pure" ignorance, without any state s, because the nature of s is irrelevant and the only excusing condition is that P did not know he would do X in s. So, in general, if P is responsible for not knowing he does X, and he then does X, *then* he is responsible for doing X. If ignorance does not excuse, then ignorance is no excuse!

The first of our two tasks has thus been accomplished. But this will be of no avail if P is never responsible for not knowing that he does X, in particular if this is the case when P is a scientist doing the kind of research we are interested in. So, let us return to Joliot and suppose that a great deal of evidence was available to him about German science, nuclear science in particular, and about German military support for that science, and so on, such that most scientists would have realized that publishing the neutron-multiplication data was too risky. But Joliot didn't. Is Joliot to blame for not realizing what (nearly) everyone else would have realized? If so, then, without any further supporting argument, we seem to be committed to saying that whenever P has evidence e that points to conclusion c, then P is to blame if he does not accept c. I will leave the meaning of "points to" vague at this stage, but intuitively it means that (nearly) everyone would make the connection between e and c. But does this principle stand up? It surely does not. There is nothing morally wrong about failing to see that evidence points to a conclusion such that P can be blamed for not seeing the connection. This could be described as "cognitive failure," or P's intellectual abilities could be questioned on this occasion, but P has done nothing morally wrong.

This invites the question of what if c is harmful, in that not realizing that c was the case meant certain moral agents were harmed. This seems relevant because it carries some moral import, but the principle still cannot be affirmed. The connection between e and c is still itself a matter of coming to know that one points to the other—still an issue of cognition and understanding. However—and this does make the difference sought here—suppose that P has some special obligation or duty to look out for things just like e and c, and P fails to do so. Now it can be said that it was clear that e pointed to c, *and* that it was P's duty to attend to this matter, so then there was a moral failing on P's part when he did not do so. Take a simple example: P is a lifeguard whose job is to look out for swimmers in distress in the surf. He fails to see one swimmer lifting his arm and waving, although these movements are clearly visible from the beach and are seen by some other beachgoers. That P does not conclude that someone is in difficulty is, in the first place, a cognitive failure, as the waving arm is visible. But in the second place, it is a moral failure because, as a lifeguard, he is specifically charged with looking out for such things, unlike an ordinary beachgoer.[8]

We can agree that if the lifeguard sits back and does nothing to aid the swimmer, then there is reason to hold him morally blameworthy, but he is still ignorant of facts about what the swimmer is doing. Suppose that, after all, the swimmer is just waving to the beach: the lifeguard sees his arm go down and then sees a confident and powerful swimming stroke to catch a wave back to the beach. The lifeguard does nothing. It would still, I maintain, have been a moral failing had the lifeguard not noticed the arm going up, because that is the signal for difficulties in the surf, and it is his duty to notice all such signals and then do what is necessary. Ignorance of certain matters of *fact* can therefore be a moral failing when these matters are indications of what agents should do to prevent harm.

Science as an Institution

Notice that if it had been conceded that moral failing only comes in when the lifeguard fails to act, then he would not be responsible for his ignorance. Recall the pertinent relationship among ignorance, action, and responsibility: P is responsible for not knowing that he does X, and therefore he is responsible for doing X. In the lifeguard example, this becomes a little more complicated: the lifeguard is ignorant of the fact that the swimmer is in difficulty and therefore that he is failing to rescue him, *and* he is responsible for being ignorant of these facts and therefore responsible for failing to rescue the swimmer. If moral failure, and hence responsibility, only came into play in regard to the lifeguard omitting to rescue the swimmer, the lifeguard could plead that he simply didn't see the waving arm and state this as his excuse. But now suppose something quite different (and extraordinary): the lifeguard says that he did not realize that he was supposed to look out for swimmers in difficulty and hence his not seeing the swimmer in question was not his fault, as this was not something he was supposed to do. This would bring the judge, jury, and prosecuting counsel up short, for the assumption is that the defendant is a lifeguard, and if he is a lifeguard, he must know what he is supposed to do—look out for swimmers in difficulty. Now let us look for the general message of this example and explore its implications for science.

It is a precondition for proper participation in the practice, role, or *institution* of being a lifeguard that one knows that there are rules of conduct and action to which one is obliged to conform. This concept of *social practice* is not novel: it is commonplace in sociology, and so it does not require vast elaboration here. However, it is worth nailing down, and to this end Peter Berger and Thomas Luckmann's *Social Construction of Reality* is helpful: "In the common stock of knowledge there are standards of role performance that are accessible to all members of society, or at least to those who are potential performers of the roles in question. This general accessibility is itself part of the same stock of knowledge; not only are the standards for role X generally known, but it is known that these standards are known. Consequently, every putative actor can be held responsible for abiding by the standards, which can be taught as part of the institutional tradition and used to verify the credentials of all performers and, by the same token, serve as controls" (Berger and Luckmann 1984, 91).

The essential point is that social practices and institutions are routinely engaged in by people who "play by the rules": without the rules, there could be no practice. This is not to say that there is never "deviance" or that it is impossible for some not to play by the rules. But that could not be the norm: unless people normally abided by the rules, the practices in question could not exist. So normally, ignorance is no excuse, because normally, it is correct to expect people to know about the rules, standards, and so on, of the practices in which they engage. If this were not true, then such institutions as lifeguarding could not exist, for they depend on people on the whole at least being aware that rules exist. Once the existence of a social institution is given, ignorance of the rules will not be accepted—of course, there may always be particular extenuating circumstances, but the onus is clearly on the plaintiff to prove his case, the presumption being that the rules are known. The argument here therefore appeals to practice. Before we turn to see if this argument fits science, it is necessary to clarify what it is for the subject or actor to be committed to the rules in so far as he takes part in the practice; this is precisely the point insisted on here—that the subject is *expected* to know the rules. Taking part in the practice without knowing the rules is possible, although as the practice of science is more complex, this will be increasingly unlikely.

Can this argument, then, be used as a model for science? Are there rules and regulations, grounded in the very practice of science, that scientists are expected to know, ignorance of them entailing moral responsibility? Certainly, myriad rules govern the conduct of scientists as members of the scientific community, ranging from guidelines for correctly dealing with data to obligations to acknowledge the contributions of subordinates. When viewed in this way, the scientific community is seen as similar to society as a whole, in the sense that it comprises persons dealing with one another in certain accepted ways, but different in that one or more special aims serve to mark it off from society as a whole, as a distinct and separate "subsystem." The scientist in society does not, by any means, identify such a tightly defined institution as the scientific community per se. Consider, however, the proposition "Science affects people"—SAP, for short. This is a general claim that expresses the notion that scientific research has outcomes that affect the public, those outside the scientific community, and underpins more specific guidelines about the effects of particular lines of research ("Nuclear physics can lead to military applications"; "Genetic engineering on seeds for staple crops is likely to have an impact on food resources and agribusiness"). Can all scientists be expected to be aware of SAP?[9]

Suppose scientist S maintains that he simply does pure research in a university and so refuses to acknowledge that he is a scientist in society. Suppose he argues further that it is a mistake to lump together all of the ways of doing science; instead of seeing science as a monolith, he says, we should recognize that the scientific community is composed of quite different parts—and his is of the most pristine kind, dedicated to pure research at a self-funding university. Suppose also that S denies awareness of SAP. We can say all sorts of things about this frank admission—we can ask S where he has been all his life—but can we argue that doing science, in whatever context, commits him, qua scientist, to SAP? Notice that making this suggestion is different from simply claiming that S ought to know SAP because it is true, obvious, a commonplace, part of what every educated scientist knows.

The realities of modern scientific research are such as to blur the boundaries between academic, industrial, and government research to such a degree that S's defense is surely implausible. These boundaries have become blurred as a consequence of several developments. One is the increased mobility of scientists from one sector to another: it is quite common for university scientists to move to industry, for government scientists to take up university posts, and so on, because the work in the different sectors is similar. Another, closely related development is the increasing participation of university scientists in the patenting process—the process designed to safeguard the inventor's rights to the commercial profits from his invention. Once upon a time, academic scientists were not supposed to do this; they were supposed to publish papers in refereed journals, not look to commercial applications. Now, however, this is encouraged in universities, often acting as a criterion for promotion.

Perhaps the most important development in scientific research, for our purposes here, is its dependence on *grants*. Virtually all experimental scientists depend on grants to finance their work. Many granting bodies have "missions," such as to promote public health, and hence direct their funding to projects that seem likely to contribute to that mission. Now this in itself is a concrete manifestation of "Science affects people." A mission to harness science for a particular aim that goes beyond the search for knowledge for its own sake—an aim that we would hope, to use Baconian language, would contribute to the relief of man's estate—presupposes SAP. Otherwise, the mission would be pointless. It must be acknowledged that not all granting bodies have a mission and that not all scientists seek grants. Yet even those granting bodies that do not have a mission do take into consideration the possible outcomes of the supposedly pure research that they are funding. It is just not *possible* to apply for a grant and not be aware of this. But what of the scientist who does not use grants, one of the tiny minority? S could be one of these people, but then he would not conform to the norm, and, like the deluded lifeguard, the onus would be on him to explain his behavior.

We can, therefore, conclude that even the "purest" researcher, the scientist who only seeks to publish papers, ought to know SAP. But SAP in itself imposes no *specific* constraints or demands on the scientist. Granted that science affects people, and we know already what kinds of ways this can happen, what should the scientist do? This is a question that falls squarely within the *ethics* of science. Thus far, I have tried not to build any particular moral requirements into the theory of responsibility, save for the minimal prohibition on gratuitous harm, which is surely a necessary constraint on the conduct of any moral agent. SAP warrants the imposition of that standard on (pure) scientific research. However, such questions—what counts as doing harm, whether it is harmful to do military research or research into the genetic or racial basis of certain behaviors, whether embryonic stem-cell research is permissible, whether it is appropriate to impose further demands on the scientist in the name of morally correct conduct—are, again, questions for a well-worked-out ethics of science that expresses and codifies the scientist's forward-looking responsibilities. I think there is room in such ethics for more or less specific demands on scientists, demands tailored to kinds of researchers and to different fields of science, all under the umbrella of SAP.

Ignoring Omissions

Omissions are less transparent than actions, as we have seen, in a number of ways. If P does X, then there is no doubt that P *can* do X and hence that P has control with respect to X. But if P does not do or prevent X, then the evidence that he could have done so must be less convincing than it is when P does X. Another practical difficulty is in imposing a distinction regarding omissions akin to that made between intended and merely foreseen actions. We may want to do this if we think that it is worse to intentionally omit to do (or prevent) X than just to note that one could do (or prevent) X and then fail to do so. Presumably, an intentional omission is one in which P deliberately does not do X—namely, he thinks about and decides against doing X. But it is not so obvious why this is worse than merely noting that he could have done X. We find it worse to do X intentionally because, under this description, P wants X to take place—he wants to feed his rabbits a poor diet rather than just foreseeing that their diet will be poor if he gives them rat food. Thus, the relevant distinction is between omitting to do X because X is an outcome that the agent (explicitly) does not want and simply not doing X. Provided—and this is some proviso—that it is possible to find out why P did not do (or fail to prevent) X, this can be built into the description of what he is responsible for: "Omitting to do X because not-X was the desired outcome," or "Omitting to do X with no particular desire for not-X." In this way, the possibility is left open of blaming P more for the former.

Whether a distinction of this kind is necessary—or indeed, whether omissions need to be taken into consideration at all—depends on what kind of responsibilities agent P has. If P only has responsibility not to do harm, and if this is not understood to imply the prevention of harm, then under that minimal moral constraint, omissions will not be blameworthy. A constraint that forbids doing harm but not preventing it seems strange, to say the least. But in keeping with the approach taken here, we want an account of responsibility that is flexible enough to cover omissions as well as acts, and this might be because there is not just a constraint on doing harm but an obligation to do good as well. In this case, responsibility for omissions will be more common than if only the minimal requirement not to do harm is in operation, and there would be responsibility for omissions to do (good) as well as omissions to prevent (harm). Further, omitting to do what one is ignorant of will become more important as well.

Not to know that one has *omitted* to do something means that one did not know that one could have done it, that one did not know that one should have done it, or both. That is how things stand when the question is about *responsibility* for an omission, rather than about whether the agent was aware that an outcome was under his control. There is only responsibility for an omission to do X if X is something that the agent should have done. SAP denotes a context in which the practice of doing science implies that the scientist knows that what he does affects people. The scope of science affecting people need not be restricted to what scientists do, to their actions, but can also encompass what they do not do. If P is able to contribute to solving pressing moral problems—perhaps by helping to provide a cheaper and more sustainable water supply by researching water conservation rather than something more personally profitable—then failing to do so may count as an omission on P's part.[10] Again, whether scientists have these positive duties is controversial. But if they do, then what SAP establishes, as before, is that a denial that science can help with pressing moral problems will not wash.

An example will help to clarify the issue: Suppose that S is an environmental scientist with expertise in the fields of hydrology, water conservation, and so on, and suppose that he is located in a developing country with water-supply problems, yet he accepts grants from companies to do work in connection with environmental-impact statements. The work is theoretical, and in that sense it is pure, but it is to be used to justify a development that will have little benefit for the local population. The alternative is for S to turn his skills directly to the problem of water supply and conservation. Furthermore, suppose that S denies that he knew that such a problem existed and that, unlikely as it might seem, his denial is sincere: S did not know that he had omitted to help solve the problem; he did not know that he had the opportunity to do such research. What do we say of S? There is, first of all, the difficult issue of whether S has a positive duty to help others, which we assume he is able to do. If he does not, there is nothing further to say. Suppose, then, that he does indeed have this positive duty. Then the situation is as follows: S cannot deny SAP, for reasons already given, and let us say further that the "cash value" of SAP in this case is that science affects people for good as well as ill and that S cannot deny this either. If S knew he was omitting to do X, then a framework is in place for holding him responsible for this omission. However, he did not know.

Do we say that S is responsible for being ignorant of the fact that he omitted to do X? This statement would seem odd, had we not prepared the groundwork for making it. If S should do X but does not do it, then he is responsible for not doing it. If S should do X but does not know that he has the opportunity to do X, then he can still be responsible for not knowing that he omitted to do X. Again, if S does not know that he had the opportunity to do X, then it is not fair to hold him responsible for not doing X without further argument. But within the framework set by SAP, *and* given the positive duty to do good, there is a basis on which to hold S responsible for being ignorant of the opportunity to do X. The positive duty to do good places quite a significant burden on the scientist: it obliges him to seek out opportunities to do good, not merely to ensure against doing harm (chapter 8 lifts this burden a little by using "common morality" as a basis for an ethics of science). It must be stressed that as yet no reason has been given for thinking that there is indeed such a duty or constraint on the scientist. The prohibition on doing harm is the minimal constraint on moral agents, without which *all* talk of responsibility would be empty. This is one reason why responsibility for actions is easier to approach than responsibility for omissions, and when ignorance is factored in, omissions seem even more remote from our everyday moral concerns. Be that as it may, however, the present account is wide enough to cover attributions of responsibility for ignorance about omissions.

"Science affecting people" means affecting their interests, making their lives better or worse in important ways. Science is a force for good and ill, and the claim here is that all scientists should know this. SAP thus becomes a kind of second-order moral principle: it informs scientists that what they do can have moral significance. The responsibilities that can be attributed to the scientist as a result of this general principle, however, concern particular acts and omissions—and ignorance of them.

This, I claim, is the final element needed to vindicate the wide view of science and responsibility: scientist S performs some action X that we suppose is harmful to some moral subjects, and he is held responsible for doing X. How? On what grounds? There are three possibilities. First, if S intends to do X, then he expresses his desire that X come about and also believes that he will do X. Because he wants to do X, then he is plainly committed to it. If X stands for "weaponizing plutonium," then Peierls was plainly committed to this project at Los Alamos, intending it to happen as a result of his work. Second, if S foresees that he also does X when he intentionally does Y, then this foresight is also grounds for holding him responsible. Suppose Fermi were really interested in achieving a critical assembly out of pure scientific interest, but he foresaw that at the same time he would be providing a source of plutonium for weapons. His preference for achieving a critical assembly outweighed any preference he might have had for not providing the material for atomic bombs, and that is why we can hold him responsible. This case is covered by the modified standard view.

Third, if S could and should have known that he was doing X, though he did not, then he no longer has an excuse for avoiding responsibility for X itself. We suppose that Joliot did not know that publishing his paper would aid the Germans by making his data available, but at his trial after the war, an exhaustive investigation found ample available evidence for this possibility, including Szilard's (unopened) telegram. Moreover, the investigation found that Joliot knew about the collaboration of German science and the military during World War 1 and that he knew that Hitler had been rearming since 1936. The jury decided that, for Joliot, ignorance was no excuse. In what follows, I will sometimes refer to the "position-to-know" test as shorthand for this third basis for holding the subject responsible.

Ignorance and Foresight in Practice

T IS ALL WELL AND GOOD TO DEMAND THAT MORAL agents should do this or that, but if they are *unable* to do what is asked of them, then such demands are pointless. It is a time-honored principle that "should" or "ought" implies "can." So, if the pure scientist is not able to look ahead and gauge where his work could lead, then we cannot demand that he should do so or, therefore, hold him responsible for anything in regard to outcomes. Thus, an ethics of science that demands that scientists look ahead and see where their work will lead, so as to minimize bad outcomes and maximize good ones, would be utopian. I call the denial that pure scientists can be in a position to know (much) about applications of their work Polanyi's Challenge, after Michael Polanyi, who sought to defend the freedom of science, as he saw it. In responding to Polanyi's Challenge, I will consider three appeals to considerations that are rather different from those relevant for deciding that it is possible for a scientist to be culpably ignorant. This practical question must be taken seriously because I believe it is important to show that the present investigation is not (or not just) an erudite exercise in philosophy but also something engaged with scientists themselves and scientific practice.

Polanyi's Challenge

In an essay called "The Republic of Science," first published in 1962 and then reprinted in 1969, Polanyi claimed that science is *doubly unpredictable.* He was referring to pure research and to what we have called outcomes—namely practical applications of pure research. This "double unpredictability" was said to be a feature specific to outcomes, in that *neither* the research's scientific result or finding *nor* any outcome issuing from this finding can be predicted in advance. Lack of "predictability" of either a finding or, given the finding, an outcome is sufficient for the outcome to be unforeseen; thus, to establish that an outcome is foreseeable, it is necessary, at the outset of the pure research program, to show that predictability of *both* finding *and* outcome is possible.[1] Yet Polanyi seems to be saying something manifestly false, considering the examples of doubly predictable outcomes that were discussed earlier.[2] For instance, during the Manhattan Project, many scientists did many things that were *highly predictable;* they completed all the steps needed to make the atomic bomb. Unless they were reasonably sure that what they were doing would take them where they wanted to go, the whole project would have been a senseless waste of time, money, and effort. It appears that Polanyi's unpredictability claims have plausibility only if we take "predictable" to mean "absolutely certain" (and then only if pure and applied research are assumed to be quite separate activities). It was not absolutely certain that the Manhattan Project would yield an atomic bomb—that is why one was tested. But certainty, in the sense of no possibility whatsoever of error, is not what we demand of science or of much else in life.

Nevertheless, Polanyi's Challenge cannot simply be dismissed. So, first a little background and clarification: Polanyi was seeking to promote a specific agenda when he wrote "The Republic of Science." He was a member of the Society for the Freedom of Science, formed in 1942 as a response to what some saw as the increasing interference of outside interests that sought to direct scientific research in particular ways; he was particularly worried about those who held up Soviet science as a model, such as J. D. Bernal (Polanyi 1969, 58). Polanyi and his fellow freedom fighters wanted to resist any overall directing of research, but at the same time they were aware that science needed support. Polanyi's essay can thus be seen as an attempt to promote a science policy that left the choice of research projects entirely in the scientist's hands. Hence he expresses the unpredictability thesis as follows: "You can kill or mutilate the advance of science but you cannot shape it. For it advances only by essentially unpredictable steps, pursuing problems of its own, and the practical benefits [outcomes] of these advances will be incidental and hence *doubly unpredictable*" (1969, 59; my emphasis).

Polanyi simply assumes that the "advance" of science is unpredictable—thus taking as given the first of the challenge's two unpredictability claims—while he supports the second claim, which attaches to "practical benefits," by an example: the discovery of the Einstein formula. Polanyi, however, frames this discovery by referring to a January 1945 incident involving himself and Bertrand Russell. Polanyi and Russell, on the *BBC Brains Trust*, were asked if they could think of an application of the formula, the irony being that this question was posed a mere six months before the Trinity test. Polanyi concludes that if he and Russell were stumped—they failed to foresee the atomic bomb—then it would have been even more difficult for Einstein himself to have done so in 1905. Of course, one example—even one no doubt thought to be especially favorable—hardly establishes the second unpredictability claim. Still, to answer the challenge, I will begin by addressing the first claim.

Polanyi does not cite any methodology to support his claim about the unpredictability of science. But some view of the way science works is necessary here, for the first unpredictability claim is a general thesis about how science advances—and that is the province of methodology. When Polanyi asserts that "you cannot shape" the advance of science, one is naturally inclined to ask what it is about the "advance" of science that makes it impossible to "shape." First, it should be noted that the term *prediction*, which Polyani uses when he declares science "doubly unpredictable," refers to something quite specific in philosophy of science.[3] Thus, here I will instead use the neutral term *expectation*. Polanyi's Challenge can then be restated as the view that scientists have, at the outset, no definite expectations about the findings and outcomes of their research. Is this claim correct? Is it true that scientists never have definite expectations about their findings? I think not, and, to support this judgment, I will appeal to the most widely accepted description of the methodology of science, Thomas Kuhn's. But first, without any appeal to methodology, it is clear that scientists must always have *some* expectations about what they will find out if they are to perform even the most basic procedure—even if they are to simply measure something.

Suppose scientist S is part of a team that is investigating the properties of a liquid *f*, such as its viscosity at given temperatures. An elementary way to do this is to determine the temperature of a sample and see how long it takes for it to run down a plane inclined at a given angle, the time being proportional to the viscosity. Temperature and time will have to be measured for a sequence of experiments on *f*. The techniques here are all extremely well-known and reliable, which means that the scientist *expects* them to work: if a mercury (or alcohol or oil) thermometer is used to measure the temperature of a bath in which the sample and the inclined plane are immersed (assuming the sample does not react with the water), then S expects to see the mercury expand quickly and reach a steady state. He will then have every confidence that the reading indicated is actually the temperature of the sample, within experimental error. He may even be able to make a good estimate of the time taken to flow down the plane. The only thing he will not expect in advance is the exact values of the parameters. While this example is simple, it is far from atypical: a great deal of scientific research is aimed at investigating the properties of things, nuclei, atoms, compounds, viruses, surfaces, conductors, bioassays, and so on, and a great deal of what appears in scientific journals are reports of such investigations. And while the techniques used are on the whole far more sophisticated than in the example just given, the same sorts of expectations are in place.

A Kuhnian Reply

In Kuhn's account of the workings of science, these expectations are vouched safe by various *paradigms*. Kuhn tells us that science is usually a mundane affair, based on paradigms and exemplars. These specify both the theoretical framework within which the scientist works and standard laboratory practice for undertaking experimental research, and they model solutions for presenting findings. Kuhn, famously, referred to work within a paradigm as *normal science*. The other type of science is *revolutionary*, and here the mold is broken—or rather, scientists are forced to acknowledge that it is, because of the accumulation of anomalies that have destabilized the old paradigm. With none of the guiding assumptions of normal science, revolutionary science is much more of an adventure. Thus, if the sequence of experiments just described were such that at a certain temperature the liquid started showing remarkable properties, which in turn revealed an unknown molecular structure, then by accident the experiments might prove to be the beginnings of a period of revolutionary science. But this is highly unlikely. What virtually every scientist does throughout his working life is normal science. And what this implies is that what virtually every scientist finds out during his career is in accordance with the paradigms.

This does not mean that a paradigm has all the answers, in the sense that they are already written down somewhere—research must find something out—but it does "guarantee" that research based on the general lines of inquiry that a paradigm lays down will have answers that can be found out.[4] This is easiest to grasp when we realize that *theories* and *laws* are elements of paradigms. The experiments on f, for example, will be conducted in light of thermodynamics, a theory that specifies that the viscosity of f will decrease as its temperature increases, unless its chemical composition or its state changes. So this is precisely what the scientist expects to happen; what he wants to find out is just how it happens—the particular manifestation of the law for f. It is, I think, helpful to express this by saying that an experiment's findings uncover or reveal an *instance* of a law or of nature, a state of affairs—the temperature and viscosity of f standing in the given relation—that conforms to the law (see Forge 1999). And again, the paradigm guarantees that the law is correct.

One might then wonder why scientists bother to discover instances of laws, why they bother to work within paradigms. If the paradigm guarantees that there are answers to the questions they ask of nature, why go to all the trouble of confirming such expectations? That is, if I may say so, a good question, and it admits several answers. One is that scientists just like doing science; they enjoy doing experiments and calculations, just as other people enjoy doing puzzles.[5] And it must be admitted that some experiments, such as huge experiments in particle physics, are very difficult to perform and require a great deal of skill. Another answer is that science is a prestigious and rewarding profession. Yet another is that science is useful: it has applications in the form of outcomes. In some respects, this third answer makes the most sense: the scientist is trying to find instances that issue in useful outcomes. Things are different in revolutionary science, but not so different that scientists working without the paradigm have no expectations.

Kuhn sometimes refers to the breakdown of normal science in terms of expectation: nature sometimes violates paradigm-induced *expectations* (Kuhn 1962, 52–53). Revolutionary science appears to be much more of a journey into the unknown, something strange and unpredictable, and so perhaps Polanyi's first unpredictability claim applies here. If so, his claim would be severely circumscribed, as little revolutionary science is done. But even when engaged in revolutionary science, scientists—great scientists like Galileo, Newton, Darwin, and Einstein—have some expectations that guide their work, although these are not strictly paradigm-induced expectations: it is not the case in revolutionary science that "anything goes." For one thing, Kuhn requires that the new paradigm resolve the anomalies—"nature's violations"— that killed off the old one. For another, the new paradigm is expected to take a certain form. For example, in physics, the paradigm is expected to codify relationships, in mathematical terms, which represent connections between the relevant quantities, such as the mechanical quantities position and momentum. This is what Newton did, systematically, in his great revolutionary work *Principia Mathematica.*

One way to underestimate the distinction between normal and revolutionary science is to maintain that the difference is only one of degree, not of kind (cf. Toulmin 1970). So in comparing Newton's discovery of the law of gravitation—an instance of what is said to be revolutionary science—with Edmond Halley's discovery of the path of a comet—using the law and hence working within the Newtonian paradigm—it might be said that both found "unknowns," although Newton's was rather more elusive. The path of a comet is represented in mechanics by a curve in space—in this instance a very elongated ellipse with the sun at one focus. Assuming that this is a two-body problem, the curve can be found by a relatively simple application of universal gravitation. Assuming further that Halley knew in advance that the finding was going to be an equation of an ellipse, his problem was "which ellipse." This was his unknown. Newton knew that the law of gravitation would be a function of mass and acceleration; his problem was "which function." This assessment of the difference between the two sorts of science, normal and revolutionary, seems plausible to me, for science certainly does not ever proceed in a vacuum, devoid of any guidance or expectations about results, even in scientific revolutions.

I think that this conclusion both seriously weakens Polanyi's thesis about the unpredictability of scientific findings and also provides some guidance as to where the boundaries of culpable ignorance might be located. Thus, for revolutionary science, where there is certainly less assurance of unknowns being found, it would appear that ignorance might at least be a better excuse than it would be for normal science. But perhaps this conclusion should not be embraced quite so quickly. An account of revolutionary science has been given, but only one such instance has been discussed, and no alternative methodology to Kuhn's has been canvassed; maybe there are others more favorable to Polanyi. The only methodology that would unequivocally support Polanyi's thesis would be one in which the scientist has no expectations whatsoever, for then findings would be truly unpredictable. There is such a methodology, going back to Francis Bacon and beyond, which holds that science begins with observation: the scientist just looks to see what is there, with no preconceptions. The latest manifestation of this view is logical empiricism, which, like its predecessors, has been thoroughly discredited and so can be easily dismissed.[6] It can be said with confidence that no viable methodology supports Polanyi's first unpredictability thesis.

Finally, while revolutionary science may be focused on addressing the anomalies that beset the old paradigms, the new paradigm may open up new and unexpected avenues. This is what happened in 1905 with $E = mc^2$. Einstein was *not* trying to find a more general conservation law that connected mass to energy; he was trying to remove what he saw as an asymmetry in the treatment of the relative motions of a conductor and an electric field.[7] The formula "fell out" of his work, as a consequence of the required (Lorentz) transformation relations. Confirming such unexpected consequences of the new paradigm has often been regarded as more important for its acceptance than the resolution of anomalies, although philosophers of science have found it hard to explain why this should be so. Quantum mechanics also has a number of implications that were not suspected by Erwin Schrödinger, Werner Heisenberg, Paul Dirac, and its other founding fathers. Here, there is clearly a difference in kind between normal and revolutionary science. It would therefore be unfair to hold a "revolutionary" scientist responsible for such new elements of the paradigm, those that are, so to speak, a side effect with respect to the resolution of the anomalies of its predecessor. The "position-to-know" test fails in such cases: the scientist did not know what these new elements would be, but he cannot be held responsible for not knowing about them.

If Polanyi's claim about pure research's unpredictability in some strong sense were vindicated, then this would evidently entail that outcomes would also be unpredictable. If the scientist had absolutely no idea what he was going to find, then it would be impossible for him to gauge where this might lead by way of outcomes—this would be true in our view of the relation between pure and applied research. But this is not how science is conducted: on the whole, the scientist has a more or less good idea where his work will lead. The "advance of science" is indeed shaped; in general terms: it is shaped by scientists' expectations that their findings will accord with the paradigm. However, Polanyi's other claim—that the outcome is unpredictable, even given the finding—remains.

Lessons from the History of Science and Technology

Here, an outcome is a technology—a way of doing something, understood very broadly. Typically, applied research leads to the production of some artifact, in which case the outcome is manifest as a product. It is possible for there to be a technology that is not in fact used—to know how to do something without actually doing it—and this will still be classed as an outcome. The reason why science underpins, generates, or gives rise to technology was explained earlier (see chapter 1), through a sketch of the realist account of the relationship between science and technology. To reiterate, science, in this account, is an attempt to describe the world, in particular to codify pervasive patterns and relationships in law statements embedded in paradigms.[8] Such knowledge can then be used to devise techniques to manipulate the world: what science finds out and the basis of technology's operations are one and the same domain—if this were not the case, then it would be more difficult to understand the relevance of science to technology. This viewpoint shows that science's giving rise to outcomes is intelligible, but it does not establish that these outcomes can be foreseen. However, it does suggest that the *histories* of science and technology are not entirely separate: a given technology will not normally come about until the relevant science is in place. Indeed, while it can be said that the histories of science and technology amounted to separate stories until the seventeenth century, they became increasingly intertwined afterward.[9] A little reflection on the history of science and technology is instructive, revealing something about what *sorts* of science and technology have been related in the past.

The relationship between science and technology was, for example, evident in the nineteenth century, when advances in organic chemistry gave rise to the dyestuffs industry, and advances in electricity and magnetism fostered such innovations as the electric telegraph and electric lighting.[10] It seems obvious here that different kinds of science were leading to different kinds of technology: it would have been strange indeed if the new organic chemistry gave rise to the electric telegraph. The point, of course, is that the workings of the electric telegraph have nothing whatsoever to do with organic chemistry and everything to do with the transmission of current via a conductor. The telegraph manifests certain laws of electromagnetism, not principles of chemical analysis and synthesis. Thus, it might appear that we can at least, based on past experience, be able to foresee what *sorts* of outcomes are more likely to be the consequences of a particular line of scientific research. Thus, research in the field of electromagnetism—say, into the insulating properties of certain substances—is more likely to have an impact in what might broadly be termed the electrical industry than in the chemical industry. But there are also electrical applications, so to speak, in the chemical industry—for example, insulators are needed in electrolytic processes—so it is by no means true that an industry draws *only* on one science. However, there is a fairly clear sense that the chemical industry produces chemicals, by synthesis or from natural products, and that such techniques as electrolysis and cracking are means to that end. So while a particular insulator may have a use in a chemical process, it is not too much of a distortion to think of this as the electrical industry's "contribution" to the chemical industry.

These general considerations about the kinds of applications that might issue from a basic research project can be supported by developing the example raised in the section before last, in connection with the liquid *f*. Let us suppose that scientist S is aware of the characteristics of a good lubricating oil: it is stable, has a high boiling point and low coefficient of expansion, and in particular does not greatly change its viscosity with increased temperatures. It is therefore by no means implausible to maintain that S can entertain an outcome in which *f* is used as a lubricant. In such cases, we may be inclined to classify S's research as applied, not pure, and we should do so if S's avowed intention is to produce a lubricant. But to classify as applied *every* instance of research in which the scientist can look ahead to the outcome would preclude *by definition* foreseeing the results of pure research, and that is obviously not helpful. However, it clearly makes sense that one can say that S can foresee that his research might lead to a new lubricant without, at the same time, committing oneself to the view that S does his research just for this reason.[11] Indeed, one can imagine that S might decide *not* to publish his work just because it would then be possible for the oil companies to exploit his findings. To embellish the example, suppose that *f* is a rare natural product only found in some environmentally sensitive area, and S judges that this area would be spoiled if the oil companies realized its worth. We might even say, in this case, that S is discharging his moral responsibility.

To summarize, if findings based on a given area or domain—paradigm—have already issued in a technology or a kind of technology or have contributed to such a technology, then it is quite possible that further work under that same paradigm might result in some development or improvement of that same sort of technology. Nuclear physics, for example, has had extensive application in weapons systems, power generation, and medicine, and one would imagine that it will continue to do so. Further, particular lines of research will tend to give rise to particular sorts of applications. Thus, research on the geometry of critical assemblies is more relevant to nuclear weapons than it is to nuclear medicine. This would appear to be a lesson that can be drawn from the history of science and technology. And this lesson has been learned by the granting bodies that fund "strategic basic research": they do so because research in the fields in question has in the past led to sought-after outcomes, and the expectation is that this will happen again in the future. Therefore to ask a scientist to become aware of the applications that his area of research has produced in the past, to try to see how his particular research project might have applications in the future, and to consider the consequences of such applications is not to ask the impossible. However, where there is true *innovation*, where the new technology is not in an obvious way a variation on what has gone before, then this demand cannot be met. This situation resembles the unexpected consequences of a new paradigm.

Where genuine innovation requires input from several different fields of science, it will be still more difficult for a scientist working in just one of these fields to foresee an outcome. Several such cases emerged in the course of an examination of some important innovations from the period 1950–70. The purpose of the study, called Technology in Retrospect and Critical Events in Science (TRACES), was to try to uncover the importance of critical events in science—the critical findings based on pure research, for innovation—in order to inform science policy. Here is a comment on the report: "[The analysis] reveals how this particular innovation [the video recorder] depended on the merging of several streams of scientific and technological activity, including control theory, magnetic and recording materials, magnetic theory, recording theory, electronics and frequency modulation. Similarly, to take another example, it was the combination of research in the fields of hormones, steroid chemistry and the physiology of reproduction that eventually led to the development of the oral contraceptive pill in the 1950s" (Irvine and Martin 1984, 18). So, if many different, and essentially independent, scientific fields are needed to provide the basis for a given technology, and if this technology is new, a genuine innovation, then it is difficult to see how a scientist working in just one of these fields could foresee that his work will contribute to the innovation. This sort of situation is clearly different from a case in which a technology is complex but already well known, and the kind of science that informs it is also well known. One of the problems that science policy, and economic policy, would like to address is how to foster genuine innovation; no one, as far as I am aware, has suggested that it is a good idea to ask research scientists how to innovate. None of this means that a research scientist might not have the vision to combine the findings of "several streams of scientific and technological activity" and produce an innovation. It just means that the scientist cannot be *expected* to have this kind of foresight—a failure of the "position-to-know" test. The lessons from the history of science and technology are thus not all of a kind: a case in favor of the second unpredictability claim could be mounted if attention were restricted to "genuine" innovation, especially where this requires input from several fields of science. On the other side, where a given research field has a track record of applications, the claim is less plausible. Of course, we should keep in mind that the second unpredictability claim is supposed to cover *all* outcomes; hence the fact that some episodes conform does not establish its truth, while, strictly speaking, any counterinstance shows it to be false.

The Argument from Patents

If scientific discoveries could be patented so that any benefits flowing from certain future outcomes would accrue to the scientist who made the original discovery, this would amount to a convincing refutation of Polanyi's second unpredictability claim: the scientist would need to state on the patent application just what the outcome would be and so, ipso facto, would be able to foresee it (although not inevitably, because the technology in question might not work). However, the suggestion that it is possible to patent a fact about the world, as the realist might put it, seems strange: patents are supposed to reward and protect the ingenuity of individuals who, to put it simply, invent something useful.[12] Nevertheless, the U.S. National Institutes of Health (NIH) attempted to do so in 1991, on behalf of Craig Venter, who enjoyed substantial support from the institution and who wished to patent certain DNA sequences called expressed sequence tags (ests). I will begin this section with some brief comments on this case—but notice that the argument from patents is about genuine novelty and so complements the previous argument against Polanyi.

Venter had been able to infer the existence of these sequences in the human chromosomes, or at least the existence of the sequences interspersed with "junk" DNA or introns, through a clever technique: he added messenger RNA (mRNA) to tissue where it would pick up the information expressed by extant proteins, extract it, and convert it into a DNA sequence (cDNA) through the enzyme reverse transcriptase. The ests are the parts of this sequence that, so to speak, do the work, comprising the nucleic-acid triplets that code for the amino acids that make up the proteins. However, while the structure of a given protein could thus be inferred, its biochemical function—what it does in the body— was not necessarily known. So Venter and the NIH were really trying to patent a scientific discovery, the assumption presumably that the proteins in question were doing *something* and that because Venter had discovered the corresponding ests, his proprietary rights over this discovery should be protected. His court case did not succeed. But it points to an *attitude* held by scientists, who are well aware that their research may have outcomes and are therefore anxious to safeguard their proprietary rights. Such an attitude is far-removed from that of the disinterested scientific adventurer of Polanyi's Republic of Science, who knows neither what he will discover nor how it will be used and (seemingly) does not care how it will be used. Now, the "argument from patents," as I will call it, denies this attitude toward outcomes, the basis of Polanyi's second unpredictability claim. If scientists are indeed concerned about their proprietary rights with respect to outcomes of their work, then this presupposes that they believe their scientific work *will* have outcomes. Later, I will make some general comments about patents, but first the argument from patents should be qualified.

Not every patent is based on some scientific discovery: some inventors still work in the traditional mold. Further, not every patent that is based on a scientific discovery is implemented by the discoverer. In many instances, perhaps even most, scientific findings are taken up and used by others. That is what happened with the Einstein formula and the atomic bomb, and it is what Polanyi takes to be the rule (in his second unpredictability claim). This "rule," however, would be directly contradicted by a scientist making a particular discovery and then immediately patenting an outcome based on his finding. For example, if Venter had been able to see the function of some of the proteins produced by the cDNA that he sequenced and had then found a means to produce these proteins by engineering the cDNA, patenting it himself, this case would convincingly refute Polanyi's claim. In practice, however, research must be funded at a high level and is usually conducted by specialist teams, which means that such individual achievement is uncommon. Funding agencies and universities now exercise a good deal of control over the intellectual property generated with the aid of their resources and administer proprietary rights by taking out patents themselves. This does not undercut the argument from patents, because scientists work—accepting grants from outside agencies, using special labs and equipment endowed by universities—with the understanding that they will not be the sole owners of their "intellectual property," although their interest is protected. The environment in which most modern scientists conduct their research is structured in this manner, with an eye fixed on safeguarding rights to outcomes. Some details will further elucidate the argument from patents.

In the preamble to a recent analysis of the citation patterns in a given class of patents, the authors remark that "to be issued, a patent must satisfy three general criteria: it must be useful; it must be novel; and it must not be obvious" (Perko and Narin 1997, 65). This straightforward statement captures the "essence" of patenting: if an invention or discovery (or, more strictly, its "outcomes") were not useful, then there would be no point in patenting it. The idea here, presumably, is that there is nothing to gain from something that is not, in the broadest sense, useful and that hence, in such a case, there are no rights that could be infringed upon. If something is not novel, then it resembles or reproduces something that is already available, and while coinvention is possible and is covered by the law, *re*invention is not.[13] The third criterion is somewhat less clear, as what is obvious is not always apparent. The general idea, however, is that the inventor must demonstrate some skill and ingenuity and not merely straightforwardly apply existing knowledge. When patents are rejected because their technology is "obvious," this is sometimes expressed by referring to the proposed patent as "state of the art," meaning that anyone acquainted with the field in question should be familiar with it. Of course, to be an "inventor," it is not necessary to be a scientist, and an "invention" need not rest on a scientific finding, but instances that do not rest on science are now extremely rare.

The patenting process is now so widespread and important that successful recent patents, such as the following, are commonly posted on the Internet:

> Wear-resistant coatings composed of laser ablated hard carbon films are deposited by pulsed laser ablation using visible light, on instruments such as microscope tips and micro-surgical tools. Hard carbon, known as diamond-like carbon (DLC), films produced by pulsed laser ablation using visible light enhances the abrasion resistance, wear characteristics, and lifetimes of small tools or instruments, such as small, sharp silicon tips used in atomic probe microscopy, without significantly affecting the sharpness or size of these devices. For example, a 10–20 nm layer of diamond-like carbon on a standard silicon atomic force microscope (AFM) tip enables the useful operating life of the tip to be increased by at least twofold. Moreover, the low inherent friction coefficient of the DLC coating leads to higher resolution for AFM tips operating in the contact mode.[14]

Microtools that wear well are (obviously) useful, so the usefulness criterion is clearly satisfied here. As for the other two criteria (that an invention be novel and "not obvious"), I think it must simply be accepted that they are satisfied as well. What is apparent from the description quoted above is that the inventors have found a *method* for depositing the material—diamond-like carbon—using lasers for making hardened tools and that they are patenting the method. Lasers (and AFMs) are now ubiquitous in modern materials-science laboratories; these inventors evidently saw a way to apply laser techniques to solve a practical problem. And clearly, the inventors foresaw the outcome of their work—namely, better microtools. As stressed earlier, to patent an outcome based upon a scientific finding *presupposes* that the outcome is foreseen.

Another example can be found in the 1994 isolation of the gene BRAC1 by a team of forty-five research workers from various laboratories, including several different labs at the University of Utah and Myriad Genetics Corporation (Miki et al. 1994). The corporation, the university, and the National Institutes of Health had all contributed money to the project, which was of considerable importance, as BRAC1 is implicated in many instances of breast cancer—that is, having the gene is highly statistically relevant to developing breast cancer. The gene is therefore said to make the unfortunate bearer "susceptible" to the disease. The isolation of the gene in itself is of only theoretical interest—showing the form of a certain abnormality on chromosome 17—and as such is simply a discovery about the human genome. If such an abnormality had been found in the genome of some animal species, then scientists might have found a use for it—perhaps using the poor animals as laboratory "guinea pigs"—or they might simply have recorded the discovery in some research publication. But of course, the nature of BRAC1 transcends theoretical interest—at the very least, it is hoped that it will provide a basis for diagnostic tests and maybe also point the way toward some treatment method. The most dramatic treatment would be to remove the gene from individual genomes (somatic gene therapy); other forms would involve investigating the gene's protein-producing functions and the associated biochemical mechanisms and pathways. The discovery of the gene, then, was a first step in all these directions.

The members of the team that discovered the gene were well aware of the significance of their work at the outset—this hardly needs to be noted. Many such biomedical and molecular genetic research projects are undertaken in the full knowledge that the findings might have important outcomes for human health; that is why the majority of them are funded. Most such projects would therefore stand alone as counterexamples to Polanyi's position as a whole, regardless of whether patents are involved. Still, the discovery of BRAC1 did lead to patents, the first regarding a diagnostic test for forty-seven mutations of the gene, granted to Myriad in December 1997. Considerable competition over proprietary rights among the principals that funded the original research over proprietary rights has followed, including legal actions. It has not, therefore, been the individual scientists but their financial backers and employers that have taken out patents in connection with this discovery; as noted above, this is common practice, "intellectual property" belonging to the funding institution.

Once a patent has been granted, then a process or product can be sold, in a variety of ways. For instance, an exclusive license to make a product could be granted to a firm for a certain time. Depending on the product, this might be quite expensive. Alternatively, nonexclusive access to a database of information might be sold to several different concerns, which can then make whatever use they can of the information. In the pharmaceuticals industry, as might be expected, there is tremendous competition over research findings, particularly in connection with gene hunters, and various patenting strategies have been tried. All of these circumstances have conditioned the context in which scientists work, making the outcome, rather than the discovery itself, the focus of attention. It might be objected that all of these examples are seemingly of applied research, whereas the research at issue is pure. This objection, however, is beside the point: the argument from patents is a response to the second unpredictability claim, which purports that once (pure) research findings are in place, outcomes are still never predictable. The argument from patents is then, I believe, a convincing refutation of Polanyi's position.

The scientist might still claim that in practice he cannot be expected to foresee where his research will lead, because of the character of scientific research and the nature of the process that leads from research findings to outcomes. Thus, a scientist who acknowledges the changed context of science and accepts SAP can nonetheless throw down Polanyi's Challenge without being guilty of inconsistency. The conclusion here is that scientists can *sometimes* be expected to see where their research will lead, not always. Specifying the circumstances in which outcomes are foreseeable—producing a formula or general method for doing so—would be a difficult task, to say the least; at best, I suspect, we would have to remain content with more case studies. Nevertheless, Polanyi's Challenge has been refuted by three distinct arguments that counter its validity.

Part 3

LOOKING FORWARD

The Ethics of Science

E OBVIOUSLY EXPECT SCIENTISTS TO DO WHAT ALL moral subjects do in their daily lives. But when mention is made of responsibilities, the implication is that something about the scientist's profession—or less formally, his role—brings with it certain *special* obligations. If we have doubts about whether any such responsibilities attach to the scientist, then I do not think that these can be satisfied by deciding whether it is proper to call scientists professionals without begging the question. Scientists are not professionals in the same way that lifeguards are because they (normally) have no special clientele (such as beachgoers). However, they do have special skills and knowledge that can be used for both good and bad purposes—this was our point of departure—and one might suppose that this is enough, given the magnitude of the effects of such special skills and knowledge, to impose responsibilities on the scientist.[1] But there are difficult questions that revolve around the issue as to just what these responsibilities are and why scientists have certain responsibilities and not others.

One way to approach this matter is to consult what scientists themselves have to say about it, either as individuals or through professional bodies and organizations. Szilard's 1939 telegram to Joliot, for example, can be seen as the former informing the latter of his responsibilities to the community beyond the laboratory doors. One manifestation of the "changed context" of science since 1945 is the formation of societies that have codes of ethics. Some of these are primarily research ethics, which are not of interest here, but others explicitly address scientists' responsibilities. For reasons I will explore later, I find it necessary to view such pronouncements by scientific bodies critically, not to take them as the last word on the matter; still, they are worth canvassing. Another approach, more likely to appeal to philosophers, is to begin with a general theory of ethics and then apply it to science, but it cannot be relied on exclusively. In the first place, we would be called upon to justify our choice of theory, evoking much controversy; in the second place, the application is likely to be distressingly uninformative—for example, "Scientists should strive to bring about the best consequences they can." Thus, I will instead appeal here to the idea of "common morality," presented in the work of Bernard Gert.

What Kinds of Responsibilities Do Scientists Have?

Morality is sometimes said to impose restrictions on the freedoms of moral agents.[2] This is consistent with the working assumption that we have been making throughout—that at the very least people should not gratuitously harm others, harm considered *gratuitous* if it cannot be justified. Of all the ways that one could act, those that harm others without justification are therefore forbidden by morality, and in this sense, the freedom of moral agents is restricted because they are not allowed to act in ways that cause harm. Deciding what is *justified* is not easy, as it is often necessary to try to balance one set of harms that the agent causes against others that his actions prevent. This question may arise directly and forcefully in the biological sciences, and it is the topic of much discussion in bioethics. For an agent to be asked to justify an action that harms someone implies that he is responsible for that harm, that the action does indeed "belong" to him. But the idea that there are some things that moral agents should *not* do because these actions adversely affect others—that moral agents' freedom is restricted—should be the starting point for all accounts of forward-looking responsibility. People with special skills or roles share this in common with all moral agents, and so scientists too are included.

An attempt to derive the responsibilities of the scientist from a basic and uncontroversial understanding of morality will not, however, take us very far. One might try to derive a richer account by seeing the limitations imposed by morality not simply as a matter of refraining from doing things that are harmful but also as a positive demand to do certain things that would not necessarily be done as a free first choice.

Morality on this understanding would not be just a matter of living a blameless life, of refraining from doing harm, but of positively seeking out good things to do. This seems an attractive option when considered together with the judgment that science is a mixed blessing: the responsibilities of the scientist in this scenario would reflect both the "bad" and the "good" sides of science, and scientists would be required not merely to refrain from research with harmful consequences but to search out opportunities to do research with beneficial consequences. But to *derive* the responsibilities of the scientist from morality in this way, I think, requires more by way of interpretation and justification than does the previous understanding—that being a moral person is simply a matter of living a blameless life. All of us can accept that. To suppose we must also strive to do good is (much) more controversial.

In the backward-looking sense, the scientist's responsibility has been taken to be *moral.* In the introduction, I noted that two other forms of responsibility—legal and social—also have currency and that, given our wide account of backward-looking responsibility, the conditions for moral responsibility and legal liability are somewhat closer than in other accounts. "Social responsibility" in the backward-looking sense has, I think, little or no circulation in normal usage, but it certainly does in the forward-looking sense. Indeed, a number of scientific associations refer explicitly to social responsibility in their codes of conduct, and some even include the words themselves in their titles.[3] This seems to suggest another way of beginning to think about the scientist's forward-looking responsibilities, perhaps one that can take us further than our uncontroversial conception of morality. This might be the case if social responsibility were both significantly different from moral responsibility and sufficiently clear as a basis on which to proceed. That is to say, if it were clear what it means to be socially responsible, and if being socially responsible were significantly different from being morally responsible, then focusing on this notion might indeed take us further, or in a different direction. Perhaps, then, the scientist's freedoms are (also) limited because he lives in a particular society?

I think that calls for scientists to be "socially responsible," repeated on many occasions in the changed context of science since 1945, are usually demands that scientists should be aware that their work can have an impact outside the laboratory. Such calls do not usually include precise and uniform specifications as to precisely how this social responsibility is to be discharged. Of course, such sentiments can be expressed again and again if need be, but such statements do not help with the details. Nevertheless, there are two other ways in which such calls could be understood. First, they might mean that the scientist's work should be directed primarily toward the maintenance and promotion of certain· societal *institutions*, rather than individuals.[4] Second (a point allied to the first), they might mean that the scientist's responsibilities are *local* rather than global: they are to be discharged with respect to a given society—British scientists are responsible to British society, Australian scientists to Australian society, and so on. In this sense, science should be done in the national interest.

Suppose that a scientist thinks that he ought to work for the Defense Department, as a defense scientist. While the Defense Department might want to develop an armaments industry in order to export arms to foreign countries, a decision that can sometimes have unfortunate consequences—as when the mujahideen used Kalashnikovs against the Soviets in the 1980s—usually this is for the home country's benefit in the form of export sales. Working for an institution, here the defense establishment, is thus at the same time to do science in the nation's interest, by strengthening its defense capability, its exports, or both. But it is evident that this scientist is not working impartially in everyone's interest, and this example raises a number of questions. First, it is so far unclear whether it is right or wrong for him to work for the Defense Department—a question that cannot be answered without more details.[5] Second, working for an institution normally means that the scientist is doing applied research. While this does not necessarily follow, as some institutions (such as Defense Departments) do sponsor pure research, they do so with the understanding that applications can follow breakthroughs in basic research. I will assume, then, that working for an institution amounts to endorsing its aims and methods, even when the actual research performed is "pure."

Another question now surfaces: what *alternatives* are there for a scientist, except to work for some institution—the Defense Department, a corporation, or a university—and hence endorse its aims and methods? Universities are something of an exception, as they are mostly the locus of pure research, so they can be set aside for the moment, and the answer becomes: if scientists have *no* alternative but to work for an institution of some sort, as science is no longer an activity that can be done at home in one's spare time, then being socially responsible means working for the *right kind* of institution.[6] And now some real alternatives *are* available. The Defense Department may be the right kind of institution because it keeps the nation strong, or corporation X might be the right kind because it earns export dollars and so keeps the nation strong.[7] Given that to be socially responsible is to work in the national interest, there can still be differences of opinion as to what counts as a strong or a good nation. However, this goal—the national interest—is not the only one that might be adopted. Other nonprofit institutions, such as the Red Cross and World Vision, provide an alternative to working for a nationally based institution, raising the possibility that the "right kind" of institution may not necessarily be nationally based.

It is clear that these are difficult practical issues. Retreating to generalities for the moment, the question becomes whether the focus is now an interpretation of the idea of socially responsible science, instead of the issue of the scientist's forward-looking moral responsibility. The fact that scientists are usually only able to work for an institution does not mean that responsibility for individual people has been usurped by the interests of the institution, for institutions of the "right kind," we suppose, are there to serve people.[8] The Defense Department does not have value in and of itself; it has value only because it organizes the defense of people who live in a particular country. This is not to say that institutions always appear to act in such a way that they realize this, but their raison d'être cannot be that they are ends in themselves.[9] The "right kind" of institution, then, is one whose goals and methods protect and promote the interests of people, not one that effectively protects and promotes only itself. To work for an institution, therefore, is not to do something quite different from discharging moral responsibilities toward individual people. The conscientious scientist who asks what he can do for his country and goes to work for the Defense Department does so because he thinks this is the most effective way he can serve his fellow citizens, not because he believes that the Defense Department is good in and of itself.

Given this way of thinking about social responsibility, it is obvious that social responsibility need not be something different from and set against moral responsibility. It is, rather, a kind of practical supplement, in that it suggests the *means* by which the scientist can come to grips with his responsibilities—namely, by signing up with the right kind of institution. Such institutions can even have global scope, if they have global reach. One might ask here whether an approach to the scientist's responsibilities that did not appeal to social responsibility would *require* that the responsibilities in question have global reach; it might be argued, in this context, that science itself is valid regardless of time and place and that morality teaches impartially, and that combined, these two observations might lead to this conclusion. I find this position attractive, but I do not think it must be accepted. A scientist who goes to work for a nonprofit institution that aims to aid development in a poor country is working locally, although perhaps not in his locale, and there is surely nothing wrong with that. In any case, a closer examination of the idea of social responsibility has led to a mechanism for *operationalizing* the moral responsibilities of the scientist, assuming that such things exist. Now we need a secure basis for identifying these in moral philosophy.

"Common Morality"

A well-known philosopher who has worked for many years in bioethics, H. Tristram Engelhardt Jr., believes that it is not possible for "reason to justify a canonical contentful morality" (Engelhardt 1996, 83). Instead, he thinks that his project—assessing the foundations of bioethics—must proceed in the face of moral diversity. For a "contentful morality" (or simply a morality), let us assume a set of principles that proscribe and perhaps also prescribe the behavior of the members of one group—moral agents—with regard to the members of another group, identified as those that deserve moral consideration—moral subjects. A morality will then serve to set limits on the freedom of the former in respect to what they can do to the latter; this is what we suppose morality does. I am not going to review Engelhardt's argument in favor of his (skeptical) conclusion, as it is detailed and drawn out, but I do want to oppose this conclusion with the position strongly advocated by Bernard Gert: that there *is* a common morality that can be supported by reason. On the first page of his most detailed exposition and defense of this position, Gert writes: "I shall present an account of morality, not of the morality of this group or of that society, but of morality. Further, I shall show that this common or universal morality is justified" (1998, 3). Engelhardt and Gert thus appear, on the surface at least, to be at odds with each other, and I think many would tend to side with Engelhardt, supposing that there can be no such thing as a universally accepted morality. However, I find Gert's account of morality appealing: he is not in fact advocating his common morality as universally accepted but as universally accept*able*.

Gert takes morality to be a *public system*, meaning that for it to work, it must be acknowledged by those to whom it applies—namely (rational) moral agents—as binding on persons such as themselves. The system cannot work behind closed doors, so to speak. In essence, common morality comprises a set of ten rules that count as prohibitions; a set of moral ideals—Gert does not specify a fixed number of these—that encourage certain behaviors but do not have the status of rules and hence are not binding on all moral agents; and a method for deciding what counts as justified breakings of the rules.[10] The rules are therefore not absolutely binding, and in this sense the system resembles W. D. Ross's prima facie duties more than it does Kantian morality. The rules are negative duties—all matters that agents should refrain from doing— and all of them prohibit harming. The first four rules prohibit "basic" or physical harms, like killing, causing pain, and depriving of freedom, while the second five prohibit things like deceiving and breaking promises. I will not reproduce Gert's full list here (see Gert 2004, 20), but I will note that as a full specification of what we have thus far referred to as gratuitous harms, Gert's first eight rules are as good as any, with what counts as "gratuitous" being thought of as breaking these rules without justification.[11]

While to say that one should not harm others may invite the question of what is meant by harm—at least if we are talking to philosophers—a more detailed specification, such as "Do not deprive of pleasure" (Gert's fifth rule), may also invite questions, such as what counts as pleasure. Bentham and Mill, for instance, famously answered this question differently. And as I have said, while there can be little doubt about what counts as an instance of some of the rules—for example, killing (Gert's first rule)—Gert admits that (some of) the rules may leave open questions of interpretation. He also does not claim that morality, as he conceives it, will provide a clear and unambiguous solution to every moral problem, one reason being that the rules are open to interpretation. For example, some people do not think that injections are painful and hence would not see having an injection as a (justified) breach of the second rule, "Do not cause pain"; most, however, would disagree. But within the broad area of agreement about what counts as harm, it is clear that all rational persons, other things being equal, would want to avoid harm to themselves and to those they care about. No one wants to be killed, to have pain caused to them, or to be deprived of freedom, unless there is some reason for these things to happen to them. If a painful injection will prevent a still more painful condition, then any rational person will agree to the injection. And if life itself is too painful to bear, then some will even allow a lethal injection of morphine to remove the pain.

Some unhappy people harm themselves or allow harms to befall them. Such people are commonly labeled crazy or, more clinically, *irrational*. Gert characterizes irrationality with reference to behavior that an agent should know is harmful to himself and yet carries out, or allows, with no good reason. "Good reason" here would include preventing other harms to himself or to others (or perhaps promoting good for oneself or for others, although such "good reasons" do not always justify breaking moral rules). Rationality is then defined with reference to irrationality: a rational person is someone who does not behave irrationally. But Gert is not *defining* morality in terms of what rational people do; he is fixing the *scope* of morality with reference to what rational people want. Given that most moral agents are rational in the required sense, then morality is binding on most of them and hence is a public system that applies regardless of time and place.

One of the pressing problems for Engelhardt, in his search for a universal contentful morality, was that people in different cultures hold different beliefs, and these led to different sorts of moral principles, especially concerning matters of religion. Fulfilling religious duties, and making others do so too, may become more important than rules against physical harm—this has certainly happened in the past and continues today. Gert attempts to get around this by placing further constraints on the "moral agents" who would assent to the system. If these agents are only taken to hold certain general beliefs—beliefs that all contending parties in different social, cultural, and racial groups share—then these differences will be factored out. These common beliefs include holding that all sentient beings can be harmed and wish to avoid harm, that persons are fallible and make mistakes, and so on (Gert 2004, 88–89).[12] Religious beliefs, however, are clearly not included in the compass of common beliefs simply because not everyone is religious.

In addition to the ten moral rules, Gert notes "corresponding" moral ideals. As before, Gert prefers not to list these ideals, although there are ideals corresponding directly to his first four rules: for "Do not kill," we have "Prevent killing," and so on. Persons are encouraged to follow these ideals but are not required to do so. They are therefore not required to *justify* not preventing harms, and they will not be punished for not doing so. However, this might not seem quite right: if I can save someone's life with little effort and no cost to myself and do not do so, do I not deserve censure and punishment? Especially if we understand this to be the kind of moral censure expressed by reactive attitudes? The intuition that I deserve censure is widespread, but so is the intuition that I do not—and notice that such an omission is not punishable by law. This is one of the difficult issues in moral philosophy. Those who incline to a rule-based system tend not to include omissions among their rules and do not require that agents prevent harms being caused to others. We *seem* to see this tendency manifested in Gert's system.[13] Consequentialists, on the other hand, are less concerned with the causal path that leads to an outcome, whether act or omission, than with the outcome itself. One aspect of Gert's system is helpful here, in that he allows that following a moral ideal may justify the breaking of a moral rule. Thus, if I have promised to meet a friend for a drink but stop to prevent a child from drowning and hence break my promise, then my preventing the tragedy justifies my breaking the rule. Every rational person would accept such a justification. The more difficult case is when I do not break the rule and walk past the drowning child to have a drink with my friend.

The question of responsibility for omissions was raised earlier, where it was noted that omissions are normally identified where there is a framework of expectations within which persons are expected to do certain things; when they don't do those things, it is appropriate to hold them to account. Recall that the lifeguard has responsibilities to beachgoers, to prevent them from coming to harm in the surf: an omission to save someone from drowning by a person who is not a lifeguard is an instance of the general problem just raised, but such an omission by a lifeguard is different, because his role commits him to more than simply abiding by moral rules. Gert recognizes this and allows that, for certain professions, moral ideals can come to resemble duties, and because there is a moral rule to do one's duty, the ideal may come to have the status of a rule (Gert, Culver, and Clouser 1997, 65). I say "resemble" here because there is a significant difference between rules and ideals that appears to prevent the latter from being "transformed" into the former in some special context; this difference concerns *impartiality*. Most systems of morality include some such demand, to the effect that moral principles should not discriminate among moral subjects or be applied in such a way that one or another subgroup is favored. One of the strengths of a system such as Gert's, which places the stress on rules that prohibit harming, is that this can be done impartially. One can be impartial by not harming both those in one's immediate vicinity, where there are accessible opportunities for harming, and those elsewhere, in distant places, where one has, so to speak, no opportunity to do harm (thus satisfying the rules "by default"). But a demand to help or provide assistance cannot be satisfied impartially, as the necessary time, resources, and opportunity to do so are not available to everyone.

The "formal" role fulfilled by common morality in our account of science and responsibility is that it provides what was earlier called (moral) *standards*, to avoid committing to any particular moral system (see chapter 3), and it gives us a justification for adopting those standards. In general, then, moral agents are accountable when they cause harm by breaking the moral rules: we expect them to *respond* and to give some justification. The standards comprise the rules and the ideals, and we can see immediately how this difference in status suggests that acting in accordance with ideals is praiseworthy. Because it is mandatory to abide by the rules, it seems that someone who does so is not praiseworthy, for it is not praiseworthy to do what one should do. But one is encouraged to follow ideals, for doing so makes the lot of others better by preventing harm—and hence here there is room for praise. In fact, it is just when people do what we encourage them to that we tend to praise them.

Science and "Common" Morality

There is a natural way to adapt Gert's common morality to professional ethics. A moral ideal cannot, in Gert's view, take on the status of a moral rule because of the issue of impartiality. But if we were to specify a particular group for the professional, namely a *clientele*, providing this group was not too large, it would be possible to treat the members of this group impartially.[14] A doctor could treat his patients impartially, helping those most who need the most. For such a group, the slogan made famous by Peter Singer can be applied: morality implies equal consideration (being impartial), but not necessarily equal treatment. Gert makes it clear that impartiality can only be defined with reference to a group (1998, 132), so this suggestion is not at odds with his understanding of the notion. What is special about a professional's particular clientele—the assumption being that each professional has *a* clientele—is that the professional is duty-bound to prevent certain harms from befalling them by using his special skills and knowledge. Of course, a professional is paid for his services, but it is generally accepted that there is also a moral dimension to the professional-client relationship—hence professional *ethics*—and adapting Gert's system seems to be a good way to capture this moral dimension. The significance of this is that the professional's particular duty toward his clientele is seen to be the professional's *responsibility*—and hence something that can lead to blame in cases of omission. Indeed, Gert's tenth rule, "Do your duty," will apply specifically to professionals.

I noted earlier that the nature of the scientist's forward-looking responsibilities will not be determined by deciding whether it is correct to *call* scientists professionals. While there are differences of opinion over just who to call a professional, with some commentators stressing the importance of special expertise and others the importance of a clientele (see note 1), scientists do not, on the whole, have a special clientele, and in this crucial respect they are not like doctors and lawyers, the paradigm professionals. A scientist might take on a particular project and offer his expertise—for instance, how to manage the water recourses in a semiarid area. If he is employed by the local council with the aim of improving the standard of living for the people who live in the area, then in a sense he does have a clientele, and his responsibility is to give the best advice possible, with their benefit in mind. I think such a case is the closest scientists can come to resembling "true professionals." We could also consider scientists who work in industry and use their skills and knowledge to further the interests of the corporation, but while these scientists resemble professionals in applying specialized knowledge, being members of professional organizations, earning salaries (as opposed to wages), and so on, they do not have a clientele. Scientists in industry are members of what J. K. Galbraith calls the "technostructure"—those holding specialized knowledge who guide the corporation in its quest to maximize growth and profit (Galbraith 1967). Corporations have customers who buy their products and hence enable them to grow, but they do not have a clientele. The responsibility of the technostructure, such as it is, is to ensure that the corporation's products satisfy the design specifications; there is no further responsibility to consumers (which is *not* to say that the technostructure is not accountable for what it does). Finally, research scientists in universities may also be regarded as professionals because they use specialized knowledge and skills and belong to professional bodies, but we would be hard-pressed to find any candidates who might fit the description of their clientele.

It is clear, I think, that scientists rarely have a clientele and that, qua scientists, they are not supposed to (and hence Gert's tenth does not apply directly to them). Perhaps we might also contrast the *education* of doctors, other health-care professionals, lawyers, teachers, engineers, and so on with that of scientists. The education of the former is specifically tailored to produce graduates for the professions and hence includes courses that prepare for practice: clinical work in hospitals, practical teaching, work experience as legal clerks, and so on. There is little comparable in science education.

If scientists do not have a clientele, then there is no particular associated group toward whom they can behave impartially in some respect. The "respect" here would be identified with the particular responsibility that the scientist would have to the proposed group (such as to prevent harm because of an inadequate water supply). The impartiality constraint is therefore an obstacle—provided we continue to work within common morality—to specifying a strong basis for the scientist's responsibilities, in the sense of things he should do. By a "strong basis," I mean one that allows us to determine things that the scientist *must* do, just as he must not harm others. We can either try to find a way around this obstacle or live with it.

Living with it would mean maintaining *either* that scientists only have certain things they should not do and that is all there is to their responsibilities, *or* that, in addition to these "negative duties," there are things that they are only encouraged to do. The second option implies that the scientist has a kind of two-tiered set of responsibilities: on one level he must *refrain* from harming others, while on the other he is *encouraged* to prevent harm. I am strongly inclined to the second option. I note again that Gert does not think that such "ideals" are of secondary importance, either for the flourishing of human society or within the system of common morality; thus, the notion of "second-tier" responsibilities does not imply a lack of significance. Indeed, given that common morality does not comprise rules that must be obeyed come what may, it is possible in principle that second-tier responsibilities to prevent harm might be cited as justification for failing to respect first-tier responsibilities—harming some to prevent harms to others.

The intuition that omitting to prevent harms, if not quite as bad as causing harms, is at least punishable in the same kind of way is strongest in instances in which little or no effort or cost might save someone's life or prevent some other great harm from befalling them—the emblematic drowning child, the colleague slumped in the fume cupboard (see chapter 4). But such omissions are not as relevant to a discussion of what scientists should do qua scientists. Scientists should do the kinds of things that their skills and knowledge enable them to do, and while these things may well prevent considerable harms, they will not involve merely the effort needed to turn on a fume-cupboard fan or lift up a child. They may, in fact, entail a commitment that involves a great deal of sacrifice in terms of career and status. To *require* someone to do these things thus leads to the sorts of unintuitive results that follow from too strict an application of the consequentialist calculus. Once one *should* prevent harm from befalling others, it becomes hard to set limits on when one should stop doing so.[15] In a well-known chapter of *Practical Ethics*, Singer considers what we—here the wealthy—should do about the poor in Africa, in Asia, and among our own citizens (1993, 218–46). In denying, or downplaying, the moral difference between acts and omissions—for instance, between taking away someone's food and letting him starve—Singer's argument leads him to suggest that "wealthy" households should give away 10 percent of their income (1993, 246). But this is just a policy proposal; the argument itself leads to the conclusion that wealthy households should give away as much as is needed to bring the poor up to their own standard of living—much more than 10 percent.

There is a difference between encouraging people to be generous, with either their money or their skills, and requiring that they be so. Indeed, if giving away 50 percent of one's income was the morally right thing to do, it would not be thought of as generosity. A kind of disanalogy between consequentialist implications for professionalization and actual practice begins to become clear here. On the whole, professionals can step out of their roles. The off-duty lifeguard is not supposed to scan the waves looking for raised arms as he walks along the beach with his family, and doctors are not on call twenty-four hours a day, every day. But if a doctor or lifeguard is able to continue preventing harm when his normal working day is done, then the consequentialist requires that he do so. Again, it is the fact that this is required that is the problem—that someone most of us would admire for his selfless act is merely doing what he must.[16] These problems stem from the demand that agents strive to prevent harm *impartially*, regardless of any special roles they play, whether as members of the professions or because of any special knowledge they may have. If this is not required but encouraged, on the other hand, then the scientist who chooses to further his own career does not do what is morally wrong, and neither does the off-duty lifeguard who fails to go back into the sea and rescue swimmers at risk from the collapsed sandbank, and neither does the household that does not give away 10 percent of its income. If, in fact, any of these agents did sacrifice the time, effort, and money to do any of these things, then we would consider them generous, morally praiseworthy, and good persons.

The suggested "two-tiered" set of responsibilities, according to which scientists are required not to do wrong by causing harm and are encouraged to do good by preventing it, therefore seems plausible. It is plausible in that it avoids the excessive sacrifice that the consequentialist, conflating acts and omissions, demands of those who have skills and resources that can be reallocated to help others—something I think we do not find in everyday morality. And it is plausible, on the other hand, because preventing harm is not seen as heroic or altruistic, or as the kind of supererogatory act that is beyond the call of duty. On the basis of Gert's common morality, the scientist who strives to prevent harm is laudable, but he is not an altruist or a superman. There is room *within* common morality for assessing such acts, and this seems to get the balance right. As to the scientist's actual responsibilities, these will often depend on his social, political, and economic situation, both at home and overseas.

Common Morality and Responsibility for Outcomes

Two kinds of outcomes of scientific research have been identified as relevant here: those that stem from technologies and those that stem from science as ideas. It is clear that outcomes from technology are appropriate items for assessment of scientists' responsibility within the framework of common morality. If technology is thought of as enabling us to do things that we cannot do unaided—as giving us access to an extended range of actions—then the provision of this additional means is surely something that morality can make judgments about: those that do harm are morally suspect, and those that prevent harm are to be encouraged. I do not find this conclusion contentious in the least. But when scientists reflect on the way the world is and come up with new theories, then they are producing outcomes in the second of the two senses. Assuming that these outcomes can be considered in themselves, not for what they deliver in terms of extending the range of human action, what can be said of this kind of outcome in terms of common morality?

Such outcomes will be assessable on the basis of common morality if they fit within the two-tiered system of responsibilities, and I believe they do. Science as ideas is science as a body of propositions, and while very few people can understand the full technical range of scientific inference, many can grasp the propositions that stand as basic conclusions. In keeping with the realist interpretation, these conclusions are statements of fact—statements purporting to be true. And given that science is the most reliable means that there is for finding out the truth, then what science tells us about the facts is preferable to what might be learned from any other purported source of knowledge. A suggestion canvassed earlier (see chapter 1) was that publishing "the truth" is good in itself. I disputed this suggestion on the grounds that what is good from the moral perspective has to do with moral subjects, and so any other (nonmoral) sense in which it is "a good thing" to publish the truth is not relevant here. In this account, the concept of the good that can be constructed on the basis of common morality differs from consequentialist notions of the maximization of happiness, and so forth. The good of common morality evidently involves not causing harm and preventing harm; hence, propositions that cause harm are bad, and those that prevent harm are good. But how can propositions *themselves*, apart from their physical effects on us via technology, cause harm?

This is only possible via their bearing on *other* propositions, in virtue of the logical relations that hold between them. If two propositions are inconsistent, then it is not possible to believe both of them. If one proposition implies another, then believing the former commits one to believing the latter. Therefore, the effects that science has on us as a body of ideas depend on how these ideas form and change our beliefs (the first of the two ways that science as a collection of propositions was said to be a mixed blessing at the end of chapter 1). The issue now comes down to whether this might be harmful, for otherwise, science as a body of ideas is *not* after all assessable within the two-tiered system. Certainly, science in this aspect can *prevent* harm. The most reliable factual knowledge is the best guide to action, all things considered. And the most reliable knowledge provides the most stable basis for belief, because (by definition) it is least likely to be refuted. Having one's activities frustrated can be dangerous, and having one's beliefs shown to be false can be upsetting; hence, providing a reliable basis for both activities and beliefs can prevent harm. If that were the end of the story, then the publication of scientific truth could indeed never be a bad thing and thus would not register on the first tier of the responsibility. Granted that whatever else (pure) scientists want to do, they always want to publish the truth, then they might, so to speak, enjoy the (fortuitous) bonus of doing the morally correct thing when they simply get on with the task of producing the "proper products" of research to the best of their ability.

Science as a collection of propositions can therefore only cause harm if the propositions lead people to give up beliefs or adopt beliefs and if this process is harmful to the people in question. There is no doubt that science's proclamations have caused many people great anguish by challenging their beliefs—during the Scientific and Darwinian Revolutions, for instance—and hence science in this sense *can* cause harm. Today, creation "scientists" are trying to defend their beliefs by using what they take to be the scientific method to come up with an alternative representation of the facts. One assumes that these attempts are sincere, motivated by great concern about the harms creationists think mainstream science can do to their faith. Others reject science altogether, seeing it as a disenchantment of nature that leaves us with a vision of the world as cold and soulless. It does not follow from the fact that such people are deluded that disillusioning them will, in the end, be beneficial. It may not be. A person may give up a false belief and be miserable for the rest of his life. Are scientists therefore obliged to try to work through the implications of their work for the beliefs of others and not publish their findings if they think some people might thus come to believe or disbelieve certain matters of fact that will cause them anguish? If so, the scientist will be hard-pressed indeed.

This conclusion, however, is *not* forced on us, the situation here somewhat different than for science as a basis for technology (where, I have argued, scientists do need to look ahead at the implications of their work). Two points are important here. First, to believe is to make a *choice*—to choose to regard a proposition as true. Sometimes such a choice seems unavoidable, as when the evidence is presented directly to the senses, but the propositions of science are not (normally) like this. One can easily avoid believing that the earth goes around the sun, for after all, the main problem for the followers of Copernicus was getting people to accept this proposition. Because it is up to the individual to accept or reject the conclusions of scientific research, the responsibility for believing is largely the individual's. On the contrary, people usually have no choice about the effects of science-based technology. Second, to repeat a point made above, the most reliable propositions are the most reliable guides to conduct and belief, and in this sense they always tend to the *prevention* of harm. Science as a body of ideas scores so highly in terms of this second-tier responsibility that it looks as if it may stand as a blanket justification for any first-tier harms caused. For these reasons, I think we can ultimately set aside the implications of science as a body of ideas when discussing the scientist's responsibilities.

Gert's common morality is, I believe, a plausible account of how normal moral persons conduct their lives. Harming without justification is wrong, and harming therefore opens the agent up to negative moral sentiments. Omitting to prevent harms, however, does not amount to a moral wrong in the same sense. Preventing harms is desirable and there- fore encouraged, but it is codified by moral ideals rather than by rules. The problem with requiring agents to prevent harm is that this cannot, as a matter of fact, be done impartially, and it can, depending on the circumstances, make superhuman effort mandatory. The overall impli- cations for scientists are clear: they *should not*, qua scientists, cause gra- tuitous harm, and it would be *desirable* if, qua scientists, they worked to prevent it.

Science and Weapons Research

ETER SINGER DESCRIBES SOME HORRIBLY CRUEL
experiments on animals (1993, 66)—experiments that are in his view,
and in mine, unjustified. I do not think it is justifiable to inflict pain on
animals just to see how they will react under conditions of extreme
stress and hardship. To inflict suffering just to acquire knowledge—just
to find out how the animals will react—is what we supposed our carica-
ture cold-hearted scientist would do. Part of the motivation for adopting the wide view of responsibility was to make sure that this
cold-hearted scientist would be deemed responsible for such deeds even
when his intention was just to gain knowledge and write a paper. The
great majority of animal experimentation is done in the name of human
interest, from drug to product testing. Bernard Gert provides a framework to evaluate such research, and there are other frameworks that also
protect animals. My own view, which I will not elaborate here, is that
some animal experimentation is justified for medical purposes.[1] For the
most part, however, scientists do not actually inflict harm or directly do
good when they engage in scientific research in the laboratory. Rather,
what scientists do is to provide the wherewithal or the *means* to do good
or evil by providing the basis for technology in the form of designs and
blueprints.

Providing the means to do evil by harming is not the same thing as
harming, or so it seems. For one thing, the means might not actually be
used to harm but just be available for doing harm—in which case applying the standards of common morality may not be straightforward.

These standards enjoin all of us not to harm without justification, and so for instances of actual harming, it must be determined whether these harms would be publicly allowed in order to decide whether they are justified. But providing the means to harm is not the same thing, so how the dictates of common morality apply in such instances must be investigated.[2] The particular case I am going to consider has already been foreshadowed: weapons research. I think this choice as a case study needs no justification: simply to point out that science has given us the ability to kill virtually all sentient life on the earth, via extensive or "heavy" use of thermonuclear weapons, should suggest that something has gone awry with the way science has been used.[3] And of course, it was the Manhattan Project, and its aftermath at Hiroshima and Nagasaki, that brought about the changed context of science in which these developments have taken place.[4]

I will argue for a complete moratorium on weapons research. I do so not in the expectation that this will actually happen, but from the perspective of the scientist who acknowledges his moral responsibilities.[5] That is to say, I want to give reasons why a scientist who would abide by common morality and who therefore recognizes that, as a scientist, he is obliged not to harm others should not take part in weapons research under any circumstances: there is *no* justification for this form of scientific research—a conclusion that some might think surprising.[6]

Science and Weapons Research

I understand "weapons research" to refer to research conducted with the *intention* of designing or improving weapons systems or the means for carrying out activities associated with the use of weapons, such as command, control, and communications. Thus, not only does research into better nuclear weapons count as war research, but so does research into better ways to encrypt communications between headquarters and commanders in the field. In general, weapons research is supposed to provide and improve the means for fighting wars; whatever other aims it might have depend on this *primary* aim. Scientific research aimed at weapons production does not make war any better—and I will say something later about "defensive weapons" and "humane weapons." What such research does do, obviously, when combined with an industrial base, is make available more powerful, more accurate, more efficient, and longer-range weapons of greater varieties, allowing countries to fight with more resources and greater intensity than was possible in preindustrial times. This means, essentially, that many more people can be killed much more quickly. In fact, the strategic systems produced during the Cold War, and still in existence, raised the specter of a kind of transcendence of war, of a war in which all sentient life on earth would be destroyed. There have thus been many calls for countries to at least limit, if not cease, weapons research. But there seem to be two reasons not to abandon weapons research altogether: first, if *self-defense* is justified, then it seems that so is weapons research for defensive purposes; second, if *deterrence* is justified because it prevents wars, then it seems that so is weapons research for deterrent purposes.

But are these grounds for weapons research in fact justified? Many different roles are associated with weapons production, but our interest here is in the scientist who actually devises, creates, or improves a weapon or produces the *knowledge* by virtue of which the weapon can be made. Such knowledge production is what happened at Los Alamos, with the weaponization of plutonium. This involved coming up with a way of sustaining a divergent chain reaction in plutonium long enough to allow a substantial release of energy, which entailed surrounding a subcritical hollow sphere of the material with an array of explosive lenses. It is clear that the Nagasaki Fat Man bomb was not a unique realization of this design. Other "Fat Man" bombs were also made in the United States, and the implosion design was discovered by Soviet, English, Chinese, French, Israeli, Indian, and Pakistani scientists, and most likely by scientists from other countries, such as North Korea and Iran. While the designs are not, I suspect, all exactly the same, they are assuredly recognizable variants on the same theme. In any case, the original Los Alamos blueprint could have been used over and over again, in different times and places, and embodied in many identical "Fat Man" bombs. Each individual realization of such a design is localized in time and place and has a limited effective lifetime, while the information on which it is based is eternal.[7]

I include as "weapons scientists" all persons who contribute to the designs on which weapons can be produced, whether their actual institutional designations are as engineers, research managers, or something else. Moreover, most of these individuals *intend* to produce knowledge on the basis of which weapons can be made. The exceptions here are "pure" scientists who accept grants from the Department of Defense to work on particular projects. Defense Departments have a history of funding "strategic basic research"—research that does not have any particular end in view, any particular artifact, although its field is regarded as having the potential to yield such applications. Nuclear physics is an obvious example of a defense science, as are the basic sciences behind communications and computing. Scientists who accept money from the Department of Defense may simply be interested in these fields for their own sake, but we now have in place a way to attribute responsibility for any harmful outcomes that flow from their work. To be sure, the very fact that his grant money comes from the Defense Department means that a scientist cannot plead that he did not know that his work might have a weapons application in the future. I will, however, be largely concerned here with the scientist who intends his work to have such application.

Harming and the Means Principle

Common morality teaches that harming others is wrong. But scientists who engage in weapons research by designing weapons are not, by their "immediate" actions, doing harm. Thus, a scientist doing a complex calculation necessary for a design is not, by that action itself—by what he is doing at the computer terminal or the drawing board—doing harm. Therefore, it seems that any case against weapons research must be "indirect": what the scientist engaged in weapons research does directly is not harmful, but he is aiding others in doing future harm. Recall that it is possible to describe actions in different ways, with some referring to relatively far-off consequences of the bodily movements that make up action-events. So, without stretching Feinberg's accordion very far, we can also say of the weapons scientist, S, that he is providing the *means* to harm: weapons do harm, and he is designing a weapon, so therefore he is providing the means to harm. It seems clear that to provide the means to harm is not itself to harm: what S is doing is not firing a gun or launching a missile, but providing the basis on which the gun or missile may be made. We must now ask whether, if it is wrong to harm (without justification), it is also wrong to provide the means to harm. I will call the substance of the affirmative response to this question the "means principle"; thus, the question here is whether the means principle is true or at least if its application to weapons research is correct.[8] If we cannot adopt the means principle, or some refined version thereof, then weapons research is not the kind of morally questionable activity that common morality proscribes.

I note that the means principle is only the first step in making a case against weapons research. If the means principle is accepted, then this implies that scientists have to accept responsibility for providing the means to harm, but it does not imply that they must accept blame: according to common morality, even if providing the means to harm is wrong, it still may be publicly allowed under certain conditions. However, if the activities S undertakes in the weapons lab can be described as "providing the means to harm," then they can also be described in other ways, such as "preventing or deterring harms." If these other descriptions are in fact correct, and we (mistakenly) charge S with providing the means to harm, then he has an excuse: he can reply that what he was doing was providing the means to prevent or deter harms, not to cause them, and if this is the case, he does not have to respond, because he did not perform the action with which we charged him. I will later consider whether and under what conditions these alternative descriptions are appropriate. Notice here, however, that this determination depends in part on what S *intends*. Weapons research is, after all, applied research, not pure. At least, S intends to design weapons. Does he therefore also intend to design the means to harm, or do these other possible descriptions mean that he can opt instead for one of them?

To begin to think about the means principle, suppose that one person, P, provides another, Q, with a gun, and then Q goes out and commits a crime with the gun—he does harm. Is P also responsible for the harm? The answer depends on how P "provides" Q with the gun. If P has the gun locked away in a safe and Q steals it, then there is a sense in which P has provided it for Q but is clearly not responsible for the harm done. On the other hand, if P is an accomplice in the crime and provides Q with the wherewithal to carry it out, including the gun, then P is responsible, both before the law and according to the dictates of morality. There are, however, possibilities between these extremes where matters become less certain. Suppose P is an illegal gun dealer who sells Q the gun, strongly suspecting, given Q's criminal record, that it will be used to harm. P would prefer that the harm not be done and certainly does not intend it, but he nevertheless sells Q the gun. The broad view of moral responsibility entails in this case that P is also responsible for the harm done. Only if P had no reason to think that Q would commit a crime, and no responsibility as a gun dealer to make inquiries about Q, could P deny responsibility. (Here, the application of the means principle requires the satisfaction of an epistemic condition and perhaps also a judgment as to whether any forward-looking responsibility is at issue.) Thus, if P is a legal gun dealer, and if he sells a gun to the criminal Q, inadvertently and having made all the required checks, only then is he not responsible for the harm done.

The Means Principle and Weapons as Artifacts

One might assume that scientist S does not necessarily have any particular harming episodes in mind when he designs a new weapon and that this makes a difference. But the means principle, I think, still survives in this case, because S is designing an artifact whose *primary purpose* is to do harm. Artifacts, by definition, exist for at least one purpose, even though they may be versatile and enable us to do several things, some a "by-product" of their primary purpose.[9] Primary purposes are therefore those things that designers and manufacturers have in mind when they create artifacts. The proverbial kitchen scissors is produced for all manner of domestic cuttings-up, but if it is sharp and pointed, it may also be used as a stabbing instrument. This purpose is *secondary* because it is entirely unrelated to the primary purpose and is not something the manufacturer intends his product to do. Now, my view is that all those involved in the design and manufacture of an artifact are committed to its primary purpose and that this entails responsibility for instances of its use for this purpose; this is surely obvious—an artifact's primary purpose is what it is supposed to do, what its creators *intend* that it do. A little more argument—although not much more, given the wide account of responsibility—would be needed to establish commitment and responsibility for secondary purposes.

Harming is hardly weapons' secondary purpose, as harming is what weapons are designed to do. The makers of artifacts are committed to instances in which their primary purpose is realized, and they are committed to these instances because this use is what they intended, which entails responsibility for such use. We would locate S the weapons researcher further back in the causal chain than P the gun dealer, as S designs the gun, but S nevertheless obviously plays a role in providing the means to harm.[10] There is then the issue of what S intends or foresees, as there was for P, but my point here is that S cannot deny that what he has done is design an artifact whose purpose is to harm, even if he can evade responsibility for some particular use. In a moment, I will suggest a way S might deny that he intends certain uses of his weapons

—those that are "unauthorized"—but it is not possible at this stage to deny *all* uses. S has knowingly, willingly, and hence intentionally designed a weapon. Surely, he cannot say that he did not intend this weapon to be used to harm. Given that his actions are properly described as "providing the means to harm," I cannot see any way to avoid this conclusion. It seems that the best bet for S is to claim, like the legitimate gun dealer, that he only intends his weapons to have "authorized uses," such as those sanctioned by the government.

There is yet a further, ultimately crucial difference between a scientist who provides the means to harm by designing a weapon and a gun dealer who provides a criminal with the means to harm by knowingly selling him a gun. S provides a *design* or *blueprint* that can be copied many times over, its products used in many different contexts, which means that any comparison fails to provide us with the *right* distinction between authorized and unauthorized use. The suggestion is that only authorized uses can be justified and that S is only responsible for authorized uses. But both subtheses may be wrong: authorized uses may not be morally acceptable, and S may also be responsible for unauthorized uses. All this invites the question of what counts as an authorized use, and whatever the answer, it presumably must refer to the wider context in which the weapons research is done and its products used. I will call this a "historical question" about weapons research: such a question cannot be answered without reference to the particular circumstances in which the weapons research is commissioned and carried out. For instance, the political situation of S's country is relevant, particularly whether it is at war or under threat. S might say, "Yes, I know I provided the means to harm, and I am committed to whatever uses my research leads to, but my country was at war." This is an attempted justification and consequently is an admission that the means principle applies. I will return to the question of authorized use when I consider historical issues about weapons research.

My claim, then, is that the means principle applies at least in some instances in which the products of weapons research are used to harm. Because the primary purpose of weapons is to harm others, S cannot deny that he knowingly and willingly provided the means to harm when he undertook weapons research. He can refuse to acknowledge some instances of harming because they are illegal or unauthorized, but all these instances cannot have this character in view of the artifact's primary purpose. The question of justification then becomes a historical one. However, one final response to this claim seeks to excuse weapons research on *ahistorical* grounds—that is, on grounds that do not take into account the particular context in which the weapons research is done—namely that the primary purpose of the weapon under discussion has been misconceived. Suppose S responds that his work is intended to prevent or reduce harm. That is, he claims to have an *alternative* description of his weapons research project, one that does not represent it as providing the means to do harm. Likewise, he maintains that the primary purpose of the artifacts he is aiming to produce is to prevent or reduce harm. He might also say that actual uses of the weapon were secondary or characterized as having some other purpose. S might urge this excuse on us on either historical or ahistorical grounds, although I consider only the latter.

We have already accepted that one and the same action may have more than one description, in line with the accordion effect, which allows us to incorporate the causal consequences of immediate bodily movements. In this regard, alternative descriptions are more or less inclusive of relatively remote consequences. However, S is doing something different. He is not merely incorporating a different range or grouping of causal consequences into the account of his action—making a different selection from the same class, as it were; rather, he is proposing a quite different class of consequences. There is then a *genuine* difference here, which depends on whether there is such a thing as weapons research that prevents or reduces harm. If there is, then it seems S has nothing to answer for, at least as far as the moral imperative is concerned.

Defensive and Precision Weapons

I believe that the only ahistorical grounds that could warrant the description of S's work as preventing or reducing harm would be the existence of weapons that were *inherently defensive* or, in the case of reducing harm, inherently more discriminating with respect to military over civilian targets. By "inherently defensive," I mean weapons whose *only possible* use is in a "defensive" war. I will assume that defense is morally acceptable and hence that weapons research exclusively directed toward producing the means to defend would not require justification.[11] An example of a discriminating weapon is precision-guided munitions. Thus, a cruise missile with a 500kg warhead is more likely to

hit its target than is a 500kg dumb iron bomb and hence is more likely
to reduce collateral damage. But we can immediately dismiss the search
for more precise weaponry as an excuse, because it is not true that the
only possible use of more precise weapons is to reduce civilian causalities—they could also be used to increase civilian causalities, as the
means for terror bombing. For S to say that his country would never
actually engage in such activities and hence that his work is justified is,
of course, to move to a historical justification.

Scientists undertake weapons research on one or more individual
systems, or more usually on parts of individual systems. These are
designed to fill certain roles in wartime, in virtue of given physical
characteristics or capabilities. But one cannot, for the reason just given,
infer the just nature or otherwise of the war from the role the weapon
is designed to fulfill. I maintain that there are no *inherently* defensive
weapons.[12] An episode of considerable historical importance took place
in the years following President Ronald Reagan's infamous "Star Wars"
speech. In 1983, Reagan called upon the scientific community to exploit
new technologies, such as lasers, to provide the basis for a defensive
shield for the United States and its allies that would render nuclear
weapons "impotent and obsolete."[13] The scientific community subsequently accepted huge amounts of money for the Strategic Defense Initiative (SDI), even though the prospects for a perfect—leak-proof—area
defense of the continental United States seemed impossible from the
very beginning. Because the system was never going to be perfect,
the Soviets interpreted this imperfect missile defense shield as part of
the means for an *offensive* first-strike capability: after a first strike at the
enemy's offensive systems, the defensive shield would mop up (most
of) the surviving missiles launched in retaliation.[14] Notice that what
the Soviets were interpreting were U.S. intentions and plans, not simply capabilities.

It was clear to all involved that the SDI was to be an attempt to establish a defensive shield to intercept as many incoming warheads as possible—everyone understood what it was supposed to do. This might
have been effected in several ways, most spectacularly, and most specu-
latively, by deploying x-ray lasers in space to shoot down warheads and
reentry vehicles in midcourse, while they were outside the atmosphere.
But while the SDI's purported role was clear, the Soviets and the Americans stated diametrically opposed views on the strategic mission the
SDI would play. Was it to defend U.S. assets after a "dying" retaliatory

Soviet second strike or to defend U.S. assets after a Soviet first strike (Lebow 1985)? No inference can be made from the job a weapon does— its "capability"—regarding the kind of war in which it will do that job.

Deterrence

Although the claim that some weapons have a certain special character—inherently defensive, for instance—does not stand up to scrutiny, perhaps S can still maintain that he is not providing the means to harm when he undertakes weapons research, because he is preventing harm by making weapons for *deterrent* purposes. While a defensive weapon— or a weapon used in a defensive role—physically prevents a population or asset from harm, a deterrent is supposed to prevent harm by keeping hostilities from breaking out at all. While it may well be true that certain weapons should only be employed for deterrent purposes— weapons of mass destruction come to mind straight away—we may now be skeptical of any claim that inherently deterrent weapons even exist. While each weapon can do a certain kind of job—evade radar detection and interceptors, hit a target with a given accuracy, liberate a given amount of blast and heat, and so on—a range of possible missions, embedded in different operations for a variety of conflicts, can be accomplished by the self-same weapon. Some of these might be defensive and hence seemingly justifiable, but others might not be. Using a cruise missile to destroy an aggressor's command-and-control center seems justified, while a preemptive attack on a school is not. However, an aggressor may decide simply to stay at home, because of the threat of response by cruise missiles, and so may be deterred.

Deterrence, again, is not a secondary purpose of a weapon, according the taxonomy of purposes used here, but a *derivative* purpose. A secondary purpose is something that an artifact can be used for, besides its intended or primary purpose; it is something quite different from the primary one, something that the artifact can be used for incidentally, because of its physical makeup, such as the stabbing scissors. A derivative purpose, on the other hand, is also something else that an artifact can be used for, besides its primary purpose, but it is something that "depends" on the primary purpose. Deterrence is in fact one of the clearest examples of an artifact's derivative purpose. Thus, cruise missiles equipped with nuclear weapons were at one time believed to have played a role in deterring a massive conventional Soviet attack on

Europe. Setting aside the actual historical evidence, suppose that huge tank armies would have invaded Western Europe had there not been cruise missiles and other tactical nuclear weapons in place. However, such weapons can only function as a deterrent if they can do what they were designed to do—hitting a target with the given degree of accuracy and releasing lots of heat, blast, and, in this case, radiation. But this *primary* purpose is independent of any deterrent one: armed nuclear cruise missiles did not need to have ever been used as deterrents. They could simply have been made and used, like the products of the Manhattan Project, or made and kept secret, like the doomsday device in the movie *Doctor Strangelove.*

Does the fact that weapons can have the derivative purpose of deterrence mean that S now has another chance to justify his participation in weapons research? Perhaps even a way to do so on ahistorical grounds, which do not refer to any political or historical contingencies? S might declare that he is working on the design of cruise missiles because they are weapons of deterrence. This, however, is a misrepresentation: cruise missiles only deter because they can hit targets with a given accuracy, and they can be used to do this without deterring anyone. The primary purpose—what the artifact is designed to do—thus has "priority" over the derivative one. S can design a weapon that will fulfill its primary purpose when it is used, but he cannot design a weapon that will *only* fulfill the derivative purpose of deterrence. For one thing, deterrence can fail for factors beyond S's control—the Soviets could have invaded Western Europe in the teeth of all the deployed tactical nuclear weapons— whereas the correct working of a weapon, given that the field commanders use it properly, *is* in S's control. For another thing, deterrence is a relationship between two or more states and as such is an *essentially historical* state of affairs. S might insist that his participation in weapons research is intended not to provide the means to harm but to prevent harm, but this statement must now be understood as referring to certain specific historical circumstances.[15] There is no ahistorical or context-free excuse or justification for weapons research.

Authorized Use

The argument against there being any ahistorical grounds for justifying weapons research begins with the means principle—that it is wrong to provide the means to harm others. One cannot design and make weapons without knowing what they will be used for. Is it the case, then, that *any* justification of weapons research must depend on the research's actual uses, including deterrent purposes, given that these are, in the above sense, authorized uses? I believe it is. I take the paradigm case of an authorized use of a weapon produced through government-sponsored weapons research to be when the armed forces of the government in question use the weapon in a conflict in which the government is legally engaged. That would rule out the use of Stuka dive bombers in the German invasion of Poland but include the use of radar by England in the Battle of Britain. This may be thought to open the door to another attempt at ahistorical justification, or justification that is "almost" ahistorical: provided that S is working for a democratic state, one that espouses human rights, freedom, and other desirable political characteristics, then everything will be fine because such states only wage wars "according to the rules." Alas, the historical record does not conform to this ideal, and the door quickly closes again.[16]

Authorized use is important because it constitutes the only possible justification for taking part in weapons research. Because we have embraced common morality, it may appear that weapons research can be justified using the method outlined by Gert—by asserting that breaches of the rules are allowed if rational moral persons would agree that they are publicly allowed—with the assumption that engaging in weapons research has been established as a kind of surrogate harming via the means principle. However, it should be clear by now that this is not a typical moral problem, and even if it were, Gert does not guarantee a way to solve it. In general terms, however, any justification for harming within the scope of common morality will appeal to the prevention of great (or perhaps equal) harms.[17] There may be limits on the ways in which harms can be prevented. For instance, torturing an enemy to death may not be justified to save two friendly agents, but perhaps it would be to save one hundred innocent civilians. Or using a tactical nuclear weapon on an enemy town to save an ally may not be justified, unless perhaps that enemy is bent on genocide. These are difficult questions—matters to be discussed by rational moral agents. As for war and providing weapons of war, prevention of harms will normally encompass self-defense and humanitarian invention.[18] In a "moral war," prevention of harm should extend to the enemy and to enemy citizens, so that enough but not too much force would be used. If North Korea were foolish enough to launch one of its modified scud missiles toward the

United States, it would be wrong for the latter to respond with the full weight of its strategic systems—at least wrong from the standpoint of common morality.

These two conditions for justifying going to war, and for providing the wherewithal to do so, have long been part of Just War Theory, which asserts that there must be just cause for going to war and that the practice of war must use just means.[19] Needlessly killing civilians is not a just means, although there has been much discussion as to what counts as "needlessly."[20] Use of strategic nuclear weapons, for instance, will inevitably cause needless civilian casualties. Just War Theory is therefore not a single unambiguous body of doctrine, but a tradition that is still evolving. Nevertheless, in broad outline, it is in concert with common morality over what is acceptable as a justification for going to war. So now this can be said: weapons research is justified if it only leads to authorized uses of the weapon in question, and S is justified in undertaking weapons research if he has good grounds for believing that its products will only be used in authorized ways. This condition for S being justified in undertaking weapons research may well need to be amended or at least clarified, but I think there will be problems with all versions thereof. That is to say, even if we take great care in spelling out how we understand just cause and just means, and so develop criteria for authorized use, it is clear that S can *never* have good grounds for believing that his work will *only* be used in such a way—unless the radical measure that I will suggest in a moment is adopted. The reason for this has already been given: S is not producing a finite batch of guns or bullets or bombs. He is producing a blueprint for making guns or bullets or bombs, and this blueprint will outlast the present "authorized" conflict—unless it is destroyed.

This observation brings us back, once again, to the Manhattan Project. We have seen how the atomic bomb had its origin in the minds of scientists like Szilard, Fermi, Frisch, and Peierls, who persuaded the British and U.S. governments that they needed to research nuclear weapons to deter any such program in Germany. But by the time the Manhattan Project ended, having produced three atomic bombs, Germany had surrendered, and it had long been clear that it had no nuclear weapons program. The bombs, then, were used on Japan, against the wishes of many of the scientists who had signed on to the program in the belief that a deterrent against the Germans was necessary. For these people, the Manhattan Project was a tragedy. What had seemingly begun as a program for developing a just means—to deter the Nazis from using "their bomb"—had become the bombings of Hiroshima and Nagasaki—what many considered war crimes on a par with any that had ever been committed. Even within the confines of this project, to use our terminology, the situation shifted radically from authorized to unauthorized use. And since that time, the implosion design has been incorporated into nuclear weapons of a destructive power and range unimaginable to the likes of Szilard, Fermi, Frisch, and Peierls. Of course, the Manhattan Project is the most dramatic illustration we have of scientists losing all control over how and where their creations will be used. But the same is true, in principle at least, for any weapons system.[21]

Science, Common Morality, and "Emergency Ethics"

I claim that even if S has good reason to believe that an upcoming conflict in which the products of his work will be used is just, in the sense that there is just cause and only just means will be employed, he has no assurance that there will be no instances of unauthorized uses in the *future*. It is not clear how one would be able to make some future projection—such as some kind of expected utility calculation—that would allow some balance between apparently authorized uses in the near future and possible unauthorized uses in the far distant future: the latter depends on contingencies not yet come to pass, disallowing any such forecast. Clearly, there was no way that Szilard, Frisch, and the others could make such a forecast in 1939. For one thing, they had no idea just how hard it would be to make an atomic bomb, nor did they know that Hitler would distract the German war effort and its scientific-technical support by invading the Soviet Union. The right lessons must be drawn from such examples, and these, I suggest, are twofold. First, the discovery of nuclear weapons produced not just three individual things—three bombs—but an enduring way of doing something, an approach that has shifted and developed and is now used in contexts totally different from those originally envisioned by those who participated in the Manhattan Project. And second, the decision the participants made, given the circumstances in which they found themselves, must be scrutinized: did these circumstances justify their agitating for and taking part in the Manhattan Project?

Many of the Manhattan Project scientists, including Szilard, stated after the event that they wished they had never taken part in the project. This regret exemplifies the first of the two lessons listed above: weapons designs and blueprints, once made, quickly exceed the reach and control of their creators. But does this mean that Szilard and his fellows should never have taken part in the project in the first place? That judgment would be a harsh one: Szilard and the other scientists were facing what Michael Walzer, following Winston Churchill, calls a *supreme emergency* (2004, 33).[22] Without being too precise about what this means, a supreme emergency can be characterized as a threat to one's life, to the lives of one's fellow citizens, to one's way of life—the kind of threat that the Nazi regime posed to Europe. During times of supreme emergency, measures may be taken that would not be allowed during "normal times." These may include suspension of certain human rights, the sacrifice of individuals for the sake of the majority, and—this is the issue that Walzer is addressing—use of tactics like terror bombing and other measures that violate the principle of just means. I understand the idea of supreme emergency in the way Walzer does, but I will use it not to try to justify the use of evidently immoral means in war, but to try to justify weapons research.[23] If one cannot engage in war research in a supreme emergency, then one may never do so.

"Emergency measures" are those that governments take in wartime, when facing terrorist threats or some other dire situation. They are understood to be *temporary*. Part of the rationale for such measures is that the very rights and freedoms that are being suspended are under threat; this would be the case in a country facing invasion by a regime like that of Nazi Germany or the Soviet Union. A terrorist threat is of a different magnitude, and it is to be expected that the measures taken would be less drastic than in wartime—suspension of habeas corpus for suspects, for example, but not conscription into the armed forces.[24] I see the idea of an *emergency ethic* as a response to such situations at the individual level—as a modification of what an individual may do when faced with exceptional circumstances. The idea that one can defend oneself, even to the point of killing an assailant, is a response to exceptional circumstances. However, I am interpreting emergency ethics to (also) apply to such things as supreme emergencies—situations in which a country as a whole is facing a threat—because it is in such situations that the case must be made for weapons research.[25] The suggestion is that weapons research is justified in situations of supreme emergency, but *only* in such situations. To introduce the idea of an emergency ethic here is not really to propose an alternative to common morality, but to identify certain kinds of situations, which moral agents face as a group, in which normal rules of intercourse with the members of other groups are suspended. In some cases, the threat posed is to common morality itself; this is likely in the cases mentioned above, where the rationale for emergency measures enacted at the government level is that the country's very way of life is at stake.[26]

Again, the crucial feature of emergency ethics is that they are temporary, in place only for as long as there is an emergency. Once the war is over, conscription ends; once the terrorists are caught, habeas corpus is restored for all citizens. And once the conflict is over, so too is the justification for engaging in weapons research. There are a host of practical and political problems here surrounding the issue of just when a country is facing a supreme emergency—when is a threat sufficiently real and dire to pose a supreme emergency? What is clearly *not* allowed here is weapons research in peacetime, done just in case a threat appears on the horizon. Again, I stress that my aim here is not to come up with accurate judgments about particular historical cases or to give a precise set of guidelines for when a country is facing a threat of sufficient magnitude for emergency ethics to apply. I assume that these matters are up for discussion and debate, but what is important, again, is that the scope of justified weapons research is to be severely limited, *whatever* the precise details and judgments about particular cases.

The Case Against Weapons Research

The general claim is that emergency ethics allow the agent to do things that are not normally allowed, things that he must stop doing when the emergency has passed. S, then, must stop doing weapons research when the supreme emergency has passed. But this is not enough. When emergency measures like the suspension of habeas corpus are lifted, the status quo is restored: things are as they were before. When the episode of weapons research is over, however, things are *not* back as they were before, because the means to make new ways of harming remains. Thus, even if no atomic bombs had been made after 1945, and even if all the industrial plants for making atomic bombs in Tennessee and Washington were decommissioned, the atomic scientists' unique contribution—the knowledge of how to make atomic bombs—would remain. The only way, therefore, to apply the idea of emergency ethics to weapons research is to ensure that when the emergency passes, things *do* return to the way they were before, and the only way to do this is to guarantee that the *knowledge* in question ceases to exist and hence that it cannot be used as a means for future unjustified harms.

The likelihood of S being assured of this happening in the "real world" is remote, to say the least. For instance, any applied scientist sells his labor, and what he produces belongs to his employer—in this case, whoever owns the weapons lab where he works. It would not be impossible for the conditions of his employment to be so arranged that he keeps control of his work, and it would not be impossible that he would then be able to destroy his results and so restore the status quo. In practice, all this sounds exceedingly far-fetched; hence, satisfying the conditions necessary for the application of emergency ethics seems equally far-fetched. In the event of a supreme emergency, then, it looks as if S would be in a very uncomfortable position: it seems he should use his special skills to defend his way of life and that of his compatriots, but he thus runs the risk of contributing to future harms. And unfortunately, the glimmer of hope presented above—of his keeping control over and later destroying his work—fades when we realize that the mere existence of a technology, demonstrated by its use or deployment, can stimulate others to produce it.

The dropping of the atomic bomb on Hiroshima demonstrated that an atomic bomb could be made, beyond doubt. When Heisenberg and the other German scientists interned at Farm Hall in England heard the news on the radio, they did not believe it at first, but the evidence became undeniable. At least some of these men, Heisenberg included, had not believed an atomic bomb could be made because of their own failed attempts, but in August 1945 such a bomb became a matter of fact, and Heisenberg quickly worked out the correct theory. Moreover, Hiroshima and Nagasaki provoked Stalin into imposing "one demand on his comrades," and so on, leading to the arms races of the Cold War. The demonstration that something is possible is a kind of limiting form of technology transfer: no details of how the artifact can be made are passed on, only the fact that it *can* be made. Thus, even were S to destroy his blueprints, others might nevertheless be able to re-create them by following the example he had set. I would argue for S's responsibility here too: the possibility of weapons scientists from one country following the example set by those of another is a central aspect of the changed context of science after World War 2.

To try to find a conclusion to this difficult issue, we must return to the two-tiered account of the scientist's responsibilities, with rules pro-hibiting harm on the first tier and the ideal urging the prevention of harm on the second. While the former does not always outweigh the lat-ter, and while it is sometimes true that preventing harm can be cited as justification for causing harm, can this *ever* be the case for weapons research? S simply cannot know what harms his work may cause in the future; he cannot know what must be justified in terms of preventing the present harm. So even if the present harm is the greatest harm that S could prevent—the harm that gives rise to a supreme emergency—he cannot know what to set this against as justification. I believe, therefore, that the conclusion best supported by the present argument is that, granted that the destruction of the knowledge in question is impossible to guarantee in practice, weapons research is not justified *under any circumstances.*[27]

What Scientists Should Do

HAVE ARGUED THAT THE TWO-TIERED SYSTEM OF THE scientist's responsibilities is such as to proscribe weapons research, a conclusion reached because the possible harms caused could not be justified. This conclusion centered on the first tier of responsibilities—the scientist's "negative duty" not to harm. But what of the second tier of "positive duties"? Do scientists have any of these?[1] To explore this possibility, it will be helpful to begin by discerning which of the harms common morality refers to might be prevented by scientists. It is worth noting at this point that the United Nations has set out an agenda known as the Millennium Project proposing an international, global effort to reduce such harms as poverty and disease.[2] This will demand investment and political will but also scientific research; in this sense, it is a program for responsible science.

CHAPTER 10

Harms: Biomedical Research

The first three moral rules refer to physical or bodily harms, proscribing killing, causing pain, and disabling.[3] The other seven rules do not refer to any such physical harm: depriving someone of freedom or pleasure is not necessarily to harm them physically, although it may do so, and the same is true of deceiving, not keeping promises, and cheating. The previous chapter focused on a scientist's "first-tier" responsibility, or "negative duty," which primarily engages the first three moral rules, those that refer to physical harms: the purpose of weapons is to cause physical harm, and scientists have the responsibility not to provide the means to harm. When it comes to encouraging scientists to prevent harms, it would appear that science's import will be similarly indirect. That is to say, the scientist is not like a lifeguard: he does not save particular individuals by intervening directly in the harm-causing sequence. He may rescue his colleague slumped inside a fume cupboard, but he does not do this qua scientist. Rather, he might provide the *means* to prevent harm, just as he should not provide the means to cause harm. Again, what scientists do is come up with *knowledge*—for instance, with the basis on which technologies can be developed. It would be surprising, then, if scientists were able to prevent breaches of the seventh rule, keep your promises. Philosophers might be better able to give reasons why promises should be kept and hence prevent breaches of this rule. Scientists, on the other hand, would seem to be much better placed in regard to the first three rules.[4]

It seems that, on the whole, the worst thing that can befall an individual is to be killed. Prevention of killing would then seem to be the moral ideal that one should be most encouraged to follow. But people are not just killed by other people, who do so intentionally or unintentionally. People are killed in many ways, especially if we understand "killing" in a wide sense that includes all the things that cause us to die.[5] One could even broaden the definition to the extent that when anyone dies, it follows that they have been killed by something or another, including failure of some vital organ in old age. This might be stretching matters, but it does make sense to say that someone was killed by a disease or by a pathogen. And it makes sense to say that someone was killed by malnourishment or exposure. Once we allow these sorts of causes of death as matters that should be prevented—and surely everyone can agree to that—then scientists can be encouraged to do many things in regard to them. And here there is first and foremost the great tradition of medicine and public health. The history of medicine, of public health measures, of (some of) the biomedical sciences in general is (or appears to be) the history of scientists seeking to prevent people from being killed or disabled by disease or ill health. The success of scientists in this regard is, I believe, the main reason why science is held in high regard. Achievements in such fields are, for the most part, the good ingredients in the mixed blessing that is science; there is not a great deal more that needs to be said about them here.[6]

To suggest that scientists should be encouraged to undertake research in the biomedical sciences or in public-health fields focused on preventing or alleviating disease is in one sense unnecessary: the very existence of these sciences expresses this ideal. But the suggestion that the biomedical sciences should have *particular priorities*—that they should be funded in certain ways and that scientists ought to work toward particular goals—is far from trivial. For instance, some measures that might prevent considerable harms may be less profitable than others that, while preventing harms, do so on a smaller scale. For example, malaria is difficult to treat, it affects large numbers of people, and it infects animals. It is estimated that malaria annually causes between 300 and 500 million episodes of acute illness and 1.1 to 2.7 million deaths, with women and children particularly at risk.[7] Tuberculosis (TB) is also difficult to treat because of past misuse of anti-TB drugs. While TB was nearly wiped out half a century ago, through improved living standards and antibiotics, it now kills nearly 2 million people a year and is especially deadly when there is coinfection with AIDS. The relative neglect of these two diseases, and others, in favor of more profitable biomedical research is a consequence of what is called the "90-10" divide, with 90 percent of available resources being spent on 10 percent of problems. The assumption here is that the problems are all equally pressing and that hence there is considerable inequity in resource distribution.

This is not primarily the scientist's fault, and blame is normally attributed to multinational pharmaceutical and biotechnology companies and to the government agencies that publicly fund biomedical research. And the explanation for such resource allocation is not hard to find: such diseases as malaria and TB primarily affect people in developing countries, African countries especially, and there are not many profits to be made in such countries. Again, the point here is not to make recommendations to companies or governments, but to scientists. It is clear, I think, that biomedical scientists should be urged to work on the 90 percent of diseases that are currently neglected, that affect the most people, and that are in urgent need of remedy.[8] From the moral, as opposed to the economic, point of view, a poor African woman with malaria counts as much as a rich Australian man with diabetes and high cholesterol, and if the former is relatively neglected with respect to the latter, it seems that the proper thing for a biomedical scientist is to offer himself to work toward cures and therapies for the former. There are, of course, practical obstacles to be considered. The very fact that the resources are allocated along the 90-10 divide means far fewer opportunities exist to research such diseases as malaria and TB. What, then, should the bioscientist do? Is he simply encouraged to look for opportunities to conduct research on the neglected side of the divide, or is he further encouraged to *create* those opportunities?

Suppose scientist S has the opportunity both to take part in the United Nations Millennium Project for research into malaria and to work for the multinational corporation Roche on a way to improve anticholesterol drugs. High cholesterol is a "condition of affluence" that most afflicts older persons living in Western countries; it is not strictly a disease but is a causally relevant factor for heart disease. If S wants to decide which post he should take solely on the basis of how to best fulfill his moral responsibility as a scientist, we would be inclined to advise him to work for the UN: it seems that he could prevent more harm through that course of action. It does not follow, however, that it would be wrong of S to work for Roche; in fact, if that was his only opportunity, we would encourage him to take it, as providing better anticholesterol drugs also reduces harm. Thus, S may have several opportunities to reduce harm as a scientist, and these may be ranked. Although one course of action may prevent harm, another may prevent greater harms. Of course, this may not be the only consideration, from S's perspective, but unless S's other concerns weigh significantly in the balance as regards preventing harms, they will not figure in the *moral* grounds for his decision.

There is a rejoinder to this. Recall that earlier (see chapter 8), the question of the *scope* of the scientist's responsibilities was raised: should these be global, as they would be if a scientist worked for an organization like the UN? Weapons research, in contrast, is "local"—done for the benefit of a particular country. (Some of the Manhattan Project scientists wanted to make the blueprint for the atomic bomb available to all, but this was to neutralize it as a weapon.) Working for Roche would also be local for S, albeit not geographically, because the research's benefit is primarily for the corporation and its owners, and only for the consumer via the opportunity to allocate his resources in a given way. Of course, the technology and know-how that arise from research are not local, or at least not usually so. It is possible that a particular malaria mosquito vector is only found in, say, Sri Lanka, and in that sense the knowledge of how to inhibit it would only have application there. But again, plans, know-how, blueprints, and so on endure in both time and place. While this does not amount to anything like a "contradiction" between scientific knowledge and local application, it does suggest that science is an optimal way of laying a foundation for tackling global problems. The life cycle of the malaria parasite goes through the same stages, wherever it is. *P. falciparum* develops in the same way in Brazil as it does in Sri Lanka, so if this development can be disrupted in Sri Lanka, it can be disrupted anywhere (assuming no local mutations).

The moral rules forbid persons to do things that harm others, and while harms are not all of a piece, this does not mean that the prohibition on killing is stronger than the one on deceiving. Assuming there is no justification, one is forbidden to kill and to deceive, tout court. Matters seem different as regards a person being encouraged to do something. S may be more strongly encouraged to work for the UN project against malaria, on the grounds that this can prevent the most harm. But if he has no opportunity to do so, or if there are other reasons against his doing so, then he can be encouraged to work for Roche, assuming that his work there will be toward drugs that reduce harms. Whatever the details, the point remains: in principle, a number of different things that scientists are encouraged to do can be distinguished, and they should be more strongly encouraged to do some than others.

The moral ideals encourage agents to prevent harm, but if they do not do harm, then they do not do wrong. Breaking the moral rules without justification counts as wrongdoing and invites punishment, but not acting in accordance with the moral ideals, when the opportunity arises, is not wrongdoing. Again, the consequentialist treats rules and ideals as convenient ways of summarizing the sorts of considerations that bear on good and bad states of affairs, and particular actings and preventings are judged right or wrong depending on whether they maximize or contribute to the best outcome. In this way, consequentialism is a complete guide for decision making, as well as a system of ethics. It takes into account the impact of S's decision on himself and his family; if he has the opportunity to maximize the good by working for the UN and does not do so, it will judge him not to have done the right thing. But common morality does not claim to factor in all considerations that bear on a decision and then pronounce on whether it was right or wrong. In this regard, it is surely a more suitable representation of the moral grounds for making such decisions; consequentialism is much too stern a taskmaster.

Harms: Lack of Resources

War and disease are two of the principal causes of harm to human beings, two of the great themes of human history. People are also harmed if they do not have sufficient resources to live, particularly food, water, and shelter. Slow starvation, chronic and recurrent disease due to water-borne infection, and cold may not be worse than death, but these are significant harms suffered by something in the order of a fifth of the world's population. There are short-term measures that can be used to alleviate acute crises, such as the 2004 tsunami in Southeast Asia, the civil war in Sudan, and the 2005 earthquake in Pakistan. Putting these measures in place is a matter of the political will of rich nations that can mobilize food, medicine, tents, and personnel to provide immediate aid. But such measures resemble supreme emergencies in that they are, by their nature, temporary. When Banda Aceh is rebuilt, the civil war in Sudan is over, and the villages of Kashmir are rebuilt, the poor of these countries will again be left to fend for themselves. Not much can be done in the long term about tsunamis, save setting up an early warning system. But something can be done about global poverty and its consequences.

One attempt to alleviate poverty, now generally considered a failure, was the "Green Revolution" of the 1960s. The aim was to increase wheat and especially rice production in Asia by means of high-yield varieties, through a program funded by the Ford and Rockefeller charitable foundations, which set up the International Rice Research Institute in the Philippines (Bridgstock et al. 1998, 214). Unfortunately, the varieties developed did not simply produce more rice than the indigenous varieties without any additional input; large amounts of chemical fertilizer and more water were needed. So while the seeds themselves were free, the means to grow them successfully were not. This led to disaster, with existing inequalities made worse, as richer farmers who could afford fertilizer and water pumps increased the productivity of their land and eventually squeezed out poorer farmers—the original targets of the aid program. What is surprising is that this was done purposefully, because natural varieties were not susceptible to fertilizer. Moreover, the Green Revolution increased not only the class divide but also gender inequality. Women had traditionally harvested the rice crop by hand, but the revolution resulted in more mechanization, with tractors introduced as harvesters.

The Green Revolution shows that even with the best intentions, aid programs can go wrong. And there is a sense in which the scientific research that underpinned the new crop varieties went wrong as well, in that the technology it produced caused more problems than it solved. This is nothing new: it was once hoped that the spread of malaria could be stopped by spraying the mosquito vectors with DDT, but the result was DDT-resistant mosquitoes, so now spraying is not effective as a short-term "emergency measure" for severe outbreaks. The worldwide upsurge of TB is so dangerous because of a multi–drug resistant strain, selected by improperly administered antibiotics. These cases resemble one another in that all were well-intentioned attempts to provide technologies, based on scientific research, to deal with the problems of poverty and disease. The causes of what went wrong in each case, however, appear to be different. The rice and wheat varieties provided by the Green Revolution were simply not appropriate; the technology was not right, and perhaps bad science played a role. On the other hand, the fact that drugs that were efficacious against TB were not administered properly is not a problem of technology and the science on which it was based; here, it can be assumed, recipients knew what to do but simply mismanaged the treatment.[9]

There are opportunities now to learn the lessons of the original Green Revolution and to provide more appropriate crops using genetic engineering. Indeed, scientists in Australia have isolated the gene responsible for the increased yield—the "semi-dwarfing" (sdɪ) gene—from the rice genome. This raises the possibility of engineering varieties that resemble local ones in all respects except for the dominance of this gene. Other proposals suggest engineering genes that naturally produce pesticides. But there is widespread opposition to the use of genetically engineered crops—partly because of the lessons of the Green Revolution, partly because much of the research has been conducted by multinational companies, but mainly because of the danger of contaminating existing native varieties by cross-pollination. So while the opportunities for reducing world hunger through scientifically based technologies are greater than they were in the 1960s, given advances in biotechnology, the dangers are also greater. What this implies for the present discussion is that it is not enough for scientists to be encouraged to participate in programs intended to alleviate the harms of poverty and hunger for the world's poorest people. They also need to assess these programs and only take part in those that are likely to be successful.

Positive Duties of the Scientist qua Scientist

This seems to place a considerable burden on the scientist: not only is he encouraged to prevent harms by taking part in programs that increase public health, alleviate world hunger, and so forth, but he is also supposed to assess these programs and ensure that they are not themselves likely to do harm. Moreover, there is the question raised above, of scientists helping to create such opportunities for good work if these are lacking. The responsibilities of the scientist must be kept to a manageable level, and I think it is most important to restrict these responsibilities to the things that he can do *as a scientist*, as someone with certain special skills. These skills bring with them responsibilities, but the latter should not, so to speak, outstrip the former: scientists should not be encouraged to do more than they can. Other members of society have responsibilities as well, especially those in government, and some of these also concern the proper use of science. So, regarding the question posed above—whether the scientist is responsible for creating such opportunities—the answer is that he is *not* responsible.

Provided scientists are not in a special position, as scientists, to create such opportunities, I do not see why they should be obliged to do so. Indeed, given that the Millennium Project and other similar initiatives require large amounts of money, the scientist is in no special position with regard to creating them. Countries, such international bodies as the United Nations, such philanthropic organizations as the Rockefeller Foundation, individual governments, and so forth must take the initiative. It is another matter, however, for scientists to point out that such initiatives are needed. Here, health matters are probably not central; science does not need to point out the death tolls for malaria, TB, and so on. But in regard to environmental questions, such as global warming and depletion of the ozone layer, scientists have stressed the severity of the problems and drawn them to public and governmental attention. The classic example here is Sherwood Rowland, who predicted the hole in the ozone layer and (rightly) was awarded the Nobel Prize for chemistry. Rowland, in making his prediction, published both technical papers, in which he gave the mechanism for ozone depletion, and popular articles that summarized his findings for the general public. Scientists *are* in a special position with regard to pointing out such serious problems—not only to solve such problems but to realize that they exist in the first place. So it *is* part of their responsibility to point them out.[10]

The position adopted here with regard to the scope of the scientist's positive duties is "narrow" in the sense that it is restricted specifically to the special skills that characterize science—namely, knowledge and understanding of the basic patterns of the natural world and (hence) how these can be used as a basis for technologies. Instead of this narrow conception, a broader view could be taken—one that sees scientists as also having a responsibility to become involved in politics and to so create opportunities. There is certainly a precedent for this view. During World War 2, for instance, both Winston Churchill and Franklin Roosevelt had scientific advisors who lobbied for weapons research. After the war, particularly in the United States, such people as Vannevar Bush and James Conant became strong advocates on behalf of science and were able to increase science funding in universities to the extent that it seemed to extend into Bush's "endless frontier." The broader view holds that individuals like Bush and Conant are effective advocates for science because they have scientific backgrounds themselves: it takes a scientist to know what science needs. In response, to begin with, the activities of advocates like Bush and Conant are better thought of as in the interests of science itself rather than focused on alleviating harm. Further, these advocates were effective because they had other skills and abilities, apart from their scientific knowledge.

There is no reason to believe that scientists are better than anyone else at creating the kinds of opportunities of interest here, just as there is no good reason to think that professors are the best people to run universities. Getting programs on the agendas of national and international bodies requires special lobbying and political skills, and these are not the same as those needed to weaponize plutonium or to find ways to interrupt the life cycle of *P. falciparum*. If one wants to argue that scientists ought to take part in such political activity, then it will be necessary to adopt some other conception of what the scientist's duties are. To maintain that scientists, or anyone else, are obliged to do good works whether or not they are particularly suited to carry out the good works in question is to move to some other sort of morality and, more especially, to move beyond discussions of responsibility. The narrow view proposed here is therefore the correct view of the responsibility *of the scientist.* And an important consequence of this is that some restrictions are imposed on what the scientist is obliged to do. His responsibilities must not become unmanageable and unbearable.

The View from Science

If the account that I have sketched of the scientist's responsibilities is a plausible one, then we would expect it to be reflected in the concerns voiced by scientists themselves. While the account does not actually stand or fall when measured against this standard, it would be reassuring if it found some agreement in practice. Given the present account, then, we would expect more emphasis on global problems, such as those that affect health and food production, and less on weapons research and science for profit. Of course, not every scientist will worry about these "external" matters. Many will be content to do pure research in the belief that it is a neutral activity or will think of themselves as scientific workers who receive a salary and have no further responsibility for their work. And there are in fact many scientific societies that try to promote science with this understanding in mind, including the two oldest in continuous existence, the Royal Society of London and the Acadèmie des Sciences of Paris, and one of the oldest in the United States, the American Physical Society.[11] All these societies, and many others like them, represent science as an activity that is good and worth pursuing in itself—just like the founders of the Royal Society did in 1660—and are dedicated to furthering pure science. There are, however, other societies whose raison d'être is a concern with wider issues. The following sample of these groups reviewed is tiny, even when restricted to those societies that focus specifically on these wider issues; my aim is simply to establish that the issues raised here are matters of concern to working scientists who take their responsibilities seriously.

First, the Federation of American Scientists (FAS) was founded in 1945 by some of the members of the Manhattan Project who were "concerned about control of the awesome new technology they had helped create" (although none of those discussed here, such as Szilard, Peierls, and Fermi, were among the founders).[12] FAS, on its Web site, has reconstructed the U.S. armed forces chain of command, setting out who is responsible for giving orders and who for obeying them, and hence who is ultimately responsible for what might occur. FAS also makes available a comprehensive list of the types of weapons systems in the U.S. armed forces. Most of the discussion papers it features are critical of U.S. weapons acquisition programs and question the purpose of U.S. stockpiles. For instance, FAS points out that the United States can only justify its huge strategic stockpile if it intends a first strike on Russia. Of course, this was one element of the (flawed) nuclear doctrine of the Cold War: that the United States could have launched a first strike on the Soviet Union. That such a stance is now both pointless and dangerous needs to be established by experts, and hence FAS is performing an important role here. Quantifying the preferred size of the nuclear arsenal, FAS estimates a *maximum* of one thousand, a number that takes into account a worst-case scenario of nuclear war. This figure has become canonical.

From this brief account, can it be said that FAS to an extent confirms our view about the negative duties of the scientist? FAS clearly does *not* encourage scientists to work for the Department of Defense or the armaments industry, but we would not expect such an organization to present the kind of argument given here (see chapter 9), one that makes the philosophical case against weapons research based on common morality, in the strongest terms. Such a philosophical argument is not intended to directly influence policy makers and the general public. For this purpose, something more pragmatic and prudent is needed—such as examinations of what possible use there could now be for six thousand strategic warheads and how these weapons represent not security for the United States but a threat. The argument I outlined earlier expresses larger and more abstract issues about the scientist's responsibilities, but this argument is surely consistent with moves to reduce present armament levels and prevent new weapons from coming into existence. Thus, we—myself and the members of FAS—are all opposed to present weapon levels and (hence) to scientists participating in making more weapons, but we express our concerns in different ways. So does the FAS confirm the view about the negative duties of the scientist? It does, by implication.

The same is true of the Union of Concerned Scientists (UCS), which was formed in 1969 at MIT. Its mission statement declares that it aims "to devise means for turning research applications away from the present emphasis on military technology toward the solution of pressing environmental and social problems."[13] These means include conveying the importance of such a shift in emphasis both to students and to other scientists and engineers and monitoring governmental use of science. UCS focuses on five areas of concern: food, vehicles, the environment, energy, and security. Health care is notably missing from this list, but scientific societies naturally group along disciplinary lines, and we would thus expect health care to instead be emphasized by societies formed around medicine and biomedical science. Indeed, were UCS to include health care among its emphases, I suspect it would be spreading its effort too thinly.

UCS, like FAS, also takes a pragmatic stance regarding nuclear weapons.[14] That is to say, given that it is impractical at the present time to demand complete nuclear disarmament, UCS seeks to reduce nuclear capabilities, both qualitatively and quantitatively, and to put in place various treaties and agreements that make nuclear conflict less likely. UCS thus wants to eliminate all tactical nuclear weapons and reduce the strategic deterrent to the canonical one thousand warheads—a number that most agree would suffice for deterrence, even members of the second Bush administration. UCS is opposed to missile defense, describing it as a "misplaced priority," emphasizing that the real priority is nuclear terrorism, a threat that UCS sees as grave, stressing the large amounts of highly enriched uranium and plutonium available in the world.[15] UCS has also published a copy of a letter recently sent to Congress in regard to "mini-nukes" in the form of "bunker busting" bombs, pointing out that there are good technical reasons why this innovation would fail—and indeed, this initiative has been abandoned, perhaps due in part to the activities of such societies as FAS and UCS.

Regarding food, UCS is equally pragmatic: "Our goal is to create a food system that encourages innovative and environmentally sustainable ways to produce high-quality, safe, and affordable food, while ensuring that citizens have a voice in how their food is grown. In so doing, the program focuses on reducing unnecessary uses of antibiotics and strengthening civil society's control of biotechnology." And in regard to biotechnology, UCS provides a short history of genetically engineered crops, again emphasizing a balanced approach, with increased yields and pest resistance weighed against potential risks of new allergens and contamination. The organization of UCS programs is also worth noting, each having a director or codirector along with various other senior scientists, analysts, or specialists. For instance, the UCS program on security includes two codirectors, an advisor on global security, a staff scientist, a program assistant, two senior staff scientists, a China specialist, a global security outreach coordinator, an assistant to the global security outreach coordinator, and finally a Washington representative. Some of these posts are fully funded from the (approximately) $10 million budget of UCS, while other office holders also work for other institutions, such as universities. UCS's budget comes entirely from membership dues and donations.

It is clear that the members of UCS believe that scientific expertise can be used to argue both for and against certain practices, such as producing polluting vehicles or setting up a missile defense system. While UCS does not explicitly argue against scientists' participation in defense programs, as I have done, the implication is that UCS would not endorse such a choice. But its pragmatic emphasis is, again, to be expected: we would not expect a scientific society to overtly state what it thinks individual scientists should or should not do—this luxury falls to philosophers, who can do so at arm's length. Instead, we would expect such a society to advocate some projects and be against others, and this emphasis on advocacy is just what we find.

Scientists for Global Responsibility (SGR), a small British-based society, is, however, far less reticent about making recommendations for scientists regarding "ethical careers in science and technology."[16] SGR's areas of concern are almost identical to those of UCS—arms control, climate change and energy, and genetically modified organisms—but SGR also includes a study group on population, consumption, and values and a program on science policy. SGR is small and thus perhaps not representative of scientists concerned with responsibility, but two of its recent reports are noteworthy here. First, a 2005 report entitled "Soldiers in the Laboratory" focuses both on providing an account of the effects of defense spending on science, particularly in the UK, and on putting forward a broadened concept of security—extending its reach to include security from water, food, and shelter shortages and security from the impacts of climate change (matters that might indeed become causes of war in the future). Under this broadened concept, security spending would be quite differently oriented than it is at present in industrialized countries. Second, an SGR report entitled "Thinking about an Ethical Career in Science and Technology" proposes careers focusing on cleaner technologies, sustainable development, and climate change. SGR, therefore, is much more explicit than FAS or UCS about the kinds of work scientists should do.

What about societies that urge graduates in the biosciences to take up careers working on diseases endemic in the poorer parts of the world, such as malaria, TB, and HIV/AIDS? If it is true that this is a pressing area of concern, then we might expect to find many health-focused equivalents to FSA, UCS, and SGR. In fact, there are not many such societies—

or at least if there are, they do not have a high profile. This seeming shortage may initially seem surprising, but there are in fact many other sources of assistance, apart from those based directly in the biomedical science community. For instance, there are international efforts, such as the UN Millennium Project, the African Malarial Vaccine Testing Network, the StopTB Partnership, and UNAIDS, along with high-profile aid agencies, such as Medicin sans Frontiers, the Red Cross, and Worldvision, and such private agencies as the Ford, Rockefeller, and Gates foundations. Nothing comparable to such a comprehensive and well-funded network of groups exists around opposition to weapons research, for example. The reason for this is not hard to find: helping to reduce and prevent such diseases is uncontroversial; it is clear that it should be done, and the only problem is with finding the resources. Everyone can agree that it is a tragedy that babies are dying of AIDS in Uganda and South Africa, but not everyone can so easily agree that there should be a sharp reduction in weapons production and research.

Science, again, is a mixed blessing: it can both cause and prevent harm. In terms of preventing, science's "good side," there is a great deal that scientists can do. Indeed, science must provide the key to reducing disease and poverty, for if it does not, then no key exists. Just how science might provide this key in practice is a difficult matter, but creating opportunities is not the scientist's task: his skills do not lie in creating opportunities but in solving problems when given the chance to do so. Scientists are also in a unique position to point out problems that need to be addressed: that the environment is suffering because of ozone depletion and greenhouse gas emission, that ecosystems are being destroyed irreversibly, that we have too many nuclear weapons. The scientist's forward-looking "positive duties" today must center around informing the rest of us that pressing global problems exist and working for solutions to these problems, where there are opportunities to do so. These are not, of course, simple tasks.

Part 4

SCIENCE AND
GROUP RESPONSIBILITY

CHAPTER 11

Group Research
and Group Responsibility

T HE PAPER REPORTING THE DISCOVERY OF THE BRACI gene had forty-five authors. Even if some of these people did not actually conduct any of the research leading to the identification of BRACI—there is a convention that dictates that those who provide funds or laboratory space or other forms of support can be listed as authors—this nevertheless looks like a *group* discovery. And, as such, the authors of the paper stand in contrast to the great scientists of the Scientific Revolution: Copernicus, Kepler, Galileo, and Newton worked by themselves, often enduring great hardship and loneliness. For example, Newton had very little contact with any other "scientist" in the twenty years before 1687, when the *Principia* was published. Up until World War 2, this kind of individual research was still the norm: Einstein himself was not even working in a university, let alone doing cooperative research, when he discovered the theory of special relativity. Times, however, have changed, and one of the notable features of the "changed context of science" is the ubiquity of group research. The Manhattan Project was one of the first group research projects and remains the largest ever. However, whether this adds up to some special concept of *group responsibility* is another matter; many philosophers deny that anything over and above individual responsibility even exists (see, e.g., Lewis 1972).[1] As a consequence, there is little on the subject in the literature.

How does, or how could, group research affect the theory of responsibility developed so far in this book? For one thing, the recognition that group research is now the norm buttresses one or more of the arguments that attempt to insulate the scientist from responsibility, arguments addressed throughout this book. On the other hand, some of these arguments are clearly unaffected by the existence of group research. For instance, it makes no difference to the argument from neutrality whether or not an artifact was discovered by means of individual or group research, and the same seems true for Polanyi's Challenge. It might be thought, in the case of Polanyi, that the involvement of many hands might complicate the picture to a degree that it would be more difficult for any one individual to have a clear expectation about the research's outcome. But against this consideration is the need for greater planning and coordination for a group project; to work together, the members of a group must have a good idea where the research is going and not proceed via haphazard and unpredictable steps. Perhaps the most interesting and important question raised by the fact of group research is whether there is a distinctive form of group responsibility and, if there is, how this sits with individual responsibility. I assume that group responsibility would *not* be distinctive or interesting if it were just the "sum" of the responsibilities (the shared responsibility) of the individuals who make up a group, for then nothing new would be involved (except how to sum individual responsibilities). How then should the question of group responsibility be approached? Defining group responsibility will surely depend on discerning instances of genuine *corporate* responsibility.

Approaches to Group Responsibility

If there is to be "genuine" group responsibility, then there must in some sense be "residual" responsibility that does not attach to some individual in the group in question.[2] Moreover, if there is only responsibility where there is action (I will not be concerned here with omissions), which is the position adopted here, *and* if responsibility only attaches to those who carry out the actions in question, then genuine group responsibility will depend on the possibility of groups themselves being able to act—or so it seems. Thus far, it has been assumed that the only agents are persons, mature human beings who are capable of forming intentions and having reasons for the choices and decisions they make. Hence it has been assumed that only individuals can act, and surely it is true that only individuals can act in the literal and unqualified sense of doing something. There is therefore no way to avoid the proposition that any genuine group responsibility (indeed, any form of group responsibility) must *supervene* on human action: that is, it is *impossible* for there to be an instance of genuine group responsibility without some relevant actions by individual human agents. An account of group responsibility will show how this works—how it is that human action can give rise to group responsibility. And one way to do this, Peter French's approach, is to define group action in terms of the actions of individuals (e.g., French 1992, 1995).

The supervenience requirement does not, however, entail that this is the only way to develop an account of group responsibility, for it also allows other approaches. Whichever approach we take here, it must be consistent with the theory proposed thus far. For instance, according to the account of moral responsibility given here, moral agents are assumed to have the capacity to make decisions in the light of the obligations of common morality. Individual human agents seem to be the only ones that have these capabilities, and when they fail to make the right choices, they can be held to account, whereas nonmoral agents cannot. Moral agents are blamed when they transgress the moral rules and harm others without justification, which amounts to expressing negative sentiments toward these agents, under the reactive attitudes interpretation. But it seems as if this places an obstacle in the path of developing an idea of genuine group responsibility: if we only hold responsible those who can make choices and reflect on these in the light of moral obligations, how can we hold a group itself morally responsible, for how can a group be said to choose?

French addresses this question by defining group action in terms of individual actions, specifically when the individuals are working for the group; he thinks it is therefore possible to impute intentions to the group. French's interest is mainly with corporations and corporate responsibility, and by interpreting the supervenience requirement in this way—in terms of group action and intention supervening on individual action and intention—he thinks corporations can be seen as agents and hence as members of the moral community. His approach might then serve as a model for genuine group responsibility, with the groups to which this applies having a kind of organization resembling that of corporations. It is therefore worth remarking that we can and do hold corporations responsible: it is assumed that there are identifiable and reidentifiable entities to which the concept of responsibility applies. Not only are these entities incorporated before the law and therefore able to hold assets, act in the legal sense, and be sued, but we also "react" to what these corporations do: we feel resentment and disgust at Union Carbide for Bhopal, at Philip Morris for promoting dangerous products, at Nestlé for dumping milk formula in Africa, at Microsoft for making us use its Internet browser, at Merck for refusing to allow the manufacture of generic drugs, at Bank of America for obscene profits, and so on. These observations do not show the corporation itself to be morally, as opposed to legally, responsible for blame that might be directed at individuals—company directors, policy makers, or shareholders. Nevertheless, a prima facie case for genuine corporate moral responsibility can be based on such episodes; those who instead favor reduction to individual responsibility must show how this is to be carried out.

Another way to understand the supervenience requirement is in terms of *vicarious liability*. For example, if Q acts for P, then under certain conditions, P can be responsible for what Q does. The point about vicarious liability is that there is transference of responsibility but no transference of action—P does not act, but he is responsible for what is done. As it stands, this is little more than a restatement of the supervenience requirement; what underpins or licenses the transfer of responsibility must be deterimined. One such example is coercion: if P forces Q to do something, then Q may be excused and P held responsible. That P forces Q to do something reflects on how P understands his moral obligations to others and hence on his "quality of will." Thus, P is responsible not only for what Q is forced to do but also for the fact that he forced him to do it. Such people are not well thought of: their behavior is deplored, and they are often perceived as "evil masterminds" who work behind the scenes. In principle, then, it is possible for someone to be responsible for an action without actually performing it. But in this example, the responsible party, P, is responsible for what Q does in virtue of being responsible for some *other* action that he does perform—the coercing of Q, whatever that amounts to. For vicarious liability to apply to groups, some other ground must be found for transferring responsibility, something besides some *other* action by the responsible party. I will eventually borrow something from both of these approaches in order to provide a framework to discuss group responsibility in science, but first we need to investigate what sorts of groups there are in science and why science demands team-based work, for it may be that scientific teams are not such as to give rise to genuine group responsibility.

Team-Based Work and Group Research

On the whole, scientists work in teams for several reasons. First, their work can be painstaking and demanding and generally too much for one person. For example, gene and protein sequencing, such as is necessary for the identification of BRAC1, is time consuming, even with modern automated methods. Second, a research project may require several different sorts of skills, more than any one person could be expected to have. Many interdisciplinary scientific projects, possible and actual, require different kinds of specialists, but different specialists are present even within the bounds of a given discipline. For instance, to identify the structure of a naturally occurring compound, experts are usually necessary for the various analytic techniques—spectroscopy, gas chromatography, nuclear magnetic resonance (NMR), and so on. Third, research is usually expensive, in part because of the demand for many hands and diverse expertise, equipment, space, materials, and support staff. One or more members of a group may be entirely preoccupied with getting grants—indeed, getting grants may itself be a special, and highly desirable, skill. A related point here is that major, expensive research is perceived as serious and desirable and of high status, particularly by university administrators.

Yet another reason for working in groups is that such work is a continuing part of the training of the scientist, particularly in experimental work. Experience in undergraduate laboratories is on the whole frustrating, the aim to get the answer that everyone knows one is supposed to get—and undergraduates are not let loose on the latest and most interesting equipment. To actually learn how to do proper scientific research, one must be "apprenticed" to an experienced researcher, a process that usually begins during undergraduate work and continues through completion of a Ph.D. One learns in the laboratory: it is not possible to be told what to do in a lecture room and then go alone into the laboratory and enjoy invariable success without on-the-spot guidance—much "tacit knowledge" must be acquired. A Ph.D. signifies that its holder can play an autonomous research role—that the period of apprenticeship is over and that the Ph.D. holder can now take on the important task of the postdoc, conducting the day-to-day business of research. Modern science, therefore, depends on a long period of training and apprenticeship, and unless scientists work in teams, it is difficult to see how this process could take place. As it is, the transition from graduate student to colleague is almost seamless. Group research is thus institutionalized in science; it is the way scientists are inducted into the scientific community.

The various grounds for forming groups inform a group's *character*. In theory at least, there are two extremes or "ideal types" of groups.[3] On the one hand, some groups have a complete division of labor, with different members performing entirely different tasks. For want of a better term, I will call these *discrete groups*. For a discrete group, it would not, in principle, be necessary for its members to be in the same place, work at the same time, or even communicate with each other in any way except by collating their results. If a set of entirely independent individual tasks is needed to complete a project, then these tasks could be accomplished by a group of people who did not work jointly at all, in the sense of sitting around and discussing the problem. On the other hand, some groups work together so closely that the project, after the event, cannot be represented as a summation of particular individual contributions. In such groups—which I will refer to as *integrated groups*—individuals define the problems they work on and the solutions they find by talking to each other. The effort is truly cooperative; there is no overt division of labor. Of course, groups do not have to be either completely integrated or entirely discrete: a kind of continuum exists between the extremes. However, in the interest of simplifying the discussion here, I will treat these as two separate types.

Looking back at the reasons why scientists work in groups, it would seem that if a project is highly interdisciplinary, the group would tend to be discrete: people in different specialties will clearly find it more difficult to discuss a problem's technical details than would people with a common background. Discrete groups, on the whole, might also be expected to be relatively short-lived—unless the work itself establishes a new disciplinary niche, as has happened with several important areas that were originally interdisciplinary. Discrete groups, therefore, would not make a substantial contribution to training prospective members of the scientific community. Integrated groups, on the other hand, tend to be homogeneous.

Two research teams from a university where I worked represent these two types of group, and they will serve as examples in what follows.[4] These two groups are typical of what can be found in universities all over the world, with their focus on pure research and their level of organization and funding below that of a full-blown research institute. While larger collections of pure researchers exist—in research institutes (private, corporate, or government-run) and in the R&D divisions of large corporations—scientists working outside the university are normally dedicated to strategic basic research (the famous Bell Laboratory was an exception to that rule).

Although the Manhattan Project was not the first government-run research organization, it was certainly the biggest, and it is thus worth reviewing its overall organization before returning to our two university groups, as it demonstrates why a complex project requires a variety of groups. While the Manhattan Project had a single overriding scientific-technical aim—to make an atomic bomb, if possible, in the shortest time—that demand required so many different tasks that the project would be broadly classified as discrete. For example, the work on isotope separation for the production of (80 percent pure) uranium-235 for Little Boy, undertaken by Earnest Lawrence at the Oak Ridge facility in Tennessee, was of an entirely different character from the work conducted at the bomb-design and -production laboratory at Los Alamos. Indeed, once Lawrence handed over the uranium-235 to the fabrication unit at Los Alamos in 1945, his work was done, and a totally different set of tasks ensued—ones that Lawrence could not have undertaken. But even Los Alamos was by no means an integrated group: there were originally four divisions at Los Alamos—the ordnance, theoretical, experimental physics, and chemistry and metallurgy divisions—all investigating different aspects of bomb design and manufacture (see chapter 2).

Even in 1944, when it had become clear that the implosion design was needed for the weaponization of plutonium, the implosion group was not integrated, containing such mathematicians as Ulam and such experimentalists as Neddermeyer, all working along different lines. Integration was, however, to be found on a smaller scale: theoreticians like Ulam, Peierls, von Neuman, Teller, Bethe, and Feynman talked to each other about the same problems. While Peierls was earlier singled out as the scientist who solved the hydrodynamical problem of implosion, this was done (as I stressed earlier) to have a useable example; it was not meant to imply that he solved the problem all on his own, in spite of his important contributions. The Manhattan Project was therefore discrete on the large scale but integrated at its lower levels, which is as we would expect.

To return now to the two groups at my own former workplace, one researched a new technique for pulsed NMR imaging that exploited correlations between the spins of the nuclei of atoms, such as carbon and hydrogen, described in an abstract of one of the group's papers as "of the type invoked in the EPR paradox" (Pegg 1989, 101). The quantum mechanics for the correlations, and the "logic gates," were done by theoretical physicist T, while the practical work of determining and analyzing actual spectra was carried out by two chemists; there were, then, three principal researchers. The group's major, influential, and much-cited paper was coauthored by all three and included a section describing the theory, appendices describing the logic gates, and sections that described experiments and data. T was convinced that one of the chemists, who kept trying to relegate the theory to the appendices, did not understand the theory at all, while T himself was not able to set up or take part in any of the experimental work.[5] This NMR group, which I shall call N, was not destined for a long association, as its desired and achieved outcome was the establishment of a new experimental technique; while the team's chemists could and have gone on to use the technique—and to set up their own groups at other institutions—there was really no further role for physicist T.

I will refer to the second group, a (still-active) laser physics group, as L. In this group, the personnel are all physicists, and the theory is well worked out. The group undertakes experiments using equipment with which all its members are familiar, so there is less division of labor than was the case with N. L's research is concerned with electron collisions induced by lasers, the data gathered by electron spectroscopy and electron detectors. The group has been in existence for over twenty years, and its research has evolved just a little; for instance, the group now conducts experiments with polarized as well as unpolarized electron beams. Its day-to-day research, as might be expected, entails choosing, designing, and performing experiments; analyzing data; performing calculations; and writing up the results. As it happens, one of the principal researchers tends to do the calculations and also has the necessary understanding of the laser-electron interaction. At present, a postdoc is responsible for keeping up with the literature in the field and making suggestions for new experiments. Ph.D. students in the laboratory actually perform the experiments. But this division of labor is a matter only of convenience and precedent, with all the members understanding all aspects of the research. *L* is well established, with lots of space and expensive equipment.

Do these scientists, in either group, display genuine group responsibility for the papers the groups produce? Papers are the "proper products" of pure research and as such represent the first step toward other outcomes. It is enough, in the cases of *N* and *L*, to consider the question of group responsibility with reference to the production of papers: responsibility for producing papers is a necessary condition for responsibility for outcomes, although on the whole papers fall into the category of things classed as "innocuous," with no reason, normally, to call their authors to account. But if there could be no group responsibility for papers, there could be no group responsibility for other outcomes. An account or scheme for group responsibility is necessary if group responsibility, in general terms, is to be differentiated from individual responsibility.

Group and Individual Responsibility

When we talk about moral responsibility, it is (normally) in terms of individuals, of so and so being morally responsible for such and such. Therefore, responsibility is normally attributed to individuals—responsibility for some action or outcome that has taken place or sometimes for something that has not taken place. As a first step toward generalizing the idea of moral responsibility, of setting out what is at stake, it can be "formalized" as a two-place relation, m. The first member of m is the subject to whom (for persons) or to which (for groups) responsibility is to be attributed. The second member of m represents what the first member is responsible for. Instances of the concept of *individual responsibility* are such that the first term will refer to individual agents; thus, we have the representation PmX: agent P is responsible for outcome X. According to the theory outlined earlier, P is responsible because he was in a position to know that what he was doing came under the description "doing X."[6] The intended contrast here, naturally, is with groups or *classes* of individuals; we are interested in whether, and in what sense, these things might stand as the first term in the responsibility relation.

To represent this (possible) state of affairs, we can write GmX, where m and X are understood as above, but the group *G* is represented by the first term. *G* is at least a class comprising more than one person (perhaps there could be some limiting case of a group with just one person, but this is not of interest here). In accordance with the supervenience requirement, that *G* can stand as the first term in m entails that some individuals can perform some actions, and the idea is that these individuals belong to the class *G*, with the class comprising all of those individuals who had *control* (the relation Con; see chapter 4) with respect to X—for example, all those who take on a causal role in regard to X. Given this, a minimum *condition* for group responsibility is that a single instance of PmX is *not* the whole story, in a given case where it is correct to attribute responsibility. There is, so to speak, a given "amount" of responsibility, not "all" of which is to be attributed to a particular individual P. A minimal *conception* of group responsibility will then be a situation in which more than one person is responsible for one and the same thing.[7]

One example that has been put forward to illustrate this (minimal) concept is the case of the two vandals. A statue is pushed over and broken, but it was too heavy for one person to move. In this case, then, the two vandals had to work in concert, granted the absence of any suitable tools, explosives, and so on. Many such examples—where the physical effort needed to accomplish some task is too great for one person—exist, and here there is a similarity with complex intellectual tasks that require a division of labor, such as those mentioned earlier. This form of group responsibility, known as *shared* responsibility (Melema 1988, 12), is such that the members of a class *R* share responsibility for X on condition that each is individually responsible for X—that is to say, for every P ∈ *R*, PmX. To fix the membership of *R*, and so develop an account of group responsibility along this line, we need only know when the relation m holds. In other words, *R* is simply the domain of m when the range is X. I will understand shared responsibility here to mean that there is no responsibility "left over": all responsibility, and hence all blame, goes to the individual members of *R*.

This concept of group responsibility does not introduce anything over and above the idea of individual responsibility, except for some details, incidental to present purposes, about how people cooperate. If it turns out that this is the only defensible conception of group responsibility, or the only one that plausibly represents the situation for science, then it will not be necessary to address any radically new issues in relation to group responsibility in science. Indeed, it might be *preferable* for things to turn in this direction: if there were some genuine or robust concept of group responsibility that did not reduce "without remainder" to individual responsibility, then this might be interpreted to mean that the scientist himself does not in fact have any responsibility *as an individual*, and hence he might feel free to act as he pleased. For instance, he might set aside his doubts about doing strategic research for the military, believing that whatever outcomes eventuate will be the responsibility of the group, of the military as a whole—this would amount to his having an excuse for doing the research in question. And he might even be right in his interpretation. This is certainly not an attractive scenario for those who would urge scientists to be more responsible, throwing much of the practical import achieved thus far into doubt. On the other hand, genuine group responsibility that was such as to *not* relieve the individual scientist of all responsibility would be more interesting.

Two ways an account of genuine group responsibility might be approached were foreshadowed earlier. Recall that for it to be the case that GmX, there must have been some instances of individuals performing some actions—this is the supervenience requirement. (Notice that this is consistent with there being *no* instances of PmX; that is, it allows scenarios such as that just outlined, in which no individual bears responsibility for X.) The approach advocated by French, as mentioned earlier, attempts to show how individual action can be "translated" into group action and hence how groups can be agents. Given that agents are responsible for their actions, this shows, in principle at least, how groups themselves can bear responsibility: they act, and therefore they are responsible. This approach seems in line with the theory of moral responsibility, because it ties responsibility to actions. Nevertheless, as I noted earlier, I have reservations about this approach because French is (or believes he is) forced to adopt a position with respect to the nature of intention that seems to be unduly restrictive, a concern to which I will soon return. First, however, the idea of vicarious liability, which lies behind the second approach, must be outlined.

In this scenario, instead of the agents' actions amounting to group action, when the group is vicariously liable, it is rather that responsibility is transferred to the group. There is a well-known precedent here whereby an agent or representative acts for a principal—traditionally known as the "master-servant" relationship of controlled employment (Fleming 1987, 342). Other examples of vicarious liability are (historically) husbands being liable for their wife's behavior and even (in the Bible) sons being responsible for the sins of their fathers. Today, these last two cases would be rejected as unfair, because the husband or son may well have done nothing wrong—may not have been *at fault*—and thus, even though vicarious liability has been institutionalized in the past, that does not make it acceptable today. The master-servant relationship looks more promising as a bona fide case of vicarious liability: by instructing the servant or agent to do his bidding, it is *as if* the principal himself acts, and so he is vicariously responsible for that action. The issue before us is whether there is an analogous group-member relationship that serves to affix attributions of responsibility or liability to the group itself. If so, then there will be license to infer from the actions of individual group members the responsibility of the group as a whole for the outcome in question, as appears to be the case for corporations.

Corporate Responsibility

French's work on group responsibility has the overall aim of showing that corporations themselves, aside from their members, can bear responsibility for certain outcomes. French does an excellent job of describing those features of corporations that enable us to move from employee responsibility to corporate responsibility. However, as I noted earlier, I have some reservations about his starting point, especially in regard to his views on intention. These come into play when he explains the three characteristics that he thinks are necessary before an "entity" can be an actor, including being capable of intending. French explains the capacity of intending as follows: "To say that something acts intentionally is to say that it has purposes, plans, goals and interests that motivate its behaviour. Essentially, to intend to do something is to plan to do it. If I intend to go to Hawaii in February, then I plan to go to Hawaii in February" (1995, 10). And on the next page: "It is to be expected that those who interpret intention on the desire-belief model would think that any talk of corporate intention (and so corporate actors) must be metaphorical and reducible to the intentions of humans who have the requisite beliefs and desires. Obviously, corporations cannot, in any normal sense, desire and believe" (11). While it might be said that corporations cannot, in any normal sense, plan either, let us accept French's last point and agree that only humans can desire things. Then, if the case for corporate responsibility depends on the capacity for corporations to act, and if that, in turn, presupposes that corporations can intend to do things, then the desire-belief model cannot be accepted as the whole story about intention.

The desire-belief model was used earlier (see chapter 5) in so far as it embodied the conative and cognitive aspects of intentional action, although no unreserved commitment to it was made. French must evidently reject *all* such views of intention, including any that replace desire with preference, such as that canvassed on the modified standard view. But this is surely a mistake: intention is involved with action in two ways—intention *in* action, as when an action is said to be intentional, and *prior* intention as guiding action to be undertaken in the future, intention as plans and premeditations (see Searle 1983, 84). But plans are not the kind of intentions that are "in" actions, precisely because they are not something like desire-belief combinations. Many—indeed most —actions are not planned activities. I did not consciously plan to make a cup of coffee at 8:45, but making it was certainly an intentional action of mine. I am responsible for precisely the actions that I do perform, regardless of whether they are preceded by prior intention specified in the form of plans. Further, I can have a prior intention to do something and not do it, so having prior intention is neither necessary nor sufficient for the attribution of responsibility.

French's agenda here seems to be similar to that of Wallace, who endorsed the standard view because he thought that it was required by the reactive attitudes concept of moral responsibility. If French could establish that corporations are capable of intentional action, then that would show that they are morally responsible for those actions that they do intentionally. The criticism made of Wallace was that acting intentionally may be sufficient for attributing moral responsibility, but it is not necessary. Nevertheless, it looks as if the *capacity* for intentional action is a necessary attribute of a morally responsible "entity." If P was in a position to know that he did X, then he should not have done X but something else. His actions should have been restrained by moral obligations to his fellows, and he should have *intentionally* acted (or not acted at all) in accordance with those obligations. By deciding not to go along with French, we leave ourselves with work still to do, by way of finding some relevant "capacity" or feature of the corporation that can tie it to the idea of responsibility.

The way forward is to show that the corporation lays down a basis for decision making and choice that its officers and employees use when acting in its name. This mechanism then, so to speak, replaces the faculties that an agent normally uses. For instance, in warfare, it is legal to kill someone; indeed, it is mandatory to do so when ordered by a superior officer. When someone enlists in the army and takes the field in battle, he sets aside his own faculty of choice, moral obligations, and "qualities of will" and conforms to the discipline of the armed forces, which tells him how to decide, what to do, and even how to think. The mature corporation is similar, as we have learned from French and from others, such as Galbraith, who discuss its anatomy, its establishment of a mechanism for decision making that employees enact. So while corporations themselves do not intend, they shape the intentions of their employees by directing them to adopt certain courses of action.[8]

It is helpful in this connection to look at one of French's favorite examples, the 1989 polluting of Prince William Sound by the *Exxon Valdez*. The *Exxon Valdez*, a single-hulled tanker owned by Exxon and under the command of one Captain Joseph Hazelwood, loaded oil at night from a port at the end of the Alaskan oil pipeline. The captain was drunk in his cabin when the ship left port, and a junior officer sailed the ship into a reef, subsequently spilling enormous quantities of oil. French wants to argue that it was right for Exxon to admit responsibility for this disaster, as it finally did, because Exxon's *actions* polluted the waterway. If the various protocols and procedures for designing tankers, loading them at night, hiring captains of dubious sobriety, and so on were all elements of Exxon's "corporate plans," then the sailing of a single-hulled vessel at night in Prince William Sound under Captain Hazelwood was, in French's account, an action in accordance with corporate intentions. But surely Exxon did not actually sail the ship; the corporation itself, whatever it might be, was not at the wheel steering the ship or giving orders from the bridge. And if "polluting Prince William Sound" is a negligent action that was a direct consequence of "sailing the *Exxon Valdez* without due care and attention," then Exxon *itself* did not perform either action. An inexperienced officer was sailing the ship; he was the actor in this case, not Exxon.

French wants to declare Exxon responsible for the accident because it was an actor in virtue of the relationship between the captain and crew, and so on, and because of its stated policies and decision-making procedures. In my view, in contrast, the latter warrants a transfer of liability to Exxon, but not a "transfer of action," in line with the idea of vicarious liability. In other words, there is no transfer of action here in any normal sense of acting. In the case of the agent acting for the principal, on the other hand, there is a transfer of action: there is an obvious sense in which the principal could have done what the agent in fact did on that occasion, because the principal was capable of setting in motion those events that constitute actions. But there is no such sense in which such an entity as Exxon can itself carry out actions, such as being at the wheel of the ship. However, there is no reason why French cannot say that Exxon acted if he *stipulates* this—if he defines corporate action as action by the employees of the corporation that are in line with its policies and procedures. "Corporate action" then becomes a special term in the lexicon that acts as shorthand for all of these things. But it does not follow that Exxon acted in the same sense that its officers acted. Captain Hazelwood, his junior officer and crew, the members of the transport division, and the executives at headquarters all had beliefs and desires (or mutatis mutandis, whatever elements of an alternative model of intention in action is adopted), but these are not transferable to the corporation. The stipulation "corporate action" fails to include the elements of ordinary human action that establish the tie to responsibility, and that is why I do not accept French's approach. Nevertheless, the structural features of the organization that French believes transfer action from individual to corporation do, I think, license the transfer of responsibility.

Vicarious liability is, as I have said, an idea that is familiar from the law. Joel Feinberg uses this as a basis for discussing group responsibility (1975)—an approach that seems promising. However, Feinberg's aim is not so much to show that there is an irreducible sense of group responsibility but to show how responsibility can be attributed to some members of the group as a consequence of the actions of others, depending on who was at fault. Still, Feinberg's formulation of vicarious liability can be useful here. Feinberg sets out a three-part "contributory fault" condition for liability: P must have done, or causally contributed to the occurrence of, the harmful thing in question; his actions must have been faulty; and finally, P's doing or causal contribution must have been connected to the faulty aspect of his conduct.[9] The assumption normally made, that someone is liable or responsible when he is at fault and when some harm has been committed that he intends, is here tightened to ensure that the faulty action actually contributes to the harm. For example, if I do something that harms you, and if I deliberately set out to harm by performing certain actions, but if the actual harm was not a direct result of what I deliberately did, then I am not in fact liable for the actual harm. For example, suppose I force you to come to a house in which I have planted a bomb, say by kidnapping your cat and holding it there. On the way, you are driving too fast and have a fatal accident. I am not liable for the car accident—at least not in the same sense as I would have been liable for your death in the house.[10]

Feinberg then introduces two more liability concepts: liability is "strict" if there is any weakening of contributory fault and the subject is still held liable. Normally, of course, liability is strict if the causal condition is held to be sufficient, but Feinberg's concept is more general. Second, liability is "vicarious" when one party is liable, but some element of the fault condition is properly ascribed to another party and hence is a species of (Feinberg's) strict liability. Again, if you are my agent and I instruct you to act in certain ways, then I may be held liable for the outcomes of your action when in fact the contributory-fault condition is not ascribable to me. According to Feinberg, "The person who did or caused the harm is not the one who is called on to answer for it" (1975, 108). Feinberg goes on to illustrate this point, including through the principal-agent relation, but he stresses that none of the actual elements of the contributory-fault condition "transfer." Thus, if you, as my agent, cause something to happen, and as a consequence I am held liable, there is no transfer of acting here. The vicarious-liability approach therefore clearly differs from French's approach. Feinberg is now in a position to define *collective responsibility:* this is the vicarious liability of "an organized group (either a loosely organized, impermanent collection or a corporate institution) for the actions of its constituent members" (1975, 111). Feinberg distinguishes four different subtypes in terms of the different ways the constituent members can act, be at fault, and so on, but Feinberg himself is not specifically concerned with our problem here, so he does not proceed to focus on what would license the transfer of responsibility from the member to the group itself.

Is the idea of vicarious liability consistent with the theory of responsibility developed thus far? The theory holds that an individual is responsible for all of his actions that he is in a position to know about. Can this be extended? In the case of the principal-agent relationship, it seems that it can. If a principal instructs his agent to do X, then clearly he *intends* his agent to do X as a consequence of his instruction and, ipso facto, he is in a position to know what is going on. If the agent did not normally carry out such requests, then he would not be an agent. These days, such relationships are governed by law, and the two parties will usually have signed an agreement that authorizes the agent to act in the name of the principal.[11] Thus, the principal does not himself act but does remain responsible, because it is *as if* he acts. This is, I think, in line with our theory. Going back to Fermi and the building of the nuclear reactor, Fermi issued instructions to his workers, showed them what to do, drew up plans, and so on. All these actions amounted to building the reactor. Had Fermi never once touched one of the graphite bricks needed to moderate the reaction but simply issued orders, he would still be the one responsible for building the reactor. This example is surely no different from that of the principal and his agent.

Group Research and
Collective Responsibility

HE AIM HERE IS TO BUILD ON THE APPROACH SUGGESTED in the previous chapter—namely to develop an account of genuine group responsibility, or collective responsibility, that locates a basis for transferring responsibility and to determine whether this applies to group research in science. It has been shown that there is such a basis for principals and agents, constituted by the practices and regulations surrounding the agent's acting for the principal. It is natural to transfer responsibility to the principal because it is apparent that he could (in the requisite sense) have acted himself and done what the agent did. Groups, however, cannot act, and so some other basis for transferring responsibility is necessary. Again, I begin with corporations.

Substituted Decision Making

The modern corporation does seem to have features that make possible the transfer of responsibility via substituted decision making. For example, it is clear that those who give orders, those in positions of authority, do not do so in their own interest, and this marks a crucial difference with the principal-agent relation. An agent acts to further the interests of the principal, but the managers of a corporation act in the interest of the corporation. At least this is true of what Galbraith calls the mature corporation. A mature corporation is one in which the sep-

aration of ownership and control is complete, such that the legal owners, the shareholders, do not exert any real control over the corporation's managers or technostructure, as Galbraith terms the mature
corporation's decision makers and policy formulators.[1] The overriding
interest of the corporation is increasing its earnings and minimizing its
costs, and the managers' actions are ultimately guided by this imperative. Were this not so, the principal-agent model would apply, and even
though there would be instances of vicarious responsibility, these would
not be such that the corporation itself was responsible. In light of these
remarks, let us go back to the *Exxon Valdez* disaster and ask again why
Exxon was responsible for it.

Peter French identifies two features of a mature corporation that he
takes to warrant attributing actions to the corporation itself. These features are part of what he calls the Corporate Internal Decision (CID)
structure (French 1995, 26), an organizational model that delineates levels within the corporation and rules that specify when a decision or
instruction is in line with corporate aims and policy. The latter (rules)
distinguish those decisions that are corporate rather than personal, and
the former (levels) specify who is in a position to make decisions and
who is to carry them out. The CID structure is therefore important, certainly for French, who needs a way to identify "corporate actions." For
present purposes, however, other elements of corporate structure are significant—elements that concern the kinds of actions undertaken rather
than who is authorized to undertake them.

Beginning with the overarching imperative to maximize earnings,
which Exxon shares with every other corporation, how, in general
terms, does Exxon further this goal? Clearly, it buys oil, ships oil in its
tankers, refines the oil, and then sells the product; provided the rev-
enues from these activities are greater than their costs, Exxon will have
(net positive) earnings. Let us say that Exxon's corporate policies specify both that this is what Exxon does and that this is how, in general
terms, it does it. Exxon's policies, then, amount to the overall ways
Exxon puts into practice the imperative to maximize earnings. These
policies are not impervious to change: Exxon might take opportunities
to expand its "core business" into other potentially profitable areas,
such as synthetic fuels and other energy sources. Just how Exxon buys
oil, ships it, refines it, and so on, day to day, will be the means by which
it operationalizes its policies and puts them into practice. If we refer to
the latter (the means) as Exxon's corporate procedures, then the proce-

dures are ways to enact policy. Procedures are likely more changeable than policies, and quite different procedures might be used to carry out the same policy.

This distinction between policies and procedures does not, of course, capture the full complexity of a corporation's activity; nevertheless, it is helpful in analyzing the *Valdez* incident. Thus, one of the contributing causes to the accident was the use of a single-hulled ship: a double hull may well have not been ruptured. I will assume that one of Exxon's procedures was to use single-hulled ships—this is how it shipped oil—and as such it seems to have been in line with corporate policy.[2] I say "seems" here because no corporation wants to adopt procedures that are too risky, because these threaten earnings. The *Exxon Valdez* accident cost Exxon billions of dollars, and a rational entity like Exxon did not want such an outcome. We can therefore assume that Exxon had a risk-assessment apparatus in place that evaluated its procedures and recommended changes where appropriate.[3] Because there was an accident, and because it was determined that this was not just the responsibility of the crew—a judgment that would have excused Exxon itself—then either the risk assessment failed or its results were ignored. In the former case, it can be said that the use of single-hulled ships in Prince William Sound was definitely in line with corporate policy, whereas in the latter, it can be said that a shift to multihulled vessels, though required, was not made; either way, Exxon was to blame. The question remaining is whether Exxon "itself" was really responsible for the accident or whether responsibility "reduces" to some subclass of Exxon employees who share (all) the responsibility—an eventuality that would rule out collective responsibility. I will now canvass some ways in which such a reduction might be possible, in order to distinguish when it might not be—when there could be genuine group responsibility.

In the first place, all the blame might have been owing to Captain Joseph Hazelwood, who was clearly derelict—that was Exxon's initial response when it tried to excuse itself. However, while Hazelwood's being drunk was a contributing cause, it was accepted that there were others besides, such as the now infamous use of single-hulled ships. Suppose that the (subclass of) executives who authorized extending the procedure of using single-hulled vessels to ship oil from Alaska were actually in a position to know that single-hulled vessels posed an unacceptable risk, yet they did not revise their procedure for shipping oil—they did not act on the risk-assessment recommendations. Then, on the theory proposed here, they are responsible for the accident: they failed to attend to or gather information that would have shown that accepted corporate procedure was too risky in that environment. In this case, is Exxon itself also responsible? Not as far as the use of single-hulled vessels is concerned, because the executives in fact failed to revise corporate procedure when they had the opportunity. It is not Exxon's fault when its employees fail to do their job (assuming that Exxon trained them properly, and so forth.). This is a second way in which the corporation might escape blame. But now suppose that the executives were not in a position to see that the risk was too high—that they acted in accordance with existing risk assessment, which dictated that single-hulled vessels were acceptable for shipping Alaskan oil, and that, as far as they could see, this would present no problems. A further reduction might still be possible, in regard to the experts who set up the risk-assessment apparatus. If those people were in a position to know that their system itself was risky because it failed to take account of parameters applying to hazardous environments like Alaska, then the responsibility would fall to them.

If this reduction is not forthcoming, one step further back might be taken to address the policies themselves—even to question the practice of shipping oil in general as a way to meet corporate goals. Perhaps J. D. Rockefeller, the founder of Exxon's parent company, Standard Oil of Ohio, was in a position to know that shipping oil is an unacceptable risk because of the likelihood of accidents such as that of the *Valdez*. The latter eventuality, however, is highly unlikely, as Standard Oil did not use tankers. This is where the reductionist strategy might fail: when the corporation reaches a certain size, its activities ever more complex, and when it has been in existence longer than its longest-serving employee, the "position-to-know" test may not be satisfied. In other words, when the corporation reaches a given stage of complexity, it will not be possible to trace corporate actions (as French would say) back to specific individuals who bear all responsibility for them.[4] It is on the historical record that Exxon, not Hazelwood or any other particular group of individuals, was responsible for the oil spill, and therefore Exxon had to pay for the cleanup. This legal judgment does not imply that there was genuine group responsibility on Exxon's part, because if a group of managers had done the wrong things and were totally to blame, Exxon would still have had to pay up. However, it is now apparent how it could have been Exxon's fault—if there was no such group of wholly responsible individuals. Suppose it is assumed that no reduction is possible

because the position-to-know test fails. Is this sufficient for the transfer
of responsibility to Exxon? It is not, because it is still possible that no
one else, or nothing else, bears responsibility. But it is now possible to
answer this question positively: responsibility is transferred when
human agents (managers in this instance) act in accordance with the
corporation's decision-making "mechanism." This is what I call "substituted decision making."

In the account of action proposed here, choices and decisions issue
in intentions that are manifest in those actions that the agent actually
undertakes—including those under descriptions he foresees or should
foresee. Thus, the process of deciding takes place before the agent acts
and involves weighing and evaluating alternative courses of action.
Some sort of evaluation must lead the agent to prefer to do one thing
rather than another; otherwise, he would do nothing.[5] An autonomous
agent—a person who is mature and who has his own projects, interests,
point of view, and so on—will have his own set of values in terms of
which he generates preferences in regard to the possible courses of
action open to him. An autonomous agent is thus a moral agent, someone who is responsible for what he does. To say with respect to such an
agent that there is substituted decision making implies that he is no
longer making decisions in accordance with his own, internalized set of
values. Thus, all instances of coerced actions are instances of substituted decision making, and it is because the agent is not able to choose to
do as he would that coercion excuses him from responsibility. Coercion
is not, however, the correct representation of the kind of situation of
interest here because the assumption is that the manager voluntarily
substitutes the decision-making mechanism of the corporation for his
own. This means that the manager acts in accordance with the aims and
values of the corporation, in particular earnings maximization. This is
not something that he could do on his own, and hence it could not be
found among his own personal values and aims; when he is acting as his
own man, he cannot pursue maximization of corporate earnings. But
does substituting the corporation's decision-making mechanism for his
own serve to excuse him of responsibility and transfer it to the corporation, as happens for coerced actions?

Of significance here is not so much whether the agent is in fact
excused—and we would prefer that he still bears some responsibility—
but rather the transfer of responsibility to the "body" in whose interests
the decisions are made. It is not in fact the case that every instance of

substituted decision making implies a corresponding transfer of responsibility. Suppose P decides to go to soccer matches once a fortnight and to act like a hooligan, drinking heavily, singing obscene songs, and fighting opposing fans—doing the things that soccer hooligans like to do. Whatever damage such a mob does is not organized, and the responsibility is simply shared: it is not genuine group responsibility. Assuming that P never normally does such things and becomes a hooligan on a whim, it follows that there is nothing else to which responsibility for his untypical actions can be transferred; there is no independent "mob responsibility." The mob of soccer hooligans, however, differs from the corporation in several ways. The corporation is specialized, whereas the mob is not: there are no specialist singers, drinkers, or fighters; everyone sings, drinks, and fights. Consequently, there is no need for explicit mob coordination and planning. Second, the corporation endures when its personnel leave and are replaced (a characteristic discussed later), but the mob dies out when its members go home. Finally, the aim of the corporation, maximized earnings, emerges from the particular activities of its members, whereas the damage caused by the mob, assuming that is its aim, is just the sum of the average damage that each hooligan wreaks. These characteristics of the corporation, I submit, are such as to warrant the transfer of responsibility when the agent substitutes the corporate decision-making mechanism for his own.

A corporation's decision-making apparatus is complicated to the degree that no individual can individually undergo the process through which a major decision is made, such as whether to use Alaskan oil, develop a new software package, design a new drug, or whatever it might be. This is because all kinds of different expertise, from science and engineering to sales and marketing, go into the process. The CEO and the board of directors will be able to grasp the overall picture but will lack the specialist knowledge that resides in the engineering or sales division (as was true of Robert Oppenheimer at Los Alamos). Thus, when a person becomes a corporate manager, he becomes part of a large and expert team, and hence "taking on" the corporation's decision-making mechanism amounts to participating in a complex chain of events. This is an important point: merely acting for another—taking on his values, making the choices he would make—is not enough to transfer or excuse responsibility. Even the agent authorized by his principal is not excused of all responsibility, although there is (some) transfer in this case. What is different about a corporation is that it requires many "agents," working cooperatively, to do its bidding. The manager and (in effect) the agent both make decisions and act on behalf of others, but the manager's actions play only a small part in a process that he cannot fully grasp. So what, in general, might the conditions for collective responsibility be like?

Conditions for Collective Responsibility

The minimal condition for group responsibility is that there is an instance of group responsibility if GmX is the case and if there is more than one instance of PmX, where $P \in G$. Earlier, the possibility was raised that for collective responsibility, GmX is the case, but there is no PmX; this is not correct, for it has just been demonstrated that collective responsibility is consistent with instances of individual responsibility. While a purely formal or extensionalist definition of collective responsibility is not possible, a little more can be said about the structure of the collective C before turning to an important nonformal condition. Thus, C should not simply be an unorganized group of agents, but an organization. That is to say, C will be a class of agents standing in certain relations to one another. The CID structure of Exxon, for example, imposes relations on the class of all Exxon employees, such relations as, "gives orders to," "is the supervisor of," and so on. From the formal perspective, then, C is a relational structure. There is, however, a complication here: if E stands for Exxon in the sense that it is the relational structure that comprises all present Exxon employees, then to say that E is responsible for polluting Prince William Sound is false. In the first place, this statement is too inclusive if it implies that every employee is responsible, for some might have nothing whatever to do with shipping oil. Second, it is too exclusive because some of those who formulated crucial policy may be no longer working for the corporation. One obvious way to address this problem would be to pick out the subclass of all Exxon employees, past and present, who played a causal role in the disaster. That may be the correct solution as far as group responsibility goes—more analysis would be needed before a final judgment—but that subclass in itself would not amount to the collective that is Exxon.

One reason why an extensionalist definition of the collective will not suffice is that it cannot cover the essential ingredient that the individual actors, those who play a causal role, are acting not for themselves but for the collective. This is an intentional matter: the actors substitute the collective's decision-making mechanism—whatever that amounts to—for their own and act for the collective. The causal contributions made by the collective's members are normally a consequence of their acting in accordance with this mechanism, not in terms of their own interests, which is the "condition of substituted decision making." It is this condition that distinguishes collective responsibility from shared responsibility. For shared responsibility, the members of class S all presumably make the same decisions and choices—otherwise they could not cooperate effectively—but these choices "belong to them," not to something else. Thus, a collective C must have some such decision-making mechanism associated with it. This in turn presupposes that C also has some goal(s) or aim(s) toward which the mechanism is directed and that supplies its rationale—all matters exemplified in the last section. So, in addition to the structure that comprises the class of relations in which its members stand, C will also have a goal or aim that is its raison d'être and a decision-making mechanism.

One might, then, think that collective responsibility could only attach to corporations. However, I believe it is possible to find examples of collective responsibility elsewhere—hence the issue of collective responsibility in science would remain open—so I will now give a (highly fanciful) example of a collective that is altogether unlike a corporation. Recall the earlier mentioned "random vandals," who ruined statues by toppling them over and breaking them. The idea was that the chosen statues were too heavy for a single vandal working on his own, so he had to find a like-minded friend to share the work. In contrast, let us imagine that the vandals are part of a long tradition of statue breaking, belonging to the infamous Cult of the Vandals. The destruction of the statue is thus far from a random incident; it is premeditated and well planned. The vandals themselves are members of an ancient cult, its origins lost in the mists of time, who believe there is some higher purpose to the destruction of certain statues on certain propitious dates; this destruction is their goal. They dedicate themselves to this purpose and train their muscles to pull and push respectively, with one working exclusively on his latimus dorsi and the other on his pectorialis major, as their fathers and forefathers did before them.

There is now a sense in which the breaking of the statue can be attributed to something other than just two individuals who share responsibility for it—namely, to the Cult of the Vandals. This cult is an organization, a class with defined relations, its vandals different from the class of random vandals. All this warrants a redescription of events as "The Cult of the Vandals strikes again." All kinds of stories can be invented about the cult's decision-making mechanism. We can suppose that the cult's elders, who have successfully served their time in the field, interpret augurs in terms of cult lore (compare Exxon's corporate policy) and determine which statue should be destroyed on a given date. This becomes the decision of the Cult of the Vandals, not of its individual members. That this may not be rational is not, of course, a bar to people accepting it—many real-life examples could be given of people submitting to irrational practices. Let us suppose that in this time of modern, as opposed to ancient, art, statues are made of such materials as glass and plastics, as well as stone and marble. Suppose that a glass statue in a museum is singled out and broken during an exhibition, and bystanders get hurt. Those who first laid down the lore of the cult could not have been in a position to know that such accidents could take place, and in this respect there is some similarity between Exxon policy makers and the use of single-hulled vessels in Prince William Sound. The cult itself is therefore to be blamed for the harm done to the bystanders.

This example, whatever one makes of it, points out another difference between shared and collective responsibility, in terms of the membership of the classes of individuals. For shared responsibility, the class S comprises just those individuals who took part in, and who have responsibility for, a particular outcome. Change the membership, and the compass of the attribution of responsibility is also changed. If the composition of the mob of soccer hooligans changes from week to week, then so does the list of individuals who share responsibility for the damage. Collective responsibility is different. It does not matter, from the perspective of transferring responsibility to the collective, who makes the causal contributions, as long as they are made by agents acting for the collective. Suppose, as a matter of fact, that the members of E_v are the Exxon employees who played a causal role in the *Exxon Valdez* episode. Classes are defined by their members, so replacing just one member of this class with someone else produces a different class. But this does not change the fact that Exxon is responsible. (This is another reason why extensionalist definitions are not appropriate for singling out these concepts.) On the other hand, adding someone to the class of those sharing responsibility for an outcome—someone who in fact played no causal role—means that it is no longer true that $S'mX$, where S' is the class with the extra member.

Collectives therefore seem more like collections of roles than classes of individuals.[6] For example, if a group cannot work without P's input, and no one can take the place of P, then I do not think the group can function as a collective. I think collectives are such as to be relatively independent of the particular individuals who make them up. This suggests that the collective must be such as to define certain types of causal roles that can be taken on by various people who take part in the collective's activities. This is in line with the idea that collectives do certain characteristic sorts of things: Exxon ships oil, Microsoft makes software, the Cult of the Vandals smashes statues, and the Blair government governs. Making complicated software, for instance, involves various tasks, which define corresponding roles. A role is defined by the performance of certain actions, duties, task-responsibilities, and so on, circumscribed by some context. So there can be various sorts of roles, allowing the activities in question to be standardized and what people do in performing their roles to be categorized. Someone might enact their role in a unique and interesting way, but that will be incidental to the performance of the role per se, because to talk about roles is precisely to make a contrast with what one does as a special and particular person. The point about roles, then, is that they can be taken on by many different people, just as many actors can play Macbeth—although not equally well. Thus, different people can take on the pushing role in the Cult of the Vandals, aside from the incumbent Espalda Gigante.

The notion that the collective is structured by roles is associated with R. S. Downie (1972), who makes useful observations about the relation of the individual to the role he takes on and identifies several ways in which moral concerns can arise in connection with roles. For instance, the question of whether an individual should take on a given role, and the morality of the role itself, is worth some comment. Downie suggests that some roles might be just plain bad, regardless of who occupies them, using the secret police as an example. If this were true in general, then it would be possible to judge the moral responsibility of the collective, and the individual, in advance: if P acts out his role as a secret policeman, then we can conclude a priori that he does wrong and, presumably, that his becoming a secret policeman was wrong in the first place. This is very nearly a reduction of collective responsibility back down to individual responsibility: suppose P knows full well just where his performance of a given role will lead, what the outcomes will be, and so on, and suppose this is true of everyone in his organization—a situation that surely reduces to shared, and hence individual, responsibility. This differs from Downie's example in that Downie does not affirm that the secret policeman knows all the details of his work—simply that whatever they are, they are not good. In this scenario, the fact that P plays a role does not suspend his normal responsibilities for intentionally and knowingly performing actions. If it did—if, say, being a secret policeman and tricking people into incriminating their neighbors suspended one's ordinary responsibilities and relieved one of any blame—and if this were true of all collective responsibility, it would be a cause for concern, for playing the role would excuse the individual from responsibility.

I do not think that it is normally accepted that actions that are "role performances" are such as to always excuse the individual. In the first place, it is assumed that the person in question has chosen, more or less freely, to take on the role—he has volunteered for the army or the secret police, he has applied for a job at Exxon, and so forth—and that he has an idea of what this means—that he has to kill, spy, enact corporate policy, and so on. In the second place, performing a role—substituting the collective's decision-making mechanism for one's own—is not completely involuntary: the agent does not give up all volition and become an automaton, for he still can choose whether to go on with the role. My view here is that role performance does not excuse responsibility, but it does mitigate blame, to a degree. Actions that are role performances still open the agent to blame, but the fact that the role was, so to speak, assigned to him and is not of his own making is mitigating. Thus, we blame the secret policeman for spying and informing, but we think worse of the person who spies and informs of his own initiative. Moreover, the more coercive the collective is, the more mitigation there is: the soldier who is told that if he does not join the firing squad he will be put up against the wall himself and shot is coerced to the degree of being excused. Where the coercive pressures are not so great, on the other hand, the agent has the choice of continuing to play the role or opting out. In general, then, role performance—action based on the collective mechanism—does not excuse the individual from all responsibility. The situation is as before: the only excuse allowed for an individual who is in control of what he does is that he was not in a position to know about the outcome in question.

Group Responsibility in Science

Can we attribute either shared or collective responsibility to groups of scientific researchers? There are different kinds of group research, as has already been shown, and there may be some correlation between kinds of group responsibility and a group's place on the spectrum from discrete to integrated, with the latter type more likely to show collective (genuine group) responsibility. So at the outset, uniform judgments about responsibility and research groups should not be expected. However, I do assume that at the very least there are instances of shared responsibility, given that someone, or something, has responsibility for producing results, and that this is a group effort requiring several hands. This, at any rate, is the situation according to the present account, for the only alternative to shared responsibility for a group is collective responsibility. The prospects for collective responsibility may seem less bright, in view of the level of organization a group must have in order to count as a collective.

There will be collective responsibility in science only if the condition of substituted decision making is satisfied (and if the position-to-know test fails) for some scientific groups. Before returning to our examples, it must be determined whether this is even possible—it could be that groups in science are so different from corporations that they always lack the structural features necessary for collectivity. First of all, the scientists in question would have to substitute the group's decision-making mechanism for their own. And second, the position-to-know test must fail. The group, it can be assumed, must have an associated "collection of roles," such that the contribution of one or more individuals is not vital to the running of the group. If a particular scientist is needed in order for the group to function, then evidently there would be no autonomous group decision making. Thus, if a group were dedicated to developing the ideas of one scientist, or if it relied entirely on the special fund-raising skills of another, it would not be a collective, its nature clearly indicated by the presence of such a scientist. In fact, I think this is the case for what we earlier called discrete groups, such as N. The aim or goal of the group must also be considered, and here I think this aim must be taken to be the publication of "high-quality" papers. Publication is not normally the subject of moral judgments, and so again some further outcome must be assumed, such as misuse of the scientific results by a party reading one of the papers, although what this is does not need to be made explicit.

It may appear that there can be no collectives in science because the first condition cannot be satisfied for any group of scientists—that is because there can be no such thing as group decision making in science. Thus, what a scientist does—which theory he uses, which technique he employs in the laboratory—is not determinable by a group: there is no "group physical theory" or "group experimental technique." However, there are problems that only scientists working in groups can tackle, such as the structure of the BRAC1 gene, as well as problems addressed by small groups like N and L. The selection of problems is thus a matter for the group, and when a scientist joins a group, he submits to the group's orientation—this warrants a shift to the group's aim with respect to the formulation just given—to publish high-quality papers that no member could produce by himself. This, of course, is not to say that a strong-minded scientist cannot change the direction of group research and dominate a group's activities. The group's decisions will then effectively be his, however, and such a group will not qualify as a collective. Beyond the selection of problems, decisions about where to publish, how to maximize grant income, and even where to work can be made by the group. It is even possible that some of the details of a scientist's work can be dictated by the group. For instance, although theoretical physicist T was familiar with "EPR-type" interactions before he worked in N, he had not investigated the particular form that these took in NMR applications. Likewise, the kind of quantum-mechanical calculations used by the members of L are determined by the particular problems their group is working on.

The second condition is the one inherited from the theory of responsibility—that a person in a position to know about the actions he performs and the outcomes he brings about is responsible for those actions and outcomes. This also applies to group research. If the members of a research group are in a position to know that their research will have X as an outcome, then this cannot be an instance of collective responsibility. But why not, if the first condition is satisfied? I think the answer is clear: if we, as a group, are aware of what will result if we make choices and decisions in line with certain procedures that we substitute for our own, then any outcome that we foresee will come about when we act is our responsibility. We cannot excuse ourselves by blaming the procedures. The situation is the same as it was for the Exxon executives who knew that using single-hulled vessels was too much of a risk. But when the position-to-know test fails for individuals, there is no question of any responsibility for the outcome unless there is collective responsibility. The question of collective responsibility arises precisely at the point where the possibilities for individual responsibility run out.

Finally, there is the action or outcome X that is such as to attract moral responsibility. Returning to L and N, I will again assume that this condition is satisfied.[7] The group N, it will be recalled, combined the diverse talents of a physicist and two chemists, who came up with a new technique for NMR. In the normal course of events, the physicist could not do what the chemists did, and vice versa, so there was a precise division of labor, and N was properly classified as discrete. The papers produced were authored by the three principals, with no students ever mentioned, and the group was short lived, staying intact for just five years. To reiterate, in order for there to be collective responsibility, there must at least be something resembling roles, defined tasks, practices, and so on that do not depend on the individual. It could be said that, in the case of N, there was the role of the creative quantum physicist and that what T did could have been done by someone else. However, no one took over T's "role," for once the main papers were written, the work was finished. To see a role operative here would be like assigning roles to the random vandals: just because something was done—something that has an accepted description ("pushed the statue over") and that, in principle, could have been done by someone else—does not mean that a role can be said to exist. For there to be a role, there must be something more to do when a particular task is completed, which might amount to doing the same thing again, doing something similar, and so on. But when the random vandals pushed over the statue, that was it—no more to do; T's research was similar. Unlike the vandals' "work," however, T's was highly creative, and perhaps no one else (or hardly anyone else) could have done it.

To be historically correct about this example, it must be acknowledged that the group did employ a technician and a postdoc (who remarked that the group "never felt like a group") and began to conduct experiments in the routine way that is characteristic of the integrated group. However, when the original research into the new technique was published and received by the peer group in NMR, the group became modestly famous, and the university felt it should do something in response. So, it appointed one of the chemists to a personal chair, which effectively ended the cooperation. That chemist, and the technician, left for another university, which set up a center for the chemist. Soon after, the other chemist left for a chair at yet another university. T stayed and finally got his own chair. These little details strengthen the claim that this was a discrete group and moreover reinforce the judgment that responsibility for outcomes is shared. *N* clearly lacked the organizational structure necessary for there to be a collective decision-making mechanism, so there was nothing the members could substitute for their own autonomous processes. I assume this is true of all discrete groups.

Turning now to the laser group *L*, I suggested that this group does have a certain structure and permanence. Unlike *N*, its reason for being was not to develop some new technique based on a special insight, but rather to carry out much more routine electron-collision experiments. The very fact that these experiments are routine and based on well-established methods means that there is much more scope for the development of roles. In fact, some of these roles were foreshadowed in the description of the group above: getting grants, dealing with laser-electron interaction theory, deciding which experiments to do next, doing the calculations, writing up, and so forth. None of these jobs requires any unique ability, and any of them could be done, more or less well, by anyone trained in the field. Indeed, over the years, a number of Ph.D. students have returned and taken over the postdoc role—one effect of this being that their names have appeared in different orders on different group publications, as this group has a tradition of putting its students' names first. *L* is an integrated group—it comprises only physicists who work in a well-defined discipline.

Suppose that this group has published two good papers a year—appearing in top journals—for the past twenty years, each coauthored by five people. This is not completely historically correct, but it is near enough true on average. Let us suppose also that a total of twenty different people have appeared as authors in the group's publications, with either or both of the principal researchers appearing on all. There is, again, at least shared responsibility for the publications, but is there more? If one of the papers has been read, and the results used for something untoward—perhaps some military purpose that no one in the group foresaw—who or what is responsible? Suppose no one was in a position to foresee this application and the position-to-know test fails;

then the answer to the question depends on whether the condition of substituted judgment is satisfied. This in turn depends on whether *L* is sufficiently similar to a corporation to qualify as a genuine collective.

L lacks a formal CID structure: no hard-and-fast set of rules lays out management reporting or relations of supervisor to subordinate; scientific groups, unlike other aspects of university life, still tend to be collegiate. And *L* does not have anything like explicit policy and procedures. The features necessary to assemble the kind of decision-making mechanism earlier outlined for a corporation appear to be lacking. But on more careful observation, characteristics of the organization of group research can be discerned that are analogous to corporate policies and procedures. For instance, a group like *L* will have accepted strategies for publication; it will aim at journals like *Physical Review A*, which publishes papers on experimental atomic physics, and avoid journals like *Journal of Magnetic Resonance*, which does not. It will apply for grants from the Australian Research Council (ARC) rather than the National Health & Medical Research Council (NH&MRC), and so on. Such strategies are general ways in which *L* seeks to further its goal of maximizing publication. And they are revisable: if polarized electron-atom collision experiments were to become the foundation of some medical technique, then *L* might look to the NH&MRC for money. These strategies are pursued by means of certain tactics, such as writing up papers in a journal's house style, tailoring grant applications to an agency's stated aims, and so forth. And again, these tactics will change in response to other changes: for instance, if the ARC begins to stress the importance of avenues of application for research in the national interest, *L* might couch its new grant request in those terms. Is this analogy strong enough to establish that *L* is a collective and that there is, or would be, collective responsibility for the untoward outcome posited in the previous paragraph? I think not.

One reason to still deny *L* genuine collective status is the suspicion that it lacks the "emergent" goal or aim that determines the focus of the collective's decision-making mechanism as distinct from those of its members. Yet the goal of publishing joint papers and doing group research obviously cannot be reached by an individual scientist on his own: to do these things, he has to join a group and work cooperatively. I thus believe that we can discern an emergent aim for *L*. Another condition for collectivity is that the decision-making mechanism is that of the group itself: it is associated with policies and procedures that have been put in place by generations of members to further the group's over-all aim. Here, I think L has not been in existence long enough for the mechanism to be "dissociated" from the group's two founding members. If these two have been involved in planning and setting up all the group's strategies and tactics, then all aspects of the group's work will be affected by their contributions. The state of affairs here resembles that of a company that is still run by its founder, before it has evolved into a mature corporation that is in the hands of the managers. I therefore believe that any responsibility for outcomes of work done by L is shared by the members of the group, with proportionately greater praise or blame due to the two founding members.

Suppose we project L twenty years into the future. It still exists and still does laser physics with electron beams, but it has had a great stroke of luck: one of its experiments was shown to have a medical application, like the work done by N, but unlike N, L did not break up. It moved from strength to strength, gaining new sources of funding. The university was approached by a large medical-equipment company that offered a joint venture in the form of a new fully equipped building, on the condition that it could patent any application of the work done for the next ten years. The building was built, many new staff were hired, and a full-time director of research was appointed. The strategies for publication were greatly expanded, due to the fame of the group and the new interest in the medical applications of laser physics. The group's aim is still the same—to publish—and this aim is still within the sphere of pure science, but the group's opportunities are greatly expanded. I think the case for collective responsibility for outcomes is now much stronger. The decision-making mechanism for the maximization of publication is no longer so closely associated with the two founding members, who have long since retired. The group has, so to speak, evolved into a mature phase in which it is no longer the creature of those who founded it.

There are research institutes of this kind in existence, the most famous including the Salk Institute and the Sloan Kettering Foundation in the United States and the Max Planck Institutes in Germany. These institutes attract large amounts of money because it is hoped that they will produce useful outcomes, but their research is still classified as pure, for they are not like corporate R&D groups. The size and longevity of these institutes are such as to make them resemble corporations more closely than ordinary university research groups do, and so the case for collective responsibility becomes correspondingly stronger. Were we to look into the development of these institutes, from their (usually) modest beginnings until the time when they began to receive large amounts of money, we would find real-life examples that fit the story just told. When the research group becomes the research institute, it becomes a "mature" organization, its aims now prosecuted by a decision-making mechanism that is fully dissociated from its founder members.

I mentioned earlier that there is a prima facie case for holding corporations responsible for the wrongs they do. We blame them: we blame Exxon for spilling oil in Prince William Sound, not the captain of the ship, the CEO, or the board of directors. We react against Exxon itself and resent its carelessness and high-handedness. I have tried to show that we are right to do so, for Exxon is responsible for its activities as a collectivity, distinct from its employees. The responsibility of corporations supervenes on the actions of their employees, because there is a transfer of responsibility to the corporation via substituted decision making. The case for collective responsibility in science depends on a similar structure being in place. I think that we can state with some confidence that collective responsibility in science is not ruled out in principle, because of the nature of science. However, I have some doubts about there being many examples of collective responsibility in ordinary scientific research in universities: such groups are still immature (not a pejorative description) and hence are not sufficiently similar to corporations. But collective responsibility is possible in science, and hence there remains the question of the responsibilities of scientists who work in (mature) research institutes.

Taking Responsibilities Seriously

HAVE ARGUED FOR A WIDE VIEW OF THE SCIENTIST'S BACKWARD-looking responsibility: not only is the scientist responsible for what he intends to do, and for what he foresees that he does, but he may also be responsible for actions and outcomes that he does not foresee. People are not in general responsible for what they do not know they do, and so in order to establish the third ground for holding the scientist responsible, it was necessary to maintain that there are certain things that he should know about and should do. Thus, backward-looking responsibility clearly cannot be all there is to the scientist's responsibility if the wide view is taken. And indeed, there is a forward-looking dimension as well, worked out with reference to common morality and giving rise to a two-tiered system of "negative duties"—things the scientist is obliged not to do—and "positive duties"—things that he is encouraged to do.

I believe that this account is soundly based and that it does not hold the scientist to impossibly high expectations—that it is in fact *possible* to be a responsible scientist. While my argument does imply certain revisions of science as it is practiced now—for instance, I believe that spending on defense science should be drastically cut—the unlikelihood of this happening does not render my account impractical or utopian. It is an easy enough matter for a scientist simply not to work for a defense establishment. In other words, at the individual level, it is simple to forego weapons research, and if all scientists did so, there would be no such science. In reality, countries will continue to spend large sums on weapons research, and scientists will continue to profit from this, but wittingly or unwittingly, they will not (usually) be acting responsibly. There are other kinds of scientific work in which there is potential for conflict as a result of the scientist's responsibilities as they are understood here, but this is not owing to the very nature of the work: weapons research is unique in this regard. I will consider what I take to be the most common way this can happen. I will also discuss what I think is a fairly radical revision, in view of the present account of responsibility, of our understanding of what it is for a scientist to do science. Both of these issues are *consequences* of the present account, consequences for the pure scientist and for the applied scientist.

The Scientist qua Scientist

What are some of the consequences of this account? We seem to have arrived, via another path than that originally taken by Richard Rudner, at the conclusion that scientists qua scientists make value judgments.[1] Rudner believed that scientists must make value judgments *as scientists* because doing science—which is all that the scientist qua scientist ever does—is always a matter of accepting or rejecting hypotheses, and because the evidence for a given hypothesis is never (hardly ever) totally convincing, a judgment that "there is enough support" must be made on each occasion. That judgment, Rudner said, is both a scientific judgment *and* a value judgment (1980, 234). Rudner rebuffed the objection that science merely assesses the degree of support for a hypothesis and then a human investigator accepts or rejects it "under some other description," qua employee or qua lecturer who needs a publication or something else. It must be remembered that Rudner's argument was made over fifty years ago, when logical empiricism still held sway and when the notion that science is in any way value-laden was hence a radical one. So when Rudner asked "under what description" people in science make value judgments, he was questioning the nature of (pure) scientific research at a time when the prevailing view was that matters concerning values were subjective, variable, unreliable, or even meaningless—in contrast with the objective character of science. The consensus about science and values has subsequently changed, although perhaps not enough; I believe Rudner's view of science as value-laden can be extended even further.

If scientists as scientists need to make judgments about whether a hypothesis has enough support to be accepted, then we can ask what *kind* of values they appeal to. To take a familiar illustration, Hahn and Strassman detected tiny amounts of barium and krypton after they had bombarded natural uranium with neutrons. They wrote to Lise Meitner, who discussed the results with her nephew Otto Frisch, and it was finally suggested that the uranium must have split apart—the phenomenon that Frisch christened "fission." Were values involved here? In Rudner's view, they presumably were. Hahn and his fellows *decided* that there was sufficient support for the hypothesis that uranium was split apart by the incident neutrons: this was the best, and seemingly only, explanation for the presence of barium and krypton. Hahn and the others were not compelled to accept this explanation; the evidence was not such as to force them to do so, and indeed, others remained unconvinced. If they were not compelled to accept the explanation, then they must have decided that they could or should do so. It seems to me that this is simply Rudner's claim: that typically scientists must decide to accept or reject hypotheses, explanations, and so on, because evidence is rarely if ever compelling and because, in the absence of certainty, they must base decisions on something else. This "something else" is values. But they make these value judgments as scientists, and as scientists they are on the whole able to make good judgments as to when to accept explanations, hypotheses, and so on.

The values that scientists are using in Rudner's account can be called "cognitive values" because they are about cognitive aspects of science.[2] Hahn and Strassman wanted to find the right explanation for their experimental results; as realists (which we can assume they were), they wanted to know what mechanism was responsible for what they had seen—they wanted to know what was really going on. As capable and experienced scientists, they checked for other sources of barium and krypton in their lab. When they found none, they realized that the only source could have been the uranium and thus looked for a way for uranium to produce these two lighter nuclei. It could be said that Hahn and Strassman were doing good science, that they knew they were doing good science (for example, by seeking causal mechanisms), and that in this sense they were making value judgments about their own work. This position represents a challenge to those who believe that science is a matter of observation followed by inductive generalization, where the former is indubitable and the latter logically secure. But no one has held that form of extreme empiricism for a long time, and today we can all accept Rudner's position without demur. The present account, however, sees science as value-laden in a different, and I think more radical, way. The value judgments that any scientist has to make do not involve just cognitive values. Do scientists make these additional judgments qua scientists or under some other description? This "description" may seem inconsequential, as long as the judgments are made, but the point is worth discussing, as it will reveal something more about the implications of the present account for our understanding of science.

Our account of science and moral responsibility deals with *all* forms of science, pure as well as applied. Those scientists who simply intend to do science for its own sake and then to publish learned articles have responsibility for the outcomes of their work as much as applied scientists do (see part i) . So in the choice and conduct of scientific research, it is necessary (at least) to make value judgments about whether the research will have foreseeable, unjustifiably harmful consequences. In other words, the first tier of forward-looking responsibility should engage *all* scientists in their choice of *every* research project, and as such it entails a revision of the traditional understanding of pure research, expressed by such people as Polanyi. It could be said that such judgments are not made by scientists qua scientists, but by scientists qua responsible members of the moral community, or something like that. But the matter must be examined a little further. Suppose S is concerned that his project in nuclear physics might aid the weapons establishment and that this is his only concern (itself a value judgment). As a nuclear physicist, S knows how nuclear weapons work and so must decide whether his proposed research will in some way make them work better. Given that he is operating within the paradigm, he has a fair idea of the results he will get, although he does not know precisely what they will be. So he speculates as to possible outcomes and how they could possibly make nuclear weapons work better. Suppose he is working on a particular aspect of the nucleus of iron—an element that, as far as anyone knows, will never have any application in weapons research. He thus concludes that his work is safe.

The decision that S is making has nothing to do with the sufficiency of evidence supporting a hypothesis; such decisions are not cognitive, in our agreed-upon sense. But they are decisions based on S's scientific knowledge. S knows how nuclear weapons work, he has a good idea where his research will lead, and he sees no connection between the two. That there is no connection is a *scientific* judgment. This becomes, or is the basis of, a *value* judgment when S affirms that, as a responsible scientist, he is morally justified in undertaking the research project. I have argued that all scientists must take responsibility for the outcomes of their research. The nature of all science is that it affects us, regardless of whether it is intended to do so as applied research or not intended to do so as pure research. So one *can* say that S judges his project morally acceptable qua scientist, because it is the very nature of science to affect our lives. To hold this viewpoint is to see an intimate relation between science as knowledge of the world and science as practice based on that knowledge. The relationship is seen as an intimate one here, in light of our account of responsibility. So I think a case can be made that scientists qua scientists must always make value judgments about the projects they engage in, if they take their responsibilities qua scientists seriously.

This account also has implications for a distinction often seen as complementary to that between scientific and value judgments—namely between objective and subjective aspects of science.[3] Science as knowledge about the world was traditionally seen as concerning objective matters of fact, while particular applications of this knowledge were viewed as consequences of subjective interests. But this distinction is not reflected in the actual conduct of scientific research. In the present account, pure and applied research are distinguished in terms of the *context* in which the work is done, as opposed to the content. Fission, for example, is the mechanism by which an atomic bomb goes off. So when Hahn and Strassman's work was replicated at Los Alamos (assuming that it was), the exact (near-enough) same things were done in that lab as had been done in Berlin three years earlier, but now the work was classed as applied. The work was the same, done to the same standards and with the same results, but the intentions and aims of the two groups of scientists were quite different. Hahn and Strassman were trying to explain why they had found barium and krypton, while the Los Alamos scientists wanted to investigate the conditions under which fission in natural uranium takes place in order to garner information for creating the mechanism for an atomic bomb. Why should investigating the properties of nuclear fission for the purpose of explaining certain experimental data be objective, value-free, pure scientific research, while doing the *exact same thing* for the purpose of making bombs be subjective, value-laden, applied research? To take another example, in 1944, the idea of using plutonium in the gun-barrel assembly was given up because predetonation would prevent a nuclear explosion. This information about the fissile properties of plutonium had never been obtained before, and the results no doubt would have been publishable as a pure scientific research paper, of interest in and of itself. In this case, in other words, the applied research preceded the pure research. Of course, pure research can be given the honorific label of "objective, value-free knowledge," but this title does not mean much at all.

Whether it is an extension of the scope of Rudner's original position or a new take on the value-laden nature of science, the present account of science implies that there must be more to doing science now than there was in the days when the scientist only needed to worry about confirming his results and their explanatory and predictive scope. In any case, one consequence of this account is that no scientist can escape making value judgments. Hence, if the scientist is obliged not to do research that will, or may, have outcomes that can cause harm to others, then he must be well informed about matters that are not, according to the traditional viewpoint, strictly scientific or strictly objective. He must know how his work can affect others and try to see if there is a significant risk that his present projects will do so. And he will certainly be strongly motivated to stay well informed if he further wants to ascend to the second tier of responsibility and do research that will benefit people. Put another way, scientists have the *responsibility* to be adequately informed about where their research may lead, and they have this because they are responsible for the foreseeable impacts of their work.[4] One obvious and practical suggestion—one that has been made many times before—is that the education of the scientist should give him this understanding about the nature of his work. Science education should not focus exclusively on the "objective side" of science, as it does almost exclusively at present. If the scientist qua scientist does other things beyond testing, explaining, and predicting, then he should learn to do these other things as well.

The Scientist qua Employee: Dual Loyalty

The majority of scientists do not work in universities and research institutes doing science for its own sake: they work for the government or in industry. The scientist who works for the Defense Department in times of national emergency will be doing applied research, as will the scientist who works for a pharmaceutical company researching the malaria parasite or the long-term effects of cholesterol-lowering drugs, as will the scientist who works for a chemical company on genetically modified organisms. I have argued that scientists have responsibility to others in view of any harmful effects of their work. But if they voluntarily sell their labor by accepting employment in government or in an industrial lab, do they not also have responsibility to their employer—a responsibility to work under the conditions stated in their contract, on the projects assigned them by their supervisors? If this is granted, as I think it must be, it cannot thus be assumed that working for an organization means that the scientist has no responsibilities at all for the effects of what he does, in view of the first tier of our two-tiered account. Again, being an employee is to have something like a role-responsibility —that is, certain obligations that people do not as a rule have. Not all beachgoers have the duty to rescue someone in difficulties in the surf, but the lifeguard does, as he has the special skills and responsibility associated with that role. Similarly, not every scientist is obliged to work for and support the aims of Monsanto, but S does because he is their employee. But again, that does not mean that *anything* Monsanto wants, S must provide: it might be said, in light of the above discussion, that S still has responsibilities qua scientist even when he is employed to do applied research. There is, however, at least the possibility of conflict between S's role-responsibility as an employee and his responsibility qua scientist, if the former requires him to do certain things that are incompatible with the latter.

In the field of medical ethics, the term "dual loyalty" is used to refer to situations in which "physicians have responsibilities both to their patients and to a third party and when these responsibilities are incompatible."[5] The worst situations in which such conflicts have occurred concern doctors using their special skills for aiding and abetting state torture, which is directly opposed to what these skills should be used for. The case of Stephen Biko, in South Africa, is one of the best known. At least two medical practitioners, prison-district surgeons, certified that they "could find no pathology" after Biko was interrogated in September 1977. Biko died five days later of massive brain damage. In this case, the district surgeons' loyalties were to the South African government and to the interests of the apartheid regime, as well as to their patient as a suffering human being. They were complicit in Biko's death in spite of the fact that the Medical Association of South Africa had signed the World Medical Association's Tokyo Declaration on torture and medical practice, which asserted that doctors should not in any way condone torture.[6] Notice that two issues arise in this case: whether Biko was in fact innocent and whether it is always wrong for doctors to use their special skills to assist in causing suffering rather than preventing it.

It is tempting to take the view that it is *always* wrong for doctors to use their special skills to cause suffering, or to be complicit in some way in condoning suffering; in that case, we would not need to worry about whether Biko was innocent or not. To extend these reflections to S and his responsibilities, it might then be said that S's responsibility not to do harm must always take precedence over his role-responsibility to his employer. I am inclined to think that this latter rule is probably one that can in fact be accepted, although I am not convinced that *all* dual loyalties can be dealt with in quite such a straightforward way. For instance, if we did accept that doctors can never condone the torture of terrorists, then we would be committed to the view that whatever any terrorists did, doctors could not be complicit in finding out their plans. But in the most extreme case, where a fanatic has hidden a timed nuclear device in a city, surely any measures that get him to reveal its location are justified. This would be a supreme emergency, during which the normal rules of common morality, and the special duties of such people as doctors and scientists, can be justifiably suspended. It would be a stretch of the imagination, however, to think that such conflicts could occur between S and his employer, because corporations are not charged with safeguarding the public and other such lofty matters, and it will thus be most unlikely that S's role performance could justify his doing harm to others.

Let us also use the term "dual loyalty" in this context to cover any such possible instances of incompatible responsibilities. How might these come about, and how might they be dealt with? Earlier, the nature of corporations (and scientific institutions) in relation to group responsibility was detailed (see part 4). The interest here is not so much in group responsibility but in how tensions can exist between the aims of the corporation/company and those of its employees. Intuitively, these tensions come about because the corporate imperative is to maximize growth (or profit), and the way to do so might come at the expense of employees, customers, suppliers, and persons generally affected by a company's products and production processes. Examples like the *Exxon Valdez* and Bhopal disasters are cited as paradigms of corporate greed and short-sightedness, but perhaps these are really not typical—they are both mistakes that the corporation would rather not have made. In fact,

I think it may often be the case that S's role-responsibility and his responsibility as a scientist pull in the same direction, as in the first example I will consider.

Short-sightedness can come about where there is uncertainty about side effects or indirect outcomes; either the corporation may be uninterested in these and so devote insufficient time and energy to further research, or it may take a stance based on an assessment of what would best suit its overall aims. For instance, suppose corporation M wants to try out a newly developed form of genetically modified canola by supplying farmers in Canada with the seed at a subsidized price. Scientist S is concerned that not enough testing has been done to ensure that the batches of seed do not contain an alternative genetic type that he came across in the lab. This alternative type could have undesirable properties, such as lower yield, susceptibility to pests, or unsuitability for consumption, which could come to infect the wild-type strains.[7] Here, surely S's responsibilities as a scientist and as an employee point *in the same direction;* it is in the interests of *both* M and M's customers *and* others affected by M's actions that the alternative genetic type not be released. Release would be bad for M because M might be liable for damages, and its reputation would suffer; it would be bad for M's customers because they would receive a bad product; and it would be bad for others if the genetically modified crop infected their own seed. So S, to the best of his ability, should point out that further testing and quality control are needed, and presumably he should do so by means of the processes and procedures within M. This is a scientific issue, and presumably scientists are the ones to say that the seed is pure; because S is a scientist, he will have some input into this process.

In this example, S has responsibilities both within and beyond M, so to speak, but these do not give rise to any conflict or dilemma, and so there are no dual-loyalty issues. There would be no point in S making his concerns public by going to a newspaper right away, because this would not be the best way to solve the problem. But now suppose that S's supervisors at M insist that the batches of seed are pure and contain no variant and that M is going to sell them to farmers. What S should do now depends on how great a risk the variant will pose if it is indeed present in the batches and on how sure S is that it is present. If the risk is great and if S is convinced that the variant is present, and if his superiors are intransigent in regard to delay in shipping their new product, then it seems that the case for S taking action outside the formal structure of M is stronger. Perhaps in this case he should go to the newspaper or make his concerns public in some other way. In any case, in such circumstances, S's responsibilities as a scientist are such as to outweigh his role-responsibility as an employee. But in this example, it seems that there must be something wrong with M. That is to say, M's processes and procedures are defective, as they were at Exxon in regard to single-hulled tankers, or some of M's senior personnel are not competent, as was the case with the managers of the Union Carbide plant at Bhopal. Indeed, this would *justify* S taking the only course of action available to him and making the problem publicly known. If M will not deal with the problem, then others must be informed about it. S's loyalty should not be to a defective or badly run company.

I suggest above that one rule for approaching dual loyalty is that the scientist's duty not to harm always outweighs his role-responsibility to act as a good employee. In the normal course of events, no dual-loyalty dilemmas would be expected, because modern corporations have learned the value of being "good corporate citizens" with positive public images (cf. Forge 2002, 28). Where such problems do exist, I think in many instances that these will be due to corporate mistakes, such as those outlined in the last example. There remains the practical question of whether S really does have sufficient evidence and confidence that something has gone wrong, but once he does, he is justified in making his concerns public. So, this rule seems acceptable and, I think, shows that the present account can often provide clear guidance. Further, I think it conforms to intuitions commonly held about the applied scientist working in the corporate world—a consequence of its grounding in common morality.

As a third and final example, suppose that M routinely pursues growth by exploiting all the opportunities, loopholes, and so on that it can—that M acts entirely like a "rational entity" in pursuit of its aims (cf. Ladd 1970). M might take all the shortcuts it can in product testing, it might dump its products on markets where there is lax consumer protection, it might give bribes for preferential treatment, and so on. As a scientist, S will not be able to do much about this. As a scientist, he might argue for better product testing, but if M's ingrained culture is to minimize costs by minimizing testing, there will be little he can do. S could try to change M from within by working his way up the corporate ladder, but then he would be forced to be complicit in his work and endorse the defective procedures. Should he therefore act as in the previous case by gathering as much information as he can about M and making this public? Favoring a positive response here is the fact that S, as a scientist, understands just where M cuts corners and so is in a special position to make this information public. Against a positive response is the view that this is not really S's problem: it is a problem for the legal and consumer-protection authorities. In any case, S should not work for M, the situation here similar to that of the agent taking on the role of the secret policeman.

Again, science is often declared a mixed blessing, with some good outcomes, some not so good, and some downright bad. Scientists, among other people, are responsible for all these sorts of outcomes insofar as they are *foreseeable:* this is the message of our wide view of responsibility. Kurt Baier tells us that the rationale for ascribing responsibility is "ultimately forward-looking, to improve the future" (1987, 103). And it can be agreed that the rationale for the wide view of (backward-looking) responsibility is to improve the future by altering this mixture in favor of more good outcomes and fewer bad ones. This is what "taking responsibility seriously" means, in the most general sense, and it is a consequence of what I believe the overriding aim of science should be— to improve the lot of human beings (and other moral subjects). The view of science adopted here is as an activity that can *always* have moral and social implications. I do not deny that such a thing as pure science exists, but that classification is just a function of the context in which the work is done: pure scientific research has no special or unique character. Thus, the wide view of responsibility implies that there is no difference between pure and applied research when it comes to responsibility for outcomes. The two-tiered system of forward-looking responsibilities further implies that it would be preferable if there were no such thing as pure research. It would be preferable if *all* scientists tried to direct their research toward projects that would make the world a better place, to do science for the sake of others rather than for its own sake. This last sentiment is not one that is likely to be realized, and it is not part of the present account of forward-looking responsibility that all scientists are obliged to do "good works."

Taking responsibilities seriously is a matter of *intending* to do research that does not issue in harmful outcomes and also, one would hope, *intending* to do research that has good outcomes. Taking responsibilities seriously means acting in such a way that responsibilities are properly discharged. I have argued that scientists can be responsible for more than outcomes that they intend. Suppose S becomes convinced that this is true. He then takes into account not just what he intends to come about—what he would have concerned himself with exclusively before seeing the truth and the light—but also what he foresees will happen. But what else could "taking account" mean here except bringing outcomes within the scope of his deliberations and plans? If S thinks that he might make possible some harmful consequence by pursuing his nuclear physics project, then he will take account of this by not taking up the project. So taking responsibilities seriously means bringing within the scope of one's deliberations possible unintended outcomes of one's work. And this means that those outcomes are no longer unintended because, taking his responsibility seriously, S *intentionally* refrains from bringing them about. The same applies to unforeseen outcomes. S accepts that he can be responsible for foreseeable though unforeseen outcomes. He therefore makes every effort to look ahead and see where his work could lead. Provided that he is able to do this—and there are practical difficulties here—there will no longer be any unforeseen outcomes. Thus, taking responsibilities seriously restores the idea that S is responsible for all and only his intended actions. One cannot, of course, assert that S is responsible for all and only his intended actions without the qualification "taking responsibilities seriously."

Notes

Introduction

1. While this is in fact the view of the majority of economic historians, Rostow seemed opposed to it. He wrote, "What distinguishes the world since the Industrial Revolution from the world before is the systematic, regular, and progressive application of science and technology to the production of goods and services" (1971, 26). This passage might be interpreted so as to exempt the Industrial Revolution—I use capitals here to refer specifically to what happened in England—as "intermediary" between the "world before" and the "world after," which would make Rostow's position consistent with the view suggested above. Whatever one makes of Rostow's view of the role of science in the Industrial Revolution, his account of its role in its aftermath is compelling.

2. Whether it is possible to apply science for the "relief of man's estate" without thereby setting in motion sustained economic growth, and possibly eventual severe environmental problems, is an important question, but one I believe must be answered in the negative. To raise people above subsistence levels is to provide goods and services, food, and housing that count toward economic growth. In this book I do not address the question of whether the Industrial Revolution will lead to so-called environmental meltdown, although the issue of sustainable development is raised in part 3.

3. I use "he," "his," and "himself" here and elsewhere in the book most advisedly. While I would normally use gender-neutral language, all the scientists I discuss here are men. This is not because I have any particular bias in favor of male scientists, but because the case studies I use, especially the Manhattan Project, only involve men. Switching between gender-neutral language when referring to the scientist in general and gendered pronouns when discussing these specific individuals would be awkward and mannered—I tried it. So, with reservations, I will use gender-specific pronouns throughout this book.

4. Scientists can also be responsible for what they *omit* to do, but I will not consider omissions until part 2. Henceforth, "responsibility" may be understood to cover both actions and omissions.

5. This example is far from science fiction, though the actual circumstances are slightly different. Progress in aerosolization has been made in order to deliver biological-control agents to pests like the gypsy moth, its intent applied research for "beneficial purposes." However, this same research has application for biological warfare, for agents like anthrax (BMA 2004, 45). This clearly raises some difficult issues for the scientists in question.

6. The direct object could also be "doing X," and the expression "P is responsible for doing X" makes perfectly good sense. Of course, when focusing on outcomes, P is responsible because he brings X about or contributes to the

production of X. What is at issue will therefore always be some action of P's. The difference between consequentialism and its rivals is that the former sees morality as concerned only with outcomes, not with the quality of actions. While I continue here to discuss outcomes, the focus shifts to actions in part 2. A note on conventions: I will use the letter P to refer to any person or agent and the letter S when I wish the agent to be specifically understood to be a scientist.

7. Conversely, in a world without responsibility, ethics would gain no purchase. To put it differently, responsible conduct is the way, or "mechanism," by means of which ethically sanctioned standards of behavior are manifested in the world.

8. The issues discussed in this book may also seem relevant for science and politics. If scientists are to be encouraged to be morally or socially responsible, then this might well imply that they need to be politically active—or perhaps "politically responsible." I would not deny the importance of such engagement, but this book does not concern how the responsible scientist engages in science policy. I also note here that issues specific to science and democracy have been discussed of late; see Kitcher 2001 and Salomon 2000. I should add that Kitcher's work is a welcome acknowledgment from a well-known philosopher that important questions about what makes science "good" cannot be answered independent of context—or what I call *historical considerations* (see part 3).

9. In fact, the "recipients" of moral responsibility should be identified as moral subjects rather than as people. This is preferable because it allows for a wider conception that does not restrict moral considerations to human persons; for instance, it allows sentient animals to be moral subjects.

10. I say "on balance" because we want to allow for the possibility that morally sanctioned action involves doing a lesser harm to prevent a greater one.

11. For example, Australia obliges citizens who witness a traffic accident to report what they saw. Most laws, however, take the form of negative duties: P is obliged *not* to do X.

12. Some have also canvassed the question of science and responsibility; see, e.g., Bernal 1939; Gustafsson 1984; Mercier 1969, 1970; Nordgren 2001; Weeramantry 1987. I will not discuss any of these works, as their approaches and projects differ radically from mine.

13. Everyone does not accept this view, because not everyone agrees that moral responsibility is the topic of the work's third chapter, the issue turning on questions of translation. However, in the most recent edition of the *Nicomachean Ethics*, by Roger Crisp, chapter 3's topic is taken to be responsibility.

14. I will not refer to any particular passage in Fischer and Ravizza 1998 to back up my gloss on their views, but it is most certainly a source to be consulted by the interested reader.

Chapter 1. Outcomes of Scientific Research

1. The phrase "basic research" is sometimes used to refer to what I call pure research, but I prefer the latter term because it connotes research that is untrammeled, disconnected from practical affairs. Because I believe that pure re-

search is often linked to practical matters, this preference perhaps reveals an unsuspected sense of irony. As demonstrated below, the phrase "basic research" is also sometimes used in a special sense to refer to research that is undertaken in the hope that it will lead to applied research, although the details of the latter are unknown.

2. I reject this point of view. However, it is quite possible for a scientist to have different kinds of responsibilities—to his employer, for instance, and perhaps also to the wider community. There is no guarantee that these will be consistent, and so a real possibility of conflict exists.

3. If I may be permitted an anecdote, I did try a long time ago to argue that pure and applied research could be distinguished on the basis of the precision to which equations, such as those expressing laws, had to be solved for the respective tasks characteristic of the two types of research. The idea was that the requirements of explanation for the pure scientist were different from those of the design brief of the applied scientist. Thus form, if not actual content, would provide the key to determine what was pure and what was applied. After my paper was rejected by two philosophy journals, with good reason, I gave the idea up. Moreover, even within pure research, the quest for a universal scientific method that distinguishes science from other activities has not been successful, especially as regards a method that embraces both the physical and the biological sciences.

4. In chapter 8, I will suggest an answer to the main question raised in this chapter, which is whether scientists need to take account of the impact of their work "as ideas" and, if so, how they are to do so. Put another way, we can ask whether scientists have responsibility in the forward-looking sense for their ideas and, if so, how they are to discharge this responsibility.

5. It is worth mentioning that Latour himself sees pure research as more than merely an activity aimed at publishing papers. On further questioning, his participants revealed that they wished to convince others, their contemporaries, that they had discovered facts—that their papers reported accurate records of how things are (Latour and Woolgar 1979, 76). Latour cannot accept this realism about laboratory activity and comes to the view that facts are constructed, not discovered. This is one point at which he comes into conflict with philosophers, and it is where I part company with him.

6. Several varieties of realism as regards science are studied by philosophers of science, which would give rise to slightly different interpretations of the relation between science and technology. Such a level of sophistication is not necessary here, which is why I refer to *the* realist interpretation. Psillos 1999 is a good introduction to recent debates about realism.

7. Again, sophisticated versions of realism introduce ideas about approximation and try to show that science is approaching the truth, and they do so to deflect the criticism that science is continuously modifying and discarding theories and hence that claims to truth are utopian. Prudent realists speak of science as "aiming" for the truth and of "intended" interpretations of theories.

8. A more recent version of this argument is called the No Miracles Argument, which differs slightly from the Ultimate Argument, which I attribute to Jack Smart, but these subtleties are not relevant here.

9. Most, though not all, philosophers of science are now realists, so here I will mention a contemporary alternative to realism but suggest that it cannot do justice to the relationship between science and technology. In 1980, B. van Fraassen proposed an "antirealist" account of science that he called "constructive empiricism," which has some notable adherents today (van Fraassen 1980, chapter 1). While an antirealist would typically deny some central tenet of realism, van Fraassen does not deny that theories and their characteristic terms should be taken literally. In this respect, then, he is at odds with instrumentalism. He does, however, deny that this "literalness" is at all important for our understanding of the workings of science. Constructive empiricism instead maintains that science aims simply to be "empirically adequate" and that it does so by "saving the phenomena." What this means, given van Fraassen's particular view of theory structure, is that theories represent phenomena by embedding them in models. However, van Fraassen makes no attempt to explain why this is possible, and he cannot do so by appealing to any realist interpretation of his models, as he denies the importance of this feature of science. He is therefore unimpressed by the Ultimate Argument (van Fraassen 1980, 23–25). It is evident, however, that constructive empiricism cannot account for the success of technology, given that such an account depends crucially on the realist interpretation. Thus, while van Fraassen may also be unimpressed by this extension of the Ultimate Argument, he would need to propose some other way to understand the impact of pure research, the problem that first led us to realism.

10. Hewlett and Anderson's remark, from their authoritative history of the atomic bomb, is interesting here: "The first year at Los Alamos [the Manhattan Project's nuclear weapons laboratory], perforce, had to be spent in determining nuclear specifications and in devising systems of assembly. This activity led the laboratory deep into basic research, but the leadership always kept in mind that the ultimate goal was a combat bomb, not just some interesting explosive device" (1962, 249). I classify this research as applied precisely because "the ultimate goal was a combat bomb." Had the work been done in peacetime at Harvard, Berkeley, or the University of Chicago, out of scientific curiosity, it would have been classified as pure.

11. I will not for the most part rely on this finer discrimination but will refer to all industrial research as "applied," although I understand it in a broad sense to include strategic basic research. I am in fact inclined to the view that there should be no pure research and that the "most abstract" research allowed should be "strategic basic research."

12. In chapter 7, I will discuss what I call "Polanyi's Challenge," after Michael Polanyi's claim that pure scientists are unable to look forward to assess possible applications of their work. I think that this challenge can be met in many instances of pure research, but perhaps the exception is such work as Hawking's.

13. Their evidence, naturally, was not of consistent "quality," with Newton, for example, writing nearly 150 years after Copernicus and so able to stand on the shoulders of such giants as Galileo and Kepler.

14. The time of this writing is shortly after the fiftieth anniversary of Einstein's death. One commentator, noting this anniversary, both lamented the paucity of girls doing physics, which he could not understand because physics "tells us about the secrets of the universe," and mentioned that the special theory of relativity—the theory that gave us $E = mc^2$—has revolutionized our understanding of space and time. The claim for relativity's "revolutionary" potential, however, is pure propaganda. In physics, one mostly just does difficult math, and moreover, relativity has not revolutionized "our" understanding of space and time, if "we" are ordinary people, that is, nonphysicists.

15. This is exemplified by Merton's thesis that Puritanism and Protestantism were crucial to the rise of modern science. Empirical work, such as that undertaken in the new experimental science of the seventeenth century, displayed qualities considered virtues by the Reformed Church, such as decent, honest, intellectual toil. In contrast to the Catholic Church, whose intellectual ideal emphasized reflection on the Bible and the works of Aristotle, the Reformed Church thus endorsed what would now be identified as modern empirical science.

16. Kant maintained that we should always tell the truth, but he was well aware that truth-telling does not always produce the best outcome. He gives the example of a murderer who asks a man the whereabouts of his best friend, with murderous intent. Kant argues that even here the truth should be told, but clearly, there would be no dilemma, and the example would not be worth raising, if no bad outcome was likely.

17. The moral system introduced in part 3, so-called common morality, is not founded on a notion of the good, and it is not consequentialist, as is Singer's, but it does lead to the same conclusion as regards the acceptability of such experiments.

Chapter 2. The Manhattan Project

1. The other Fat Man bomb manufactured at Los Alamos was tested in July 1945 in New Mexico. The third and final atomic bomb produced by the Manhattan Project, codenamed Little Boy, was dropped on Hiroshima.

2. Still, the following quotation from Richard Feynman is instructive: "After the thing [Trinity] went off, there was tremendous excitement at Los Alamos. Everyone had parties, we all ran around. . . . But one man I remember, Bob Wilson, just sat there moping. I said, 'What are you moping about?' He said, 'It's a terrible thing we made.' I said, 'But you started it. You got us into it.' You see, what happened to me—what happened to the rest of us—is we *started* for a good reason, then you're working very hard to accomplish something and it's a pleasure, it's excitement. And you stop thinking, you know; you just *stop*. So Bob Wilson was the only one still thinking about it, at that moment" (Badash, Hirshfelder, and Brioda 1980, 132). This is surely an important lesson for those who do applied research: however interesting the problem might be, the use to which its solution will be put must be kept firmly in mind. If the situation changes, as it did during the course of the war, the German bomb project turning out to be a chimera, then the whole project should be reevaluated by its participants.

3. This is a presupposition of the argument of chapter 6, where I maintain that scientists can be responsible for ignorance that their work might lead to certain outcomes and even for omissions.

4. I am using *context* here a little differently from the way I used it previously, but no confusion should result. To clarify, the context that determines whether research is pure or applied depends on the scientist's aims, intentions, and so on. By research's "overall context," however, I am simply referring to the historical period into which the work falls, which is informed by accepted commonplaces about the nature of research, such as that it routinely underpins outcomes. The virtuosi of the Royal Society of London in the seventeenth century, the "amateur" scientists of the interwar years, and the well-funded professionals of today all work in different contexts. See note 23.

5. The coming sections are undeniably technical, although they include no mathematics. I encourage the reader who would normally give up on such matters to struggle on through. I have added some diagrams that I hope will help elucidate the discussion.

6. The probabilities of these events for a given element are known as cross-sections. An example of a nucleus absorbing a neutron would be a uranium-238 nucleus absorbing a neutron to form unstable uranium-239, which immediately emits an electron to yield the new element plutonium-239, in a process known as beta-decay. See note 14.

7. The periodic table arranges the elements—the building blocks of chemical compounds—into groups, with members of the same group having similar properties. The basis of the differences in the elements' chemical activity is each element's number of protons, or atomic number (and hence its number of complementary electrons). The range of naturally occurring elements comprises atomic numbers 1 to 92. Differences in the physical properties of so-called isotopes of the same element, most obviously differences of mass, are due to the presence of different numbers of neutrons in the nucleus.

8. I will make no attempt to explain this, in view of my promise not to introduce any mathematics.

9. I will return to Szilard's letter to Joliot in chapter 4.

10. Frisch and Peierls were much more perceptive in this matter than the scientists who remained in Germany for the duration of the war. The leading light of the German "Uranium Club," Werner Heisenberg, only managed to think about a nuclear weapon in terms of a "reactor bomb." See Rose 1998, especially chapters 5 and 7, for the contrast between Frisch and Peierls and Heisenberg.

11. After they performed their calculations, Peierls reports, "we were staggered by these results: an atomic bomb was possible, after all, at least in principle. . . . For all we knew, the Germans could already be working on such a weapon and the idea of Hitler getting it first was most frightening. It was our duty to warn the British government of the possibility" (Peierls 1985, 154).

12. Frisch eventually became head of the "critical assemblies" group in the weapon physics division at Los Alamos (Hawkins 1946, 231).

13. Thus: $^{92}U_{238} + n \rightarrow {}^{92}U_{239} - e \rightarrow {}^{93}Np_{239} - e \rightarrow {}^{94}Pu_{239}$. There are in fact two

electron emission events here, with the intermediary element Np unstable. Note that the effect of electron emission is to leave the atomic weight the same but increase the atomic number by 1, which is just what happens when a neutron becomes a proton: electrons do have mass, and so there is in reality a slight change in mass, and hence atomic weight, after the electron is emitted.

14. Reactor neutrons are called thermal neutrons to distinguish them from fast-fission or bomb neutrons, both resulting from the fission of uranium-235. The cross-sections differ by a factor of 10^2.

15. Kistiakowsky was unequivocal in his assessment of Neddermeyer's contribution: "The man who deserved full credit for developing the concept of implosion, necessary to explode a plutonium weapon, is S. Neddermeyer" (Badash, Hirshfelder, and Brioda 1980, 49). There were originally four divisions at Los Alamos: the ordnance division, the theoretical division, the experimental physics division, and the chemistry and metallurgy division.

16. A thorough account of the scientific principles involved in bomb design could be found at http://www.fas.org/nuke/Nwfaq at the time of writing, with the technical details of implosion described in sections 3.7 and 4.1.6. When I last checked, however, many of the technical details had been removed, I assume censored.

17. Kistiakowsky, having given Neddermeyer credit for the idea of implosion, relates that it was von Neumann who convinced their boss, Oppenheimer, that the idea would work (Badash, Hirshfelder, and Brioda 1980, 62).

18. There were also some further refinements, such as coating the explosive to increase the shock, but I will not document all of these here.

19. Ulam, in his autobiography, makes some pertinent remarks about implosion: "I talked a lot [at Los Alamos] with von Neumann and Calkin about problems of hydrodynamics, especially those concerning the process of implosion. Somewhat to my surprise, I found the abstract, intellectual habits as a mathematician immediately useful in the work with these more practical special and tangible problems. . . . A discussion with von Neumann which I remember from early 1944 took several hours, and concerned ways to calculate the course of an implosion more realistically than the first attempts outlined by him and his collaborators. The hydrodynamical problem was easily stated but very difficult to calculate—not only in detail but even in order of magnitude. In particular, the questions concerned values of certain numbers relating to compression vs. pressure [which had to be known to a specified degree of accuracy]" (1976, 153–54).

20. Peierls took over the hydrodynamics group in the theoretical division from Teller, when the latter went off to think about the "super," reporting that his knowledge of shock waves was very useful (Peierls 1985, 199–200). In March 1944, Teller was head of group T-1, "Hydrodynamics of Implosion, Super." In June 1944, Peierls took over a reorganized implosion group, with the super hived off (Hawkins 1946, 84). I will note here that I will use "Peierls," in the chapters that follow, as an example of the person who solved the equations that showed that implosion was possible in theory. While I believe that it is historically correct to say that Peierls made a major contribution to the solution, it was not his alone. I would further stress that I do not in any way want

to single out the real historical Peierls for any special attribution of blame or responsibility. These comments also apply to the real historical Fermi, in view of the fact that I single out "Fermi" as the scientist who provided the fuel for the plutonium bombs. On the other hand, my later remarks about Szilard do, I assume, reflect the opinions of the real, historical Szilard.

21. A sense of neutrality that I will not consider here directly concerns "equal empowerment" and conversely the claim that technology is not neutral if it empowers selectively. It seems to me clear that much of modern technology is not neutral in the sense that only those with the right resources can access it. Lacey also mentions this sense of nonneutrality (1999, 188).

22. This will not be of much concern in what follows. While it is hard to find an instance that fits the example, if the radiation from a plutonium sphere were found to have some unexpected medical application, that would count as a secondary purpose.

23. This is the third and final sense of *context* in this book. I first discussed particular research contexts, which determine whether work is pure and applied, and then the overall "changed" context of scientific research. Now I am referring to the overall historical and political situation in which both researchers and nonresearchers alike find themselves—the second and third senses of the term's use here are close. Chapter 9 will address historical and nonhistorical justifications of weapons research, with the former taking account of the context of research in this third sense.

Chapter 3. On Responsibility

1. These are sometimes referred to as *passive* and *active* responsibility. Backward-looking responsibility is termed passive because, unlike forward-looking responsibility, it does not allow a determination of what P should do: all P can do in regard to X is make his excuses and justifications (see below).

2. I construe "facts" very broadly here. Thus, I take determining what *caused* the village's destruction to be a matter of finding out the facts, although I accept the Salmon-Dowe causal process account of causation. See chapter 5.

3. Animals differ from volcanoes in that they are conscious beings capable of complex behavior. Nevertheless, animals are not classified as agents and are not responsible for what they do. Thus, if a laboratory rat, having tunneled out of its maze onto a shelf in the advanced organic chemistry laboratory, knocks what turns out to be one component of a nerve gas into the other and so "discovers" sarin, the rat is still not declared responsible for the discovery of sarin. That dubious honor goes to Dr. Gerhard Schrader and his coworkers. Rats cannot form the *intention* to do anything complicated, like chemistry. While it is argued in this book that forming the intention to do X is not a necessary condition for responsibility for X, something like the *capacity* to form intentions is necessary, as we will see in the next chapter.

4. This point is similar to the one made in the previous paragraph regarding standards and norms.

5. The classic discussion here is Austin's "A Plea for Excuses" (1970).

6. Wallace's discussion of the "economy of threats" approach to responsibility is a specific instance of this way of relating backward- to forward-looking responsibility (1996, 55). I note also that Wallace describes this approach as having a "recognizably utilitarian character."

7. Goodin assumes that all sorts of responsibility are normative, and as a consequentialist, he derives (what he calls) blame-responsibility from (what he calls) task-responsibility, claiming that "this makes better sense of the way in which we actually assign credit and blame than does the deontological model" (Goodin 1995, 81). I use "backward-looking agent responsibility" and "role-responsibility" instead of Goodin's terms. I refer to Goodin here not only to provide another example of a consequentialist (in addition to Smart, discussed next) but also to show that some philosophers are only interested in responsibility in connection with normative considerations and so are not willing to step back a nanometer from such issues.

8. Indeed, van den Beld, taking Smart completely out of context, posits that the passage means that the supposition that a person is ever responsible for his actions is metaphysical nonsense (2000).

9. Moreover, the historian need not be interested solely in causes, in which move led to which outcome. He might wish to restore the posthumous reputation of Captain Lapointe, who he believes was unjustly blamed for allowing a Russian breakthrough late in the day by a mistaken deployment of his horse artillery.

10. In light of all this, I think Smart's "metaphysical nonsense" comment applies just to the notion that there can be attribution of *the* responsibility in a grand event like a battle. Smart is not, I believe, saying that the idea of backward-looking responsibility is nonsense.

11. Different systems of standards would select different subclasses from, though not necessarily partition, {X}.

Chapter 4. Actions, Consequences, and Omissions

1. A view that is wider still would attribute responsibility to the scientist for *all* the outcomes of his work, *regardless* of whether he foresaw or could have foreseen them—this would lead to yet another way of interpreting {X}. But I agree with nearly everyone else who has considered this issue in holding that no one can be held accountable for matters that he could not have been expected to know about. This still wider view is known as "strict liability," but I do not think it can be defended.

2. This view, among the possible alternatives, will therefore have the most impact on scientific research, insofar as scientists take their responsibilities seriously.

3. Mackie writes: "It is a factual, psychological question whether an action is intentional or voluntary, but it is a moral or legal question whether or in what ways an agent is to be held responsible. But an initially plausible proposal would relate these matters directly, yielding what we may call the straight rule of responsibility: an agent is responsible for all and only his intentional actions" (1977, 208).

4. There is a sense in which I can be doing this now, even though the book only reaches the top of the list after my death. In a thorough and deep discussion of the issues that will occupy us in the second and third sections of this chapter, Ruben considers what he calls "a puzzle about posthumous predication"—namely the predication of actions to a subject at a time after the subject has died. As I say, there is a sense in which this is possible, and those interested

should read Ruben's book (2003). Here, all I wish to say is that there are so-phisticated philosophical accounts, such as Ruben's, that provide a firm basis for accepting Feinberg's proposal.

5. One of the few voluntary moratoriums scientists imposed on themselves, in addition to the one Szilard initiated, was agreed to at Asilomar in 1975. It concerned research into certain viruses with recombinant DNA techniques. See Paul Berg's lecture at http://nobelprize.org/medicine/articles/berg/.

6. Joliot's attitude was therefore quite different not only from Szilard's but also from Otto Frisch's. Frisch did a calculation that showed that the critical mass of (naturally occurring) uranium was on the order of tons, which meant that a bomb would not be possible in an assembly in which a chain reaction was realized. For this reason, Frisch *was* willing to have his paper published (Rose 1998, 92).

7. Joliot's data collection was, of course, one of the causes of the paper being published, where the latter is taken to be an event that takes place after the former. Again, what is being entertained here is the "incorporation" of later consequences into the description of what the agent does at a particular time.

8. A further objection to the effect that Crazy Horse is the only human agent who causes the death of Standing Bear can be easily overcome by amend-ing the example to include another human agent who plays an incidental causal role, something I will not do here.

9. Alas, this is a simplification. Suppose that, simultaneous with the arrival of Crazy Horse's arrow, another fatal arrow fired by Running Bull hit (the clear-ly unpopular) Standing Bear. Now neither singly is necessary for killing Stand-ing Bear. Such issues of causal overdetermination have been discussed both in the literature on cause and in the literature on responsibility. These are clearly special cases that occur only rarely in the real world, but they do shed light on both concepts. I will not address them here, as this discussion is not primarily concerned with what Fischer and Ravizza—addressing them well and at length—call the control conditions for responsibility (1998). As far as responsi-bility goes, the upshot of their account is that both Crazy Horse and Running Bull can be responsible for killing Standing Bear.

10. We are more interested in stretching than in squeezing the accordion. An example of the latter would be a minute description of the way Crazy Horse aimed his arrow.

11. This idea of a causal process was made clear, though not first intro-duced, in the work of Wesley Salmon in connection with causal explanation. See in particular his book *Scientific Explanation and the Causal Structure of the World* (1984). The counterfactual formula I have used is derived from some ideas of Phil Dowe (see, e.g., Dowe 2001, 132).

12. Computers can solve these problems, provided that they are put in the form of difference equations, and, of course, there is much interest in the idea that the brain itself is a computer. These two issues should not be conflated. Peierls certainly did not solve the hydrodynamic equations as a computer would, by performing lots of calculations very quickly. He would have used heuristics, guesses, and other professional tricks—precisely the sort of things that are difficult to represent in the computer model of the brain.

13. The definition of *professional* used here will determine who is classified as a professional. I think professional is best defined with reference to specialized knowledge and to clients for whom a service is being provided. This, however, still does not determine whether scientists are professionals. I return to this issue in part 3.

Chapter 5. Intention and Responsibility

1. Ronald Dworkin claims that it is "uncontroversial" that no one wishes to deny that a person can be responsible for what he foresees but does not intend (1988, 347). If Dworkin were correct, then it would hardly be worth discussing the standard view or taking it seriously. However, as I have already indicated, the standard view has a venerable pedigree, as it was put forward by Aristotle and still enjoys support among his followers. Among several other traditions that have loaned support to the standard view, we should mention Strawson, who put forward the "reactive attitudes" interpretation of moral responsibility some forty years ago (1962). R. J. Wallace's vigorous defense and elaboration of this viewpoint appeared in 1996. Contrary to what Dworkin thinks, the standard view has been alive and well for many years and continues to attract supporters today—it is far from being a "straw man."

2. The most frightening of these concern applications for biological warfare stemming from civilian biological-control measures (see chapter 9).

3. It is also far from true—siding with Dworkin this time—that there is a consensus *in favor* of the standard view. Dewey, Sidgwick, and Bentham, three eminent moral philosophers, rejected it with the following statement from Dewey being explicit about responsibility for foreseen outcomes: "There is no responsibility for any result which is not intended or foreseen. Such a consequence is only physical, not moral. But when any result has been foreseen, and adopted as foreseen, such result is the outcome not of any external circumstance, nor of mere desires and impulses, but of the agent's conception of his own end" (Dewey 1962, 160). However, the "wide view" extends the compass of responsibility beyond what is "intended or foreseen."

4. One might here add a third level—or, perhaps better, another sense—of intentions as plans. This idea is associated with Michael Bratman, who has criticized the "received account" of Davidson and Goldman for not accommodating plans (Bratman 1987).

5. Wallace sees Austin as also holding the standard view, introducing it in his book by discussing the essay referred to above, "A Plea for Excuses" (Austin 1970; see Wallace 1996, 120–22). In what follows, I refer to Wallace, not to Strawson's original piece.

6. One of many pertinent examples from literature is Rashkolnikov's feelings about himself and his anguish after he murders the pawnbroker in *Crime and Punishment.*

7. Any assimilation of being responsible to being held responsible should still be resisted. Thus, for the reactive-attitudes approach, it can be said that it is "appropriate" to display reactive attitudes to P if he is responsible for X. Another interpretation is Michael Zimmermann's so-called ledger view (Zimmermann 1988, 38–39). In order not to be committed to this assimilation,

Zimmermann holds that P's being responsible for X means that his responsibility is recorded in some ledger. But this cannot be some real ledger in the world, as perhaps no one knows what P did. Just what the ledger is and where it resides is obviously a problem, and this is why I say that the reactive-attitudes interpretation gives us a simple, straightforward account of the "cash value" of responsibility. Moreover, as long as the agent is honest with himself, he will experience reactive attitudes toward himself even if no one else does, so agents, given this interpretation, might always be held responsible.

8. This indicates a distinction between intentions and intentional actions: P can form the intention to do X tomorrow, having deliberated and made his choices, but that does not entail his actually doing X. But if P does X intentionally, P must do X. "Intention in action" is thus not the same thing as having an intention. Moreover, P can act intentionally without forming any prior intention to act in that way, such as when he does something spontaneous. I am going to gloss over this distinction and assume, in the cases in which we are interested, that P forms the intention to do X and then does X. I will thus suppose that having the intention to do X, doing X intentionally, and acting with the intention to do X all amount to the same thing, although the distinction becomes relevant in chapter 11.

9. Reference can be made here to Glover, who also accepts the standard view: "It may be said that to disapprove of people is just to disapprove of their actions and characteristics. But his objection misses a vital feature of the disapproval of people that constitutes blame. For purposes of blame, we identify a person with some of his characteristics rather than others" (Glover 1970, 64–65). These are characteristics "internal" to the person, like his intentions. Glover goes on to discuss a morality of intentions, which he adopts, and a morality of consequences. The position adopted here, to repeat, is that the role of intentions is not determined by the sort of morality to which one subscribes.

10. Indeed, if "unsought intentional action" were explicated as referring to actions filling in the "in spite of" schema, lower down in the preference ranking, then it may be possible to resurrect an interpretation of the standard view associated with Bentham, Mackie, and others who have a heterodox understanding of intention. For instance, Mackie follows Bentham in talking about "oblique" intention, where P obliquely intends X if he foresees that he will do X but does not intend to do X in the "full" sense. I think it is therefore clear that Mackie would adopt the modified standard view, but he would still owe us a theory of action, for oblique intention is not sufficient for getting P to do anything.

11. I see no good reason to exclude conditional intentions, especially because reasons for action can have a qualified or conditional form: although P realized that his action would bring about Y, this was not strong enough to stop him from doing X, because his "positive" desire for X outweighed his "negative" desire for Y. In the recent literature, intentions are sometimes said to represent the "balance of reasons" in favor of an action.

12. There are to this day still examples of gratuitous cruelty to lab animals:

one recently reported case involved "spare" mice from an experiment on amphetamines that were subjected to heavy metal music while "on speed." The mice all died. This experiment has no conceivable benefit to anyone, except as a means to publication for some scientists.

13. Surprisingly, given what I have just written, I am ultimately able to accept the standard view, with the proviso that the scientist "takes his responsibilities seriously," but it will be necessary first to establish what these responsibilities are. We will not be in a position to rehabilitate the standard view until the end of the book.

Chapter 6. Ignorance and Responsibility

1. Dates are helpful here. Thus, if in April 1939 Joliot was obliged to assess how his work might affect events and he failed to do so, and if his work aided the Germans in, say, 1940, then in 1945 he can be blamed for what happened in 1940.

2. In a more detailed study, or one with a different emphasis, all this could be couched in the language of *risk*, as could some of what has been said about foreseen outcomes and actions. Thus, we could say that P believes that the risk of what he does leading to X is unacceptable or negligible, when it is neither, or that he was not aware that there was any such risk at all. I will assume that what I have to say about ignorance, actions, and outcomes can be expressed in terms of risk, typically by substituting "P is ignorant of the risk of X" for "P is ignorant of X." In one sense, risk can be understood as recording objective degrees of ignorance regarding undesirable outcomes and, as such, is a useful tool in decision making. However, couching the present discussion in terms of risk would, I think, introduce a range of interpretational and other problems that would distract us from the focus.

3. This implies that being ignorant of doing X is a necessary but not sufficient condition for being responsible for X, which I think is a safer formulation than one that makes the condition both necessary and sufficient. However, I will not be greatly concerned with any instances in which this is not also a sufficient condition.

4. Being in s excuses P because, under the hypothesis, P is "not himself" when in s. He is drunk, or drugged, or hypnotized—such that his actions, such as they are, do not "belong" to him. His bodily movements are not in control of his will, and his actions do not express his qualities of will—or so the story goes.

5. By using *extent* here, I am not, of course, implying that there are degrees of responsibility.

6. A test for this is to imagine that P was forced into state s—for instance, made to take some incapacitating drug and then placed behind the wheel of a car. P would then be excused for whatever harm he did with the car, as it was not his fault that he was in s. And the same would be true, I suggest, if he had taken the drug without knowing its incapacitating effects.

7. This becomes clearer with an actual example: Suppose P habitually does stupid things when drunk, although he has never done X. He has been warned

about getting drunk, fined, put on probation, and so on, and so has ample evidence for realizing that he should not get drunk in public. So when he goes and does X, his plea of ignorance is not accepted. One assumes that this is the kind of case Aristotle had in mind. But notice that what P is responsible for is doing something *like* X—namely, some harmful act—and not X itself. This is all we need: at issue is the fact that X is harmful to others, regardless of how else it is described.

8. I prefer to use this example here rather than the ones used in chapter 2 in relation to role-responsibility (e.g., the captain of the ship), although I note that this example would have served as well.

9. I do not want to suggest that the principle SAP suddenly became apparent to scientists in 1945. Much of the history of science, at least since Archimedes of Syracuse, is the history of scientists doing things that affect people—Archimedes, for example, used his knowledge of mechanics to prepare the defenses of his city against attack.

10. I take providing sustainable water to be a moral problem, not simply a social or environmental one, because it is a basic requirement that moral agents, including animals, have enough water.

Chapter 7. Ignorance and Foresight in Practice

1. Polanyi's Challenge can be expressed in terms of actions as well as outcomes, given the symmetry between these modes, although the latter is more convenient in this context. In terms of actions, Polanyi maintains that P cannot know that he does Y, where "doing Y" stands for achieving a given scientific result, or that he does X, where X is an outcome in our sense. Thus, Peierls could not have known what solution he would get for his imploding shockwave calculations nor that this would weaponize plutonium—at least according to Polanyi.

2. Harvey Brooks, writing in the 1960s, like Polanyi, believed that planning in science is a fact of life in the 1960s (Brooks 1968, 54).

3. Here, a possible confusion about terminology must be avoided. Methodologists, particularly philosophers of science, usually reserve *prediction* to refer to the process of drawing out the *observational consequences* of a scientific theory. A prediction in this sense is a "prognostication" about something that is open to observation, and it is usually discussed in connection with theory *testing*. One famous account of how science works, that of Karl Popper, essentially amounts to just this: scientists test theories by deducing predictions from them, and this is how science advances. But I take it that this is not quite what Polanyi meant: he did not mean to restrict his claims about science just to the process of drawing out the observational consequences of theories.

4. Just what underwrites the guarantee here is a matter of some dispute in the literature. For realists, such as myself, the guarantee is conditional on the accuracy of the paradigm's laws, theories, and so on. For social constructivists, the guarantee is based on (something like) the fact that scientists accept the paradigm as correct. The realist then naturally tends to ask just why the paradigm is accepted, for surely there must be some independent grounds for ac-

ceptance, besides the fact that the paradigm just works. It is not necessary here to buy into this debate, for we are interested in the perspective of the scientist. As long as the scientist thinks that the paradigm guarantees the answer, that is all that matters.

5. I believe this is the reason why most scientists do science.

6. See any textbook on methodology for a comprehensive demolition—for instance, Chalmers 1999.

7. One can ask here, as one can in connection with Copernicus's dissatisfaction with Ptolemy's use of the equant, how widespread the anomaly was. According to Kuhn, the accumulation in anomalies is supposed to induce a sense of crisis in the scientific community that uses the paradigm, which motivates scientists to look for a replacement. It is not clear, however, that there was such a crisis either in astronomy at the beginning of the sixteenth century, when Copernicus began his work, or in electrodynamics at the beginning of the twentieth.

8. Perhaps this is not the best way to characterize the biological sciences, where the search for laws is not so important as it is in the physical sciences. However, I still believe that the biological sciences seek to uncover pervasive patters in the natural world.

9. Not all historians of science would agree that science and technology developed separately before 1600. Of course, science and technology did not suddenly begin to influence one another over night, but a case can be made that their mutual influence was not significant until the beginnings of (so-called) modern science in the seventeenth century. Some historians of science, a small minority these days, would argue that reflection on the history of science and technology provides a conclusive refutation of Polanyi's overall position. For instance, materialists who follow Marx, and maintain that social and economic questions and problems call forth responses from such intellectual disciplines as science, would quickly dismiss Polanyi's Challenge. For them, the history of science is necessarily "externalist," and science is not an autonomous discipline. This style of history of science became influential after Soviet historian Boris Hessen's trip to a conference in London in 1931—and Bernal, for one, adopted Hessen's viewpoint. However, to embrace this view of history here would be, in my view, to beg the question.

10. Kranzberg and Purcell (1967) covers these developments.

11. That is, P can conceive of what he does under more than one description.

12. Patent law is by no means the same in different countries; there are, for instance, significant differences between the situation in countries like the United States and Australia, on the one hand, and China, on the other. There is therefore no simple answer to the question of whether discoveries can be patented. Part of the problem here revolves around the definition of a "natural product." I am interested in patents that cover intellectual property, rather than substantial inventions. Note that the idea of intellectual property is now commonplace, implying acceptance of the view that one can patent ideas.

13. I refer here to "General Information about 35 U.S.C. 161 Plant Patents,"

a document produced by the Honorable Commissioner for Patents and Trademarks.

14. U.S. patent 5,747,200, at http://www.freepatentsonline.com/5747120 .html.

Chapter 8. The Ethics of Science

1. As noted already, whether or not science is a profession depends, naturally, both on what one takes a profession to be and on how one sees science. For instance, it is generally agreed that professions have, on the whole, a number of characteristics, and some believe that if an institution has "enough" of them it may then be held to be a profession (see Resnick 1998, 38). Or, on the other hand, professions may be taken to have one or two "core attributes" that represent necessary conditions (see Goldman 1992, 1018). Some institutions qualify as professions according to Resnick but not according to Goldman. But taking sides here does not determine whether scientists have special responsibilities *unless* it is maintained that all and only professionals have such responsibilities, and to maintain this, of course, would beg the question.

2. Many references could be given here. Mackie, for instance, simply states that morality is a particular sort of constraint on conduct (1977, 106).

3. A Society of Social Responsibility in Science existed in Australia from 1970 to 1985. The British Society for the Social Responsibility in Science is still in existence.

4. The term *organization* would work as well here as *institution* does.

5. My answer, as might be expected, is that work for the Defense Department or for any organization involved in war and weaponry is only justified, if at all, in the most special and restricted circumstances.

6. If a scientist engages only in the purest of pure research and produces some revolutionary ideas, then this can have great impact on people, and in the past, it was possible to do this in one's spare time. Einstein, for example, worked on the special theory of relativity, and much else, in his spare time. I am mostly concerned here with science as a basis for technology, but I will have something more to say later in this chapter about the impact of science as ideas.

7. Corporation X will have its own interests at heart and will only incidentally support the economy of countries where its activities are located. It is not easy to make the case that working for the private sector can satisfy any positive obligation of the scientist.

8. We suppose this. Some institutions, like transnational corporations, are notorious for transcending the interests of their employees, shareholders, and customers. It is, however, unlikely that these are obvious candidates for employing socially responsible scientists.

9. At least this is the position adopted here. I do not deny that others might see certain institutions as valuable in themselves.

10. The *justification* of any such system as a universally acceptable morality is the task of moral philosophy.

11. I further note that it would certainly be possible to quarrel about the

particular harms that Gert identifies and about his inclusion of the last two rules, which enjoin us to obey the law and do our duty. Not abiding by these rules, however, will not necessarily give rise to any harms.

12. Engelhardt, on the other hand, is seeking a basis for bioethics that would in fact be acceptable to everyone, and hence the opposition between him and Gert is not substantive, as the two have different aims.

13. I note my thanks to Bernard Gert in the preface, for his comments on the present chapter. The main points he raised concerned this paragraph and my understanding of his system as "rule-based"—points that I am now trying to correct. The first of his objections concerned my remark that his rules do not cover omissions. Gert maintains that, for instance, the tenth rule, "Do your duty," may require action when one is in a unique position. I am still inclined to think, however, that this functions a little bit like an escape clause that can be appealed to in difficult cases, and I feel that the idea of a "duty" needs to be spelled out. Gert's second objection concerned my description of his system as "rule-based," and here I quote his response: "It is common to characterize my account of common morality as 'a rule based system,' but I do not agree with this characterization. First, the system is not based on the rules; rather the rules are part of the system. Second, the system contains other features, such as the ideals and the procedure for justifying violations of the rules, which are not based on or derived from the rules. Consequentialism, at least act consequentialism, is not a public system, that is, it does not require that what you morally ought to do is what you ought to publicly teach people to do, e.g., you ought to cheat in certain circumstances when you would not publicly endorse people cheating in those circumstances. I would prefer if you characterize my account of morality something like the following. 'The alternative to morality as a public system in which rules play an essential role, as Gert describes it, is some form of consequentialism.'" (Gert 2005, private communication with the author).

14. Such groups are not too large for professionals like doctors, lawyers, and teachers, because they are comprised of people who engage the professional.

15. It becomes hard because each person counts as much as any other from the moral perspective, and the maximizing calculus of the consequentialist/ utilitarian sums over all moral subjects (as regards happiness, preference satisfaction, needs satisfaction, or whichever property defines the good). Hence, if I am able to increase this "sum" by shifting some of my resources to others or by doing certain things, then I should do so, whatever the personal cost. This is not so much a crude statement of the consequentialist position as one that gets to its bare bones.

16. This brings us to another notorious problem with consequentialism: what the agent is required to do may (well) be due to circumstances entirely out of his control. If natural forces cause a sandbank to collapse, leaving many swimmers in difficulties, then anyone who is a strong swimmer, including our off-duty lifeguard, is obliged to go and help. If a scientist's particular skills would be best suited to preventing harm in Ulan Bator for the next ten winters because the harvest failed again on the Mongolian steppe, then that is where he should go, regardless of his feelings about extreme cold, yaks, and yurts.

Chapter 9. Science and Weapons Research

1. For instance, Robert Koch used about thirty "test animals" to discover the bacillus that causes tuberculosis. A huge amount of suffering, to both humans and animals, was thereby prevented. This is one of those episodes much loved by consequentialists, where a relatively small sacrifice accomplishes a great deal of good.

2. This is one reason why an absolutist pacifist morality—difficult even to state coherently—is not helpful when it comes to weapons research. Because weapons research does not actually harm, it is immune from pacifist strictures.

3. Not everyone would agree that virtually all sentient life would be destroyed, as this scenario relies on a nuclear winter resulting from debris and smoke remaining in the upper atmosphere for years. I find the modeling convincing.

4. Defense R&D in the United States, which I will take to be a rough measure of weapons research, is about 10 percent of the U.S. defense budget; as that was $500 billion in 2006, defense R&D expenditure was $50 billion. This is a lot: it is more than half the total U.S. government money spent on R&D. And while I will focus here on nuclear weapons, one should not forget research on weapons development being done in the biological sciences (BMA 2004).

5. It is quite a different matter to provide reasons for restricting weapons research that will have purchase at the political and policy level, but that is not my goal here.

6. This is not the conclusion that I reached in an earlier article, "What Are the Moral Limits of Weapons Research?" (Forge 2007b), a shorter version of this chapter's argument. There, I concluded that a supreme emergency did justify participation in a weapons research program, but now, after much thought, I have resolved that the argument does not support this position. But also see note 27.

7. I believe it is possible to build torsion catapults from the blueprints that have come down to us from around 300 B.C.E.

8. Most agree that if X is the means necessary for Y, and P intends Y and does Y, then he intends and is responsible for doing X. When one agent provides X and another does Y, the situation is more complicated, but the means principle still holds when the former intends that Y be done.

9. Dual-use technologies are a hot topic of discussion at the moment. For instance, aerosolization techniques for producing biological control agents can be used to weaponize anthrax (see introduction, note 5). What is the status of such technologies? They may seem similar to the "generic" technologies, such as aircraft engines, mentioned in chapter 2, but for something new, such as aerosolization techniques, I maintain that their primary purpose depends on their makers' intentions. This would make weaponization a secondary purpose. However, the primary purpose does not justify the scientist who publishes information about aerosolization in a climate where it is clear that his work can be bent toward weaponizing anthrax.

10. I think that the person who actually creates the means to harm—who works out how to harm on the drawing board, applying his understanding of

science to produce weapons—is actually more complicit and more to blame than the arms dealer. But this point is not necessary for my argument.

11. A recent episode of scientists seeking to defend civilians and civilian assets is worth noting here. In December 2005, Britain bought a quantity of Russian surface-to-air missiles in order to see how they work—to "reverse engineer" them—and thus develop countermeasures, in the belief that terrorists might acquire them to attack commercial aircraft. This is, of course, entirely justified, but it falls within a specific context. In another context—in a time of a projected war with Russia, say—this same research could have a quite different aim and hence lack justification.

12. This conclusion is supported by the author of a recent paper on "nonoffense defense." A more recent initiative is the notion of "nonoffensive defense," in which forces are configured in such a way as to have a "structural inability to attack." For instance, in the "spider and web" configuration, such mobile forces as tanks are available, but they are so dependent on the web that they cannot be used offensively. However, Moller notes that "the offence/defence distinction does not apply to individual weapons or weapons systems, as every weapon can be used both for defence and attack. What matters is intentions, activities, plans, options and capabilities." I agree. For Moller's work, see http://www.copri.dk/copri/researchers/moeller/bm.htm.

13. See *New York Times*, Mar. 24, 1983.

14. If it perfectly protected against the full might of the Soviet strategic arsenal, then the United States would not have needed to launch a first strike. Perfect defense against any attack would still not justify the research, which could provide perfect cover for an offensive operation.

15. This claim was staked in chapter 2. There, a derivative purpose was allowed to "override" a primary purpose in a given context—in given historical and political circumstances—considered specifically in the case of deterrence. So, nuclear weapons can be developed to deter but not to be used, and in this sense deterrence provides the rationale for acquiring them. But of course, these are, to use the present idiom, essentially historical concerns.

16. In the remarkable film *The Fog of War*, Robert McNamara is candid about the mistakes the United States made in Vietnam and elsewhere. He recounts a conversation he had with Curtis LeMay, head of the Eighth Air Force, which bombed Japan, to the effect that both would have been indicted as war criminals had they been on the losing side. The same can be said of Air Marshall "Bomber" Harris of the Royal Air Force.

17. Unlike most versions of consequentialism, common morality does not make any appeal to providing "positive" benefits, and hence, the sacrifice of some for an outcome that gives pleasure to many can never become an issue. So, there is no alternative but to treat justifications in this way.

18. Resistance may cause more harm in the long run. Again, this is a practical issue that would require discussion.

19. Walzer's book on Just War Theory (1977) is regarded as a classic. Temes (2003) is a recent and more popular account.

20. Those discussing this include philosophers, who have endlessly compared the intentions of the "terror bomber" and the "strategic bomber."

21. Another example is the Kalashnikov assault rifle (see Forge 2007a).

22. Gert also discusses the ways in which emergencies can justify behavior that would, in normal times, be regarded as violations of the moral rules. See, for instance, Gert 2004, 72–73.

23. This does not mean I agree with the position that Walzer is discussing—that unjust means can be used in supreme emergencies. I do *not* endorse this view.

24. In 2005, the Blair government in the United Kingdom passed the Prevention of Terrorism Act. This allows for terrorism suspects to be placed under indefinite house arrest and hence is just the kind of suspension of normal democratic rights that authorities seem to call for in times of supreme emergency, with Blair himself talking about "our way of life" being under threat. And as might be expected, the legislation has been controversial, with some members of the governing Labour Party voting against it and the House of Lords rejecting it several times. One sticking point was whether the legislation will lapse after a certain time—that is, whether it is temporary.

25. The political situation in which certain rights and liberties are temporarily suspended might also be thought of as the basis for an *analogy* with a situation in which weapons research is justified. However, I think the point is somewhat stronger. The states of affairs in which weapons research is allowed are themselves political situations and hence are of a piece with those in which rights or liberties may be suspended. The point, again, is that once the emergency, whatever it is, has passed, normality must prevail.

26. Common morality is at stake, for instance, in a society where racism is government policy.

27. Responses to Walzer's discussion of a supreme emergency allowing for immoral means *in bello* would also seem relevant here, given the analogy I have drawn between the scientist doing war research and the statesman ordering proscribed methods of fighting. Orend's response (2006, 146–58) is a good example. Of the five options Orend discusses, I have opted here for the one analogous to his third option. The only alternative for us here is Orend's fifth option: in our terms, this would mean that S would do wrong whatever he did, whether or not he did war research and aided his country. Orend calls this a "moral tragedy." I don't believe our two-tiered account of responsibility allows us this option.

Chapter 10. What Scientists Should Do

1. I shall use the term *positive duty* to refer to the things scientists are encouraged to do by the ideals expressed in common morality.

2. The agenda can be found at http://www.unmillenniumproject.org/goals/index.htm. The summary states that "the Millennium Development Goals (MDGs) are the world's time-bound and quantified targets for addressing extreme poverty in its many dimensions—income poverty, hunger, disease, lack of adequate shelter, and exclusion—while promoting gender equality, education, and environmental sustainability. They are also basic human rights—the rights of each person on the planet to health, education, shelter, and security."

3. Remember that there is no canonical list of moral ideals, in particular no such list that coincides precisely with the moral rules. However, the rules serve to catalog the types of harms that the ideals are supposed to prevent; hence, by beginning with rules, the harms can be discovered.

4. I will restrict discussion henceforth in this chapter to physical harms. However, I will note two other possibilities, one that is raised by another rule and one that is not. Scientists have provided effective means to deceive—the seventh rule is "Do not deceive"—in that modern media and communications are products of science that can be used to deceive in the wrong hands. But the qualification "in the wrong hands" is needed here, because modern media and communications are also an example of what I earlier labeled a "generic technology" (see chapter 2)—a technology that is so "general" that it can be used for many different purposes; a neutral tool, for all intents and purposes. The second possibility concerns science as ideas, as opposed to science as the basis for technology, which will not be addressed further (see chapters 1 and 8).

5. Following is something of a technical exercise to ensure that the scope of the moral ideals includes harms that come about naturally, even though the moral rules only cover harms caused by moral agents. What is crucial about the prevention of harms is simply what these harms are, not how they are caused.

6. There is, however, a great deal to be said about the actual practice of medicine and the biosciences from the moral point of view, particularly whether bioscientists have a duty to do biomedical research and what the overall features of this duty are.

7. These figures for malaria and TB are from data gathered for the UN Millennium Project; see http://www.unmillenniumproject.org/reports/. A more recent report suggests that a third of the world's population is at risk from malaria.

8. However, this is not recommended under every system of ethics, as the following variant on the "utility monster" shows: Suppose that 10 percent of the world's population has the potential for exquisite happiness for a lifetime, which could be triggered by a drug that would result from a huge research effort—say 90 percent of resources. Certain utilitarian calculations—dependent on how utility is "measured"—would endorse this allocation as morally correct, even though 90 percent of the population would be relatively neglected, as they are now. This is yet another reason why common morality is more efficacious here, focusing as it does on the prevention of harms, rather than on the promotion of good states of affairs.

9. Supplying a particular technology to people who are unable to use it, however good the technology is, would be yet another kind of mistake.

10. Szilard, of course, pointed out that it seemed possible to make an atomic bomb and that this was an "opportunity" that should be explored.

11. The latter does make statements about research ethics and about human rights—see http://www.aps.org/statements/index.cfm—so it is not concerned exclusively with promoting scientific research. But its fellowships, prizes, and lobbying are mostly directed at pure scientific research.

12. See http://www.fas.org/main/content.jsp?formAction=325& projectId=7.

13. See http://www.ucsusa.org/ucs/about/page.cfm?pageID=1006.

14. And hence it takes a different stance from that taken here. My aim, of course, is not to recommend politically expedient action but to give the morally correct analysis of scientific responsibility.

15. I would add that I am less worried about terrorists making an atomic bomb, given how hard it is to do so—it took the Manhattan Project three years. Of more concern is terrorists buying a recently made nuclear device, but they would need to know how to set it off, and that is not easy. On the whole, I do not think we need to worry about this kind of nuclear terrorism.

16. See http://www.sgr.org.uk/.

Chapter 11. Group Research and Group Responsibility

1. In this chapter, I will use *group responsibility* as a general term; thus, whenever more than one person is responsible for one and the same thing, I talk about group responsibility. "Genuine" or "irreducible" group responsibility is group responsibility such that the group itself bears some responsibility. I will refer to such situations as cases of *collective responsibility*, whereas I will refer to instances in which all responsibility is reducible to individuals as *shared responsibility*. *Corporate responsibility*—that of corporations—may be either collective or shared. If corporate responsibility cannot be shown to be collective, then it is unlikely that there is any such thing as collective responsibility. This chapter draws on some ideas from my earlier article "Corporate Responsibility Revisited" (Forge 2002).

2. While this is a helpful way to introduce genuine group responsibility, I should stress that I do not believe that responsibility is quantifiable in the sense that there is in every case an "amount" or "slice" of responsibility that can be apportioned out. Blame, on the other hand, can come in degrees, but again I do not think there is a fixed amount of blame associated with an outcome. For instance, if a murder is committed by three men, then each one of them can be just as blameworthy as would have been the case had only one of them done the deed—each is not one-third as blameworthy as the man who acted alone. If one of them was an accomplice, then his would be a lesser degree of blame. In this case, it seems that we have the option of saying that the accomplice is less responsible for the crime, but this judgment tracks blame. In deciding blame we decide, first, who is open to blame—that is, who is responsible. Once all the facts of the matter are assembled, judgments about blame and guilt can be made, and *then* retroactive judgments of degrees of responsibility can be made.

3. We may note in passing that some information about a group can be gained just by a superficial study of its proper products. For instance, the frequency and amount of its publications attest to a group's vigor and longevity, and the number and ranking of a publication's authors tell us about a group's composition and the relative importance of its members.

4. I found that I had to do a little of my own "sociological research" into groups, in view of the dearth of such work in the literature. Differences in kinds of research groups seem to be a subject that has not been much investigated.

5. I note in passing that the sociologist Hagstrom has reported that in such instances no one likes to be relegated to the role of "technician," as this detracts from recognition and may even warrant exclusion from authorship. It is interesting in this case that the issue of relegation was over theoretical input.

6. The conventions I use here, which are not standard, is to let capital letters P, Q, and so forth stand for individuals; capital letters X, Y, and so forth stand for outcomes; lower-case letters m, n, and so forth stand for relations; and italic capitals *G*, *R*, and so forth stand for sets.

7. The "more than" need not signify that at least two people are involved, for it could be that P and *C*, the collective to which P belongs, and no one else, are responsible. Or, more interestingly, *C*mX could hold without there being an instance of PmX.

8. By analogy with the master-servant relation, in which it is "as if" the principal acts, we might say that it is as if the corporation acts. Here and elsewhere, it may seem that there is little difference between the vicarious-liability approach and French's approach. However, I would again stress that the former does not entail any imputation of corporate action or intention, and I do not believe that such imputation is always harmless. For example, it is not harmless if it leads to an underestimation of the difference between genuine group and shared responsibility and hence allows a putative instance of genuine group responsibility to be too easily reduced to shared responsibility.

9. The first two parts of the condition for liability can be thought of as, respectively, the *actus reus* and the *mens rea* elements of fault before the law, while the third part ensures that these are properly related.

10. I can be said to be causally responsible for your death, because you would not have driven so quickly in a car with faulty brakes in the rain were it not for my threat. But by hypothesis, I did not know about the bad brakes or the bad weather. On the other hand, suppose I did know, and suppose the call was a hoax, aimed at getting you to drive too fast and have a fatal accident. In this scenario, the "faulty" aspect of my conduct is directly causally connected to the harm. It can be noted in passing that the example used in the text is also an instance of a "wayward causal chain," such as has been frequently cited as a counterexample to the desire-belief model of intention.

11. Moreover, and more generally, if the principal is in a position to know that his agent will do Y as a result of his intention to do X, it seems that we can make the case for the principal being responsible for Y.

Chapter 12. Group Research and Collective Responsibility

1. This is one of the themes of Galbraith's *The New Industrial State* (1967).

2. Single-hulled ships carry 10 percent more oil than multihulled ships and so are cheaper to run.

3. This is sometimes called, as for news corporations, the internal audit process. Most modern corporations apply risk assessment to all aspects of their operations.

4. This consideration is reinforced by Galbraith's analysis of corporate policy making. In the mature corporation, policy is made by committees, not by individuals, because of the specialized nature of the information needed to run

a mature corporation (Galbraith 1967, 75–86). Committees themselves are groups, but the main point to be made here is that it is by no means clear that individuals sitting on committees that contribute to general policies about such matters as risk assessment are in a position to know about *all* the contingencies to which those policies apply—in particular, to those where the policies will fail.

5. Having said this, I commit myself to the view that even in instances of apparently spontaneous action, as when I put my hand up to stop myself from falling on my face, I have evaluated the situation.

6. Clearly, these roles are not the same as those discussed in connection with role-responsibilities.

7. I believe that this assumption is warranted in the case of *N*, whose work has been applied in medical technology—it is relevant to the development of MRI scans. I'm not so sure about *L*.

Conclusion: Taking Responsibilities Seriously

1. Rudner's paper was short but influential (see Rudner 1980).

2. I think we can classify values along various dimensions, one of which is their "content," which signifies what the value is about. I call Rudner's values cognitive in the sense that they have to do with the quality of hypotheses, explanations, and so on. A philosopher like Popper, for instance, would prefer a highly falsifiable hypothesis because such rank high on his system of cognitive values, while Salmon would favor a hypothesis that refers to causal mechanisms.

3. At the end of his paper, Rudner writes, "What is being proposed here is that objectivity of science lies at least in becoming precise about what value judgements are being made and might have been made in a given inquiry" (1980, 236).

4. The argument here resembles that given in chapter 6 in regard to ignorance and responsibility. P can only be responsible for something that he is ignorant of if he is responsible for being ignorant of that item. Likewise, if P is responsible for the outcomes of his research, then he is responsible for being properly informed about what sort of impacts his research can have.

5. See the World Medical Association ethics unit archive for September 2004, at http://www.wma.net/e/ethicsunit/whats_new_archives05.htm.

6. The first clause of this states that "the physician shall not countenance, condone or participate in the practice of torture or other forms of cruel, inhuman or degrading procedures, whatever the offence of which the victim of such procedures is suspected, accused or guilty, and whatever the victim's beliefs or motives, and in all situations, including armed conflict and civil strife."

7. Monsanto did in fact recall batches of seed that contained traces of an alternative genetic type in 2001. In the previous year, in the Starlink debacle, genetically modified corn containing traces of an unapproved variety was released by Aventis CropScience, costing the company a great deal of money.

References

Aristotle. 2000. *Nicomachian Ethics*. Ed. R. Crisp. Cambridge: Cambridge University Press.

Austin, J. 1970. "A Plea for Excuses." In *Philosophical Papers*. Oxford: Oxford University Press.

Australian Science and Technology Council (ASTEC). 1981. *Basic Research and National Objectives*. Canberra: AGPS.

Badash, L., J. Hirshfelder, and H. Brioda. 1980. *Reminiscences of Los Alamos*. Dordrecht: Reidel.

Baier, K. 1987. "Moral and Legal Responsibility." In M. Siegler, ed., *Medical Innovation and Bad Outcomes*. Ann Arbor: Health Administration Press.

Bennett, J. 1995. *The Act Itself*. Oxford: Oxford University Press.

Berger, P., and M. Luckmann. 1984. *The Social Construction of Reality*. Harmondsworth: Pelican.

Bernal, J. D. 1939. *The Social Function of Science*. London: Routledge.

Bratman, M. 1987. *Intentions, Plans and Practical Reason*. Cambridge: Cambridge University Press.

Bridgstock, M., et al., eds. 1998. *Science, Technology and Society*. Cambridge: Cambridge University Press.

British Medical Association (BMA). 2004. *Biotechnology, Weapons and Humanity* 11. London: BMA.

Brock, T. 1988. *Robert Koch: A Life in Medicine*. Berlin: Springer.

Brooks, H. 1968. *The Government of Science*. Cambridge: MIT Press.

Bush, V. 1945. *Science, the Endless Frontier*. Washington, D.C.: U.S. Government Printing Office.

Callahan, D. 1976. "Ethical Responsibility in Science in the Face of Uncertain Consequences." In M. Lappé and R. S. Morrison, eds., *Ethical and Scientific Issues Posed by Human Uses of Molecular Genetics*. New York: New York Academy of Science.

Cardwell, D. S. L. 1972. *Technology and Science in History*. London: Heinemann.

Ceulemans, C. 2002. "The NATO Intervention in the Kosovo Crisis: March–June 1999." In B. Coppieters and N. Fotion, eds., *Moral Constraints on War*. Lanham: Lexington Books.

Chalmers, A. 1999. *What Is This Thing Called Science?* 3rd ed. St. Lucia: Queensland University Press.

Club of Rome. 1972. *Limits to Growth*. London: Earth Island.

Davidson, D. 1963. "Actions, Reasons, and Causes." *Journal of Philosophy* 60: 685–700.

Desmond, A., and J. Moore. 1991. *Darwin*. London: Michael Joseph.

Dewey, J. 1962. *Critical Theory of Ethics.* New York: Greenwood Press.

Donagan, A. 1970. *A Theory of Morality.* Chicago: University of Chicago Press.

Dowe, P. 2001. *Physical Causation.* Cambridge: Cambridge University Press.

Downie, R. 1971. *Roles and Values.* London: Methuen.

———. 1972. "Responsibility and Social Roles." In French 1972.

Dworkin, R. 1988. "Intention, Foreseeability and Responsibility." In F. Schoeman, ed., *Responsibility, Character and the Emotions.* Cambridge: Cambridge University Press.

Engelhardt, H. T. 1996. *The Foundations of Bioethics.* Oxford: Oxford University Press.

Feinberg, J. 1965. "Action and Responsibility." In M. Black, ed., *Philosophy in America.* Ithaca: Cornell University Press.

———. 1975. "Collective Responsibility." In J. Feinberg and H. Gross, eds., *Responsibility.* Encino: Dickensen.

Finnis, J., J. Boyle, and G. Grisez. 1987. *Nuclear Deterrence, Morality and Realism.* Oxford: Oxford University Press.

Fischer, J. 1999. "Recent Work on Responsibility." *Ethics* 110, no. 1: 93–139.

Fischer, J., and M. Ravizza. 1998. *Responsibility and Control.* Cambridge: Cambridge University Press.

Fisher, D. 1985. *Morality and the Bomb.* London: Croom Helm.

Fleming, J. 1987. *The Law of Torts.* Sydney: Law Book Company.

Forge, J. 1998. "Industrial Revolution." In M. Bridgstock et al., eds., *Science, Technology and Society.* Cambridge: Cambridge University Press.

———. 1999. *Explanation, Quantity and Law.* Aldershot: Ashgate.

———. 2000a. "Moral Responsibility and the 'Ignorant Scientist.'" *Science and Engineering Ethics* 6: 341–50.

———. 2000b. "Science, Moral Responsibility and the 'Straight Rule.'" *Revista Patagónica de Filosofía* 2: 5–21

———. 2000c. "Science and Moral Responsibility." In R. Cross and P. Fensham, eds., *Science and the Citizen.* Melbourne: Melbourne University Press.

———. 2002. "Corporate Responsibility Revisited." *International Journal of Applied Ethics* 16: 13–32.

———. 2004. "The Morality of Weapons Research." *Science and Engineering Ethics* 10: 531–42.

———. 2007a. "No Consolation for Kalashnikov." *Philosophy Now* 59: 6–9.

———. 2007b. "What Are the Moral Limits of Weapons Research?" *Philosophy in the Contemporary World* 14: 76–87.

French, P., ed. 1972. *Individual and Collective Responsibility.* Cambridge: Schenckman.

———. 1992. *Responsibility Matters.* Lawrence: University of Kansas Press.

———. 1995. *Corporate Ethics.* Fort Worth: Harcourt Brace.

Galbraith, J. 1967. *The New Industrial State.* Harmondsworth: Penguin.

Gert, B. 1998. *Morality: Its Nature and Justification.* Oxford: Oxford University Press.

———. 2004. *Common Morality.* Oxford: Oxford University Press.

Gert, B., C. Culver, and D. Clouser. 1997. *Bioethics: A Return to Fundamentals.* Oxford: Oxford University Press.

Glover, J. 1970. *Responsibility.* London: Routledge and Kegan Paul.

Goldman, A. 1992. "Professional Ethics." In L. Becker, ed., *Encyclopedia of Ethics.* New York: Garland.

Goldman, A. I. 1970. *A Theory of Human Action.* Princeton: Princeton University Press.

Goodin, R. 1995. *Utilitarianism as a Public Philosophy.* Cambridge: Cambridge University Press.

Gorovitz, S. 1991. "Professions, Professors and Competing Obligations." In E. Pellegrino et al., eds., *Ethics, Trust and the Professions.* Washington, D.C.: Georgetown University Press.

Greenberg, D. 1999. *The Politics of Pure Science.* New ed. Chicago: University of Chicago Press.

Gustafsson, B. 1984. "The Uppsala Code of Ethics for Scientists." *Journal of Peace Research* 21: 311–16.

Hall, L. 1960. *General Principles of Criminal Law.* Indianapolis: Bobbs-Merrill.

Hart, H. L. A. 1968. *Punishment and Responsibility.* Oxford: Oxford University Press.

Hawkins, D. 1946. *Manhattan District History Project Y.* Los Alamos: Los Alamos National Laboratory.

Hewlett, R., and O. Anderson. 1962. *The New World, 1939/1946.* Vol. 1, *A History of the United States Atomic Energy Commission.* University Park: Pennsylvania State University Press.

———. 1969. *Atomic Shield.* Vol. 2, *A History of the United States Atomic Energy Commission.* University Park: Pennsylvania State University Press.

Hughes, J. 2002. *The Manhattan Project.* New York: Columbia University Press.

Irvine, J., and B. Martin. 1984. *Foresight in Science.* London: Frances Pinter.

Kenny, A. 1978. *Freewill and Responsibility.* London: Routledge and Kegan Paul.

Kitcher, P. 2001. *Science, Truth and Democracy.* Oxford: Oxford University Press.

Koestler, A. 1964. *The Sleepwalkers.* Harmondsworth: Penguin.

Kranzberg, M., and C. Purcell, eds. 1967. *Science and Technology in Western Civilisation.* New York: Oxford University Press.

Kuhn, T. 1962. *The Structure of Scientific Revolutions.* Chicago: University of Chicago Press.

Lacey, H. 1999. *Is Science Value Free?* London: Routledge.

Ladd, J. 1970. "Morality and the Ideal of Rationality in the Modern Corporation." *Monist* 54: 488–516.

Latour, B. 1987. *Science in Action.* Cambridge: Harvard University Press.

Latour, B., and S. Woolgar. 1979. *Laboratory Life.* London: Sage.

Lebow, R. 1985. "Assured Strategic Stupidity." *Journal of International Affairs* 39: 22–29.

Leopold, A. 1949. *The Sand Country Almanac.* New York: Oxford University Press.

Leslie, S. 1993. *The Cold War and American Science.* New York: Columbia University Press.

Lewis, D. 1986. *Philosophical Papers: Volume 2.* Cambridge: Cambridge University Press.

Lewis, H. 1972. "Non-Moral Notion of Collective Responsibility." In French 1972.

Mackie, J. 1977. *Inventing Right and Wrong*. Harmondsworth: Penguin.

Marsden, E. 1971. *Greek and Roman Artillery: Technical Treatises*. Oxford: Oxford University Press.

Mele, A. 1997. *The Philosophy of Action*. Oxford: Oxford University Press.

Melema, G. 1988. *Individuals, Groups and Shared Moral Responsibility*. New York: Peter Lang.

Mercier, A. 1969. "Science and Responsibility: An Essay on the Theory of Values." Part 1. *Studi Internazionali Di Filosofia* 1 (Summer–Fall): 5–76.

———. 1970. "Science and Responsibility: An Essay on the Theory of Values." Part 2. *Studi Internazionali Di Filosofia* 2 (Summer–Fall): 65–115.

Merton, R. 1973. *The Sociology of Science*. Chicago: University of Chicago Press.

Meyer, S. 1993. *Aristotle on Moral Responsibility*. Oxford: Blackwell.

Miki, I., et al. 1994. "A Strong Candidate for Breast and Ovarian Cancer Susceptibility Gene BRAC1." *Science* 266 (7 October).

Montmarquet, J. 1999. "Zimmermann on Culpable Ignorance." *Ethics* 109: 66–71.

Multhauf, R. 1967. "Industrial Chemistry in the Nineteenth Century." In Kranzberg and Pursell 1967.

Nordgren, A. 2001. *Responsible Genetics*. Dordrecht: Kluwer.

Orend, B. 2006. *The Morality of War*. Peterborough, Ont.: Broadview.

Organisation for Economic Co-operation and Development (OECD). 1991. *Choosing Priorities in Science and Technology*. Paris: OECD.

Pegg, D. 1989. "Some New Techniques in Nuclear Magnetic Resonance." *Contemporary Physics* 30: 35–42.

Peierls, R. 1985. *Bird of Passage*. Princeton: Princeton University Press.

Perko, J., and F. Narin. 1997. "The Transfer of Public Science to Patented Technology: A Case Study in Agricultural Science." *Journal of Technology Transfer* 22, no. 3: 65–72.

Polanyi, M. 1969. "The Republic of Science." In M. Greene, ed., *Knowing and Being*. Chicago: University of Chicago Press.

Pritchard, H. A. 1949. *Moral Obligation*. Oxford: Oxford University Press.

Psillos, S. 1999. *Scientific Realism*. London: Routledge.

Resnick, D. 1998. *The Ethics of Science*. London: Routledge.

Rhodes, R. 1986. *The Making of the Atomic Bomb*. New York: Simon and Schuster.

———. 1995. *Dark Sun*. New York: Simon and Schuster.

Rose, P. 1998. *Heisenberg and the Nazi Atomic Bomb Project*. Berkeley: University of California Press.

Rostow, W. W. 1971. *Politics and the Stages of Economic Growth*. Cambridge: Cambridge University Press.

Ruben, D-H. 2003. *Action and Its Explanation*. Cambridge: Cambridge University Press.

Rudner, R. 1980. "The Scientist qua Scientist Makes Value Judgements." In E. Klemke et al., eds., *Introductory Readings in the Philosophy of Science*. Buffalo: Prometheus.

Salmon, W. 1984. *Scientific Explanation and the Causal Structure of the World*. Princeton: Princeton University Press.

Salomon, J-J. 2000. "Science, Technology and Democracy." *Minerva* 38: 35–51.

Searle, J. 1983. *Intentionality.* Cambridge: Cambridge University Press.

Sharlin, H. 1967a. "Applications of Electricity." In Kranzberg and Pursell 1967.

———. 1967b. "Electrical Generation and Transmission." In Kranzberg and Pursell 1967.

Sidgwick, H. 1981. *Methods of Ethics.* 7th ed. Indianapolis: Hackett.

Singer, P. 1993. *Practical Ethics.* Cambridge: Cambridge University Press.

Smart, J., and B. Williams. 1973. *Utilitarianism.* Cambridge: Cambridge University Press.

Spier, R. 2001. *Ethics, Tools and the Engineer.* Boca Raton: CRC Press.

Strawson, P. 1962. "Freedom and Resentment." *Proceedings of the British Academy* 48.

Temes, P. 2003. *The Just War.* Chicago: Ivan Dee.

Toulmin, S. 1970. "Does the Distinction between Normal and Revolutionary Science Hold Water?" In I. Lakatos and A. Musgrave, eds., *Criticism and the Growth of Knowledge.* Cambridge: Cambridge University Press.

Ulam, S. 1976. *Adventures of a Mathematician.* New York: Scribner.

Van den Beld, T. 2000. *Moral Responsibility and Ontology.* Dordrecht: Kluwer.

Van Fraassen, B. 1980. *The Scientific Image.* Oxford: Oxford University Press.

Wallace, R. 1996. *Responsibility and the Moral Sentiments.* Cambridge: Cambridge University Press.

———. 2002. "Scanlon's Contractarianism." *Ethics* 112, no. 3: 429–70.

Walzer, M. 1977. *Just and Unjust Wars.* New York: Basic Books.

———. 2004. *Arguing about War.* New Haven: Yale University Press.

Weeramantry, C. 1987. *Nuclear Weapons and Scientific Responsibility.* Wolfboro, N.H.: Longwood.

Zimmermann, M. 1988. *An Essay on Moral Responsibility.* Totawa, N.J.: Rowman and Littlefield.

———. 1997. "Moral Responsibility and Ignorance." *Ethics* 107: 410–26.

Index

3